From Washington and Adams
to Hillary and Trump

The Stories behind the Story of Every Presidential Election

With Special Focus on the *Volatile* Presidential Election of 2016

Everett E. Murdock PhD

H.O.T. Press

H.O.T. Press
Los Angeles, California
www.hotpresspublishing.com

Publishing fine books since 1983

ISBN: 0-923178-31-7
ISBN-13: 978-0-923178-31-4

For Zoe,
Without whom this book would not exist,
and without whom I would not exist.

Acknowledgments

I had planned to acknowledge all of the books on U.S. history that provided me with background information while I was writing this book, but I soon realized that would be an impossible task because I've been reading books on U.S. history all my life. Let me just say I am truly indebted to anybody who has written anything about U.S. history. I assume they did it simply because they are, like me, interested in the history of our country.

I am also indebted to those who took the time to put information about U.S. history on the internet. Once again, I started to list them, but found the list growing into the hundreds (and even then I knew I was leaving a lot of them out). So I will just say this: if you've ever put anything about U.S. history on the internet, I probably read it while researching this book, and I am therefore, indebted to you.

Books by Everett Murdock (Partial List)

• **Obama Won but Romney Almost was President:** How the Democrats Targeted Electoral College Votes to Win the 2012 Presidential Election

• **How to Write Fiction:** Tools and Techniques (with original stories as examples)

• **The Pain Artist**: An American Hikikomori

• **My Vietnam War:** A Novel

• **A Psalm for Cock Robin**: A Harp and His (Dead) Mother Mystery

• **Crueltown**: A Drew Steele Los Angeles-Las Vegas Mystery

• **The End of the Civil War**: A Drew Steele Civil War Mystery

• **Who Owns Arizona**: A Drew Steele Civil War Mystery

Contents

Introduction

They say if you want to know what the future will bring, study the past. You might think studying the history of past presidential elections would do little to prepare you for what happened in the presidential election of 2016; but actually it would. While it is true that the presidential election of 2016 was "different," many previous U.S. presidential elections also had their share of strangeness and chaos.

Maybe the biggest difference is that in the past, much of the drama took place behind closed doors. But in the twenty-first century, in the age of 24-hour cable TV news and the internet, there is no such thing as closed doors. In 2016, every aspect of the presidential election played out in plain view, either on America's TV screens or on the internet. Every statement by every candidate was analyzed and discussed, often in dismay, but sometimes in outrage and even unrestrained anger.

Every four years, presidential elections bring out attitudes and opinions that seem to have been existent, but hidden (some might say they have been "festering"). And in 2016, some of those hidden attitudes and opinions surfaced, and that resulted in the Republicans nominating a surprise candidate, a businessman and TV entertainer that had absolutely no experience in politics. Donald Trump has been described as a candidate that "came out of nowhere" (politically speaking), but soon after he announced his candidacy, he began to demonstrate an approach to campaigning for president that was unlike anything the country had ever seen before.

However, everything happens for a reason. In this book, I will show that the presidential election of 2016 was an evolution of processes that began a long time ago.

If you looked at my list of published books in the front matter of this book, you will have noticed that although I published a book on the presidential election of 2012, I'm mainly a novelist.

I'm a storyteller, and that's how I look at presidential elections: there is always a story that made the voters vote for one candidate and not the other. Therefore, this book will be a book of stories— not fictional stories, but stories about what actually happened behind the scenes, the stories that, in the end, determined which candidate ended up being elected president and which candidate was relegated to the lonely halls of history.

Often the story that determined the winner was about war or some other national crisis. But sometimes it was simply the story of what one candidate did (or didn't do). Watch for "**story boxes**" that tell those stories, in detail, along with an explanation of how they influenced the outcome of an election.

Presidential elections are also influenced by "the rules"—for example, the rules of the Electoral College, or newer rules that have been passed by Congress (often in the form of amendments to the U.S. Constitution). Watch for "**comment boxes**" that describe in detail how the decidedly odd rules that govern how we elect our presidents can sometimes end up determining which candidate wins.

Let's begin by looking at how the very odd "rules" of our presidential elections were created.

Chapter One
The "Rules" of Presidential Elections are Created

How did our "founding fathers" approach the issue of how to choose a national leader, and why did they come up with such a strange way of doing it? Why didn't they just let the people vote for their president? To better understand how and why that happened, we need to go back and look at the first meeting of representatives from the original thirteen states.

The Constitutional Convention

In 1787, a **Constitutional Convention** was convened to lay out a governing structure for the newly formed united states. The document that came out of that convention was the **United States Constitution**.

Getting agreement as to how the new government should be organized was not an easy task. There was considerable controversy about the issue of slavery and much disagreement about how members of the governing bodies should be elected. Even after they had agreed to maintain the British concept of a two-house legislature, there was great difficulty in deciding how the two houses should be structured. Eventually, it was decided that the **House of Representatives** would be apportioned according to the population of a state (the total population, not just voters or legal citizens). That meant the states with larger populations would have more representation in the government, and that led to **contention over how the states with smaller populations would be fairly represented**.

To better understand the process, we need to remember that the Constitutional Convention was made up of a delegation from **each of the states.** Each state was given one vote. That meant **the least populated states had as much decision-making power at the convention as the more populous states**. The delegates from the smaller states felt the larger states would dominate the government; therefore, at the convention, they often stuck together when voting. They were able to force a compromise that gave them more voting power in the Congress: **the Senate** would be made up of two senators *appointed* from each state, no matter how large or small the population of the state was.

Of course, the big states didn't like that idea one bit, because it meant states with much smaller populations would have equal clout in the Senate. But no other solution could be agreed upon, so that method was adopted.

One major area of contention that arose regarding the apportioning of seats in the House of Representatives had to do with slaves. The Southern **slave-holding states wanted to count their millions of slaves as part of their apportionment** even though the slaves were not considered to be citizens of the United States. There was also the issue of taxes. Because slaves were legally the property of the slave owner, the Northern states said they should be taxed as property. The Southern states disagreed, saying they were not property, but living beings. In other words, the Southern states wanted to have it both ways.

Neither side was willing to budge and it looked as if the convention would be bogged down in the slavery issue forever. But then, in what would be the first of many compromises with the Southern slave states in order to get the government-making process moving again, it was decided, for purposes of representation in the House of Representatives, slaves would count as three-fifths of a person. It was a decision that would have long lasting effects. It is estimated that before the Civil War, there were about nine million free whites living in the South, as compared to about four million slaves. Based on the Three-Fifths Compromise, that meant **the South was given credit for an extra 2,400,000 people** when the number of seats in the House of Representatives were assigned. If the apportionment had been based on free population, the slave states should have been apportioned 33 seats in the House of Representatives, but **by including their slaves and counting them as three-fifth of a person, they got 47 seats**.

Originally, the only national office that was elected by public vote was for members of the House of Representatives, and even then, **only males were allowed to vote.** In many states, only **men who owned property could vote.**

Even the members of the U.S. Senate were selected by political leaders.

COMMENT

The original method of **appointing senators, rather than electing them, continued to be in force until 1913** when a constitutional amendment was proposed to require direct election of senators. Many political leaders fought against the proposed amendment, and it took a year before it was finally ratified by 37 states (one more state, Delaware, ratified it in 2010). Alabama, Florida, Georgia, Kentucky, Maryland, Mississippi, Rhode Island, South Carolina, and Virginia *did not* ratify it, and **Utah made a point of explicitly rejecting it** (Some members of the legislature in Utah are still trying to overturn that amendment).

However, once it was made the law of the land, even the states that didn't ratify the new constitutional amendment had to allow direct election of senators.

The difficulty of getting three-fourths of the states to ratify such a common-sense concept as the direct election of senators *by the citizens of their state* probably tells us how difficult it would be to get three-fourths of the states to go along with the idea of getting rid of the Electoral College system of electing presidents and vice presidents.

Dispute over How the President Should Be Chosen

Perhaps the most contentious dispute at that original **Constitutional Convention** revolved around how the president was to be elected. As a result, it was one of the last issues to be resolved.

Some of the delegates thought Congress should choose the president. Others felt there shouldn't be a national leader; instead, there should be **a presiding committee.**

Although most of the delegates felt the people ought to be allowed to elect their president, a dissenting minority wouldn't go along with that idea, and they wouldn't budge.

The dissenting delegates had two reasons for being against a popular vote: first, the delegates from the smaller states knew the more populous states would control the presidential elections, and second, Many of the delegates didn't trust the people to make *the right* decision.

The first point, that the smaller states would get outvoted by the states with larger populations, was true then and is still true today. Some states have much larger populations than others, and if the president was elected by popular vote, the larger-population states would have more say in who got to be president.

Because **the delegates from the Southern states often voted together to stymie the wishes of the larger Northern states,** a compromise had to be found that would give the smaller Southern states more voting power (proportionally). The delegates had already agreed to give the slave states more voting power in Congress, and this new compromise meant they also had to give them more power in electing the president and vice president. **The second point,** that they didn't trust the voters, is less defensible in a democracy. There were a lot of reasons put forward as to why the president should not be directly elected by the people, but they all came down to the same point: **the delegates at the Constitutional Convention did not believe the people were informed enough to make such an important decision**. While the delegates believed the people perhaps had enough information to elect their state representatives, they did not believe the people understood federal and international issues well enough to choose a national leader.

After much contentious debate, in order to come to *some* agreement, the majority gave up on their idea of a popular vote for president. The people *would not* be allowed to vote for their president; instead, the political leaders in each of the states would decide who they wanted to be president and vice president. The states would then choose electors who would get together with the electors from the other states to hash out who the president and vice president should be.

After even more haggling, the delegates decided each state would be assigned **one electoral vote for each of the states' representatives in Congress. (The gathering of those state representatives to vote for a president has come to be known as the "Electoral College."** It is still how presidents are elected today.) That method meant the Southern states were given extra electors in the Electoral College, and as a result, for many years, Southerners dominated the Presidency, the House of Representatives, and the Supreme Court.

STORY

As a direct result of giving the South disproportionate voting power, **ten of the first twelve presidents were slave holders.**

George Washington, the first president, was a wealthy Virginia plantation owner who owned more than 200 slaves before, during, and after he was president. The selection of Philadelphia to be the nation's capital presented a problem for Washington: he brought some of his slaves with him, and Pennsylvania had passed a law that said slaves that lived in the state for six months automatically became free. Washington got around the law by transporting his slaves across the state border and back again every six months.

The second president, **John Adams**, was from Massachusetts which was not a slave state. However, some years before he became president, he was given a slave as a gift. He used her as the family cook.

Thomas Jefferson, the third president, owned a 5,000 acre plantation in Virginia and owned more than 100 slaves, including one woman, **Sally Hemings**, who was rumored to have been his mistress after his wife died. It was said she bore several of his children while he was president, all of whom, by law, remained slaves. Modern DNA evidence and analysis of the timing of his visits to his estate at Monticello seem to have proved the truth of that rumor.

James Madison, the fourth president, owned a large tobacco plantation in Virginia. He inherited hundreds of slaves and continued to hold them throughout his life.

James Monroe, the fifth president, was a Virginia plantation owner and owned many slaves.

John Quincy Adams, the sixth president, being from Massachusetts, was bared by state law from owning slaves.

Andrew Jackson, the seventh president, bought his first slave, a young woman, when he was only 21 years old. He later became a businessman, and for a while, he was in the business of buying and selling slaves. At one time, he owned more than 300 slaves.

Martin Van Buren, the eighth president, was from a slave-holding family, but he personally owned only one slave.

William Henry Harrison, the ninth president, was from a Virginia plantation family that owned many slaves. Harrison was said to have illegally taken several of them with him when he traveled to states where slavery was against the law.

John Tyler, the tenth president, was also a Virginia tobacco plantation owner who owned many slaves.

James K. Polk, the eleventh president, was a slave holder from North Carolina.

Zachary Taylor, the twelfth president, was born into a slave-holding family in Virginia. Although he chose a military career, he held onto his slaves. While he was president, he held about 100 slaves.

After 1850, the rapidly increasing populations of the Northern states began to break the stranglehold the Southern states had on electing presidents. At the same time, owning slaves became much more controversial in the North. As a result, political candidates for national office, even those from Southern states, tended to transfer their slaves to a relative before running for office.

The fact that small states get proportionally more electors in the Electoral College violates one of the most basic principles that guided the framers of the constitution, that all voters should be equal. Today, legal scholars say the Electoral College could be ruled unconstitutional if it wasn't specifically laid out in the constitution.

The method of selecting electors was left vague. It simply said "the states" would choose their electors and those electors would get together to choose the president and vice president. There was no provision for assessing the people's wishes.

COMMENT

There are several aspects of the Electoral College system that are relatively unknown. For example, many do not know that **according to the Constitution, the electors do not have to vote for the candidate that won their state** in the general election (and over the years, many electors have refused to do so). **In fact, there is nothing in the Constitution about a "general election."**

Today, most people expect the outcome of the Electoral College vote to be the same as the voting in the general election.

However, several times in U.S. history, that has not been true. As recently as the 2000 presidential election, **the winner of the general election was not the winner in the Electoral College vote**. In the 2000 president election, **Al Gore won the general election by more than half a million votes but didn't get to be the president** because he suffered a very narrow loss in the Electoral College.

With the country growing ever more polarized, **it was only a matter of time before it happened again**. In the volatile presidential election of 2016, **Hillary won the popular vote, but Trump squeaked out very narrow wins in the elector-heavy "rust belt" to win in the Electoral College**. And **there are strong indications that the same thing is going to happen more often in the future**.

Today, most Americans can't understand why we need an Electoral College. They ask why they can't just vote for president like they vote for every other political office. Public opinion polls repeatedly show **most Americans favor abolishing the Electoral College**, and there have been more than 700 proposals introduced in Congress to reform or eliminate the Electoral College. **In fact, more constitutional amendments have been introduced to abolish the Electoral College than on any other subject.**

But they all failed. After 240 years, Americans still do not get to directly vote for their president.

At first, most states did not hold presidential elections. In the first presidential election in 1789, only 6 of the 13 original states held any sort of popular vote for president. Even if an election for president was held in a state, the Electoral College system meant it was still the political leaders of the state that decided who they wanted to be president.

Understandably, the people of the United States were not happy that they had no say in who their president would be. They brought political heat to bear on the politicians to allow a popular vote for president. Eventually, all the states began to hold general elections in which the people could cast votes for their preferences for president and vice president. However, under the Constitution, the results of those popular president elections had no legal status.

COMMENT

Much later, *some* states passed laws that stated an elector could be fined if he or she did not vote for the candidate that won their state's popular vote. Nevertheless, in the 56 past presidential elections, there have been 156 instances in which an elector *did not* vote for the popular vote winner. These electors are referred to as "faithless electors." Later, I will discuss what motivated those 156 faithless electors.

To make sure the electors didn't just vote for their state's local candidate, it was written into the Constitution that the electors had to vote for at least one candidate from outside their state.

The votes of all the electors from the states would be tallied and added together, and the candidate that got the most votes would be named president. The candidate that came in second would be named vice president.

COMMENT

As stated in the Constitution, a candidate has to gain an absolute majority of the state electors or else the decision gets sent to the House of Representatives. Some have speculated that the framers of the Constitution assumed that such an approach would result in a variety of candidates being put for-

---

ward by the electors and no one candidate would ever get the required majority. Therefore, the decision would always come back to the House, the body of Congress in which the number of members are determined by state populations. That way, they thought the wishes of the people would be better served. In other words, they assumed the vote of the state electors in the Electoral College would be considered *nominations* from which the House of Representatives would choose a president and vice president.

But it didn't turn out that way. The Electoral College (the term "Electoral College" does not appear in the Constitution but began to appear in newspapers sometime in the early 1800s) was created at a time when political parties did not exist. Later, when two political parties emerged in the late 1700s —the **Federalists** and the **Democratic-Republicans**—they immediately got involved in the selection of electors to be sent to the Electoral College. It became crucial for both political parties to *try* to make sure the electors they chose were loyal **to the party** and would vote the way the party wanted them to.

Today, the two main political parties in the United States, the **Democrats** and the **Republicans**, pretty much control the election process. As a result, the election now almost always comes down to a face-off between the candidates nominated by those two parties. So far, the two major parties have been able to squeeze out any other candidates. For that reason, one of the major party candidates always wins the required absolute majority of the Electoral College votes, and therefore the decision never gets sent to the House of Representatives. If a third-party candidate was to get a significant number of electoral votes, **no candidate would get an absolute majority of electoral votes and the decision would be sent to the House of Representatives.**

The rules of the Electoral College system can't be changed without changing the U.S. Constitution. That would require a constitutional amendment to pass both houses of congress and the approval of three-fourths of the states. Of course, that would mean the states with fewer voters would have to give up their proportional voting advantage. Most observers think that is unlikely to ever happen.

Another Electoral College rule was written into the Constitution to keep electors from voting for their own local friends. It says electors cannot vote for a president and vice president from the same state. Although that requirement is still in the Constitution, it has been all but forgotten (in the election of 2000, the Republican nominee for president, George Bush, and the Republican nominee for vice president, Dick Cheney, were both from Texas).

Today the electors in 48 of the 50 states (all except Maine and Nebraska) are *supposed to* (but are not required to) give 100% of the electoral votes to the candidate who wins a state's popular vote. A candidate who wins the popular vote **by even a single vote margin, gets *all* of that state's electoral votes**. That means, when the Electoral College members vote, **the votes the less popular candidate received in the general election are thrown out**. It is as if those people never voted at all.

This **"winner-take-all"** method is not written into the Constitution, and originally only three states used that method, but in the mid 1800s, with the emergence of political parties, more states began to adopt the winner-take-all method in order to give their state more control over the election process. That decision was to shape all presidential elections to come.

As more states were added to the Union, the number of members in the Electoral College increased, and in 1961, a constitutional amendment (the Twenty-Third Amendment) allotted three Electoral College votes to the District of Columbia.

COMMENT

Today, the total number of members of the Electoral College has been permanently set at 538. How many electors each state gets is rebalanced after every census. (Note that the rebalancing is based on the census, not on the number of voters or even on the number of legal residents in the state. As a result, states that have had an influx of illegal immigrants have been gaining electoral votes, and the states whose populations have not been growing in population have been losing electoral votes.)

Half of 538 is 269. That means, to win the presidency, a candidate must win 270 Electoral College votes (the majority).

How Well Has the Electoral College System Worked?

In the nation's 56 past presidential elections, the Electoral College method of selecting the president has concurred with the popular vote 93% of the time.

You might ask, only 93%? Shouldn't the winner of the popular vote *always* get to be president?

Yes, but then there would be no need for the Electoral College. The truth is, as we shall see, the Electoral College system is so archaic and so flawed, it's kind of surprising it only fails seven percent of the time.

The sections that follow describe each of the U.S. presidential elections, what influenced them, and the role the Electoral College played in the outcome.

Chapter Two
Presidential Elections without Popular Elections

The Presidential Election of 1789

In the first presidential election took place in January of 1789. Most citizens of the new country felt **George Washington**, a Virginia planter and slave holder, deserved to be the first president. As commander-in-chief of the **Continental Army,** he had led the country's military through the **Revolutionary War.**

When the members of the Electoral College cast their ballots in the spring of 1789, **Washington got 69 electoral votes and John Adams got 34 electoral votes.** Based on the Electoral College rules at that time, it meant Washington would be president, and Adams, the person who came in second, would be vice president.

There was little or no discord about it because at that time there were no political parties as such, and even most of the other aspiring candidates agreed that Washington should be the first president.

STORY

George Washington was not all that eager to take on the role of being president of the new country. After years of war, some said he might have been content to retreat to his comfortable home in Mount Vernon. But he eventually agreed to serve and made the seven day trip to New York City, then the nation's capital, to be sworn in.

He was carried across the Hudson River in a boat with red, white, and blue decorations, and there were many celebratory cannon firings from the boats in the harbor as he passed. On April 30th, after the politicians had worked out how the formal inauguration should be conducted, Washington was escorted to Federal Hall on Wall Street where he was sworn into office by a local judge. Washington took the oath of office wearing a brown suit (the only one he could find that was made in America), and as befitting a military general, he had a fancy sword hanging from his side.

The Presidential Election of 1792

In the second presidential election, held in 1792, **Washington** again received the most electoral votes and was reelected president. **John Adams** again got the second most votes, which meant he would continue to serve as vice-president.

STORY

When the presidential election of 1792 was held, there were **15 states in the union**, the 13 original states plus two new states, Vermont and Kentucky, which had been added only a short time before the election.

As before, every member of the Electoral College cast his vote for Washington. However, for the first time, there was some **discord among the Federalists** (the only political party at that time). **Treasury Secretary Alexander Hamilton** thought there should be strong federal government, but **Secretary of State Thomas Jefferson** disagreed: he felt the power should lie with the states.

The dispute arose over Hamilton's creation of a national bank and his proposed stronger role of the federal government in the economy. In response, Jefferson, along with **James Madison**, a U.S. Congressman from Virginia who had participated in the development of the U.S. Constitution, put together a new political party known as the **Democratic-Republi-**

cans. **George Clinton**, the governor of New York, allied with them and the new party put his name up as a vice-presidential candidate against Adams. He got very few votes, and in fact, some of the electors that favored the Democratic-Republican position voted instead for Jefferson

It was later learned that Washington had been thinking about retiring after his first term, but when the dissonance within the Federalist Party arose, he decided to run for another term in order to try to bring the two sides together. He was unable to do that, and the "states rights" versus a strong centralized government argument continued.

In 1792, only two states, Maryland and Pennsylvania allowed popular voting, but the concept of a general election was becoming established, and in future elections, more and more voters would demand the chance to cast a vote for their national leader, even if the Electoral College made their vote meaningless.

The Presidential Election of 1796

In the third presidential election, George Washington chose not to run for reelection. As a result, there *was* contention for the office, and as a result, political parties were to play a major role in this election. Vice President John Adams ran for the office as a representative of the **Federalist** Party. Former Secretary of State Thomas Jefferson and Senator Aaron Burr ran on the **Democratic-Republican** ticket.

STORY

The Federalist Party—originally the only American political party—believed the United States should maintain good relations with Britain. They had negotiated, in 1794, a treaty with Britain that became known as the Jay Treaty.

The **Democratic-Republicans** were strongly opposed to the Jay Treaty as well as most of the other Federalist policies.

The Federalists found most of their support in New England and in the larger cities, while **the Democratic-Republicans found support in the rural south.**

In seven of the states, Connecticut, Delaware, New Jersey, New York, Rhode Island, South Carolina, and Vermont, the electors were chosen by the state legislatures. That meant **whichever party controlled a state's legislature controlled the selection of state's electors.**

In some states, elections were held to vote for electors (after the electors said which candidate they were backing).

In Kentucky, Maryland, North Carolina, and Virginia, the voters in each district **got to vote for one elector.**

Georgia and Pennsylvania held a statewide election to select electors. Massachusetts, New Hampshire, and Tennessee used a combination of general election approaches.

The political leaders of the states were not bound by the outcome of those popular votes, but they served as a guideline as to who the people wanted.

In 1796, for the first time, the vote of the Electoral College was close, with 71 votes going to Adams and 68 going to Jefferson. By the rules in place at that time, it meant John Adams would named be president, and his opponent, Thomas Jefferson, would be vice president. It would be **the only time in U.S. history that the president and the vice president came from different parties.**

Chapter Three
Political Parties Evolve

The Presidential Election of 1800

Details of the 1800 presidential election read like a fictional novel of intrigue, and much of the intrigue was due to the structure of the Electoral College. With the advent of popular voting in some states, a few of the candidates actually campaigned. They got on their horses (literally as well as figuratively) and set out to meet the voters. Today, we are so used to national presidential campaigning it is hard to imagine that not much national campaigning took place in the early presidential elections. Politics was something that was usually done in Philadelphia (the Capital of the nation at that time).

The emergence of two opposing political parties set the stage for a new level of antagonism in the 1800 election. **The Federalist party put up John Adams** and Charles Pickney for vice president; **the Democratic-Republican party put up Thomas Jefferson** and Aaron Burr for vice president.

Most of the antagonism was over the Federalist's continuing alignment with Britain and their plan to build up a centralized federal government and create an army. There was a concern that the Federalists wanted to create a military in order to help Britain in its ongoing war with France. Despite the Federalist's well-entrenched position in the seat of national power, **the Democratic-Republicans were better organized at the local level**.

STORY

In 1800, there was a long and bitter campaign for electoral votes. The campaign established many of the campaigning methods we see in modern presidential elections, including the invention of **the smear campaign.** Jefferson was seen as a philosopher, so the Federalists tried to paint him as being against religion. They claimed God was on their side and that a vote for Adams was a vote for God and a religious presidency, while **a vote for Jefferson would be a vote against God**.

In return, the Democratic-Republicans tried to paint the Federalists as **against the common man** and in favor of the rich and powerful (sound familiar?). They also attacked the **Alien and Sedition Acts** that had been passed by the Federalists in congress and signed by the Federalist President Adams. The acts, supposedly enacted because of a perceived threat from France made it more difficult for immigrants to become U.S. citizens, and gave the president the power to deport immigrants if they were deemed "dangerous to the peace and safety of the United States." The acts also gave the president the power to limit freedom of speech, again if in the president's opinion such speech was "dangerous to the peace and safety of the United States." The Democratic-Republican attack on the acts was fairly successful because many citizens felt the acts went too far, especially when most people felt the chance of an attack from France was unlikely. The Democratic-Republicans said some aspects of the acts were clearly unconstitutional in that they violated the first amendment which states, "Congress shall make no law respecting an establishment of religion, or prohibiting the free exercise thereof; or abridging the freedom of speech, or of the press; or the right of the people peaceably to assemble, and to petition the Government for a redress of grievances."

However, **all of the members of the Supreme Court had been appointed by Washington and were seen as Federalists.** Therefore, most people felt there was no chance of getting the

Supreme Court to overturn the acts even if they were blatantly unconstitutional.

Jefferson came right out and said **the acts had been created as a way to keep the Federalists in power** by quashing any criticism. In fact, the Federalists did use the acts and the threat of war to restrict what newspapers printed. They had some newspaper editors arrested and some newspapers were shut down. The newspapers that were shut down were almost always publications that leaned toward the Democratic-Republicans. That fact was especially important because newspapers were just beginning to play a more important role in elections than word of mouth.

One result of the Democratic-Republican fight against the Alien and Sedition Acts was that they had considerable success in getting the newly arrived immigrants on their side, especially those from France and Ireland. It was the first election in which candidates tried to appeal to **special interest groups**.

In 1800, there was a great deal of focus on the Electoral College. Both sides saw the flaws in the Electoral College system and so they tried to manipulate those flaws to their own advantage. Both political parties also promised significant political favors to states that could swing electoral votes their way.

One or the more notable manipulations of electoral votes occurred during this 1800 election. Virginia was one of the states in which the voters **in each congressional district** voted for one elector. Thomas Jefferson realized that if his home state of Virginia would have allocated **all** of its electoral votes to him in the 1796 election, he would have been elected president. Therefore, before the 1800 election, he convinced the Virginia state legislature to **change to a system in which the candidate that won the most electors, got all the electors**. It became known as the **winner-take-all** system of allocating electoral votes. Other states realized they would have to do the same or else states that used the winner-take-all method would have more power in presidential elections than they did. Over the next fifty years, the winner-take-all method gradually became the standard way of allocating electoral votes. **Today, only Maine and Nebraska allocate electoral votes proportionally.**

STORY

In 1800, each state could choose its own election day. Therefore, the election that year went on for seven months. The last state to vote was South Carolina, and the word went out that Adams and Jefferson were tied in the Electoral College. The electors from South Carolina were solidly behind the Democratic-Republican party, meaning Jefferson and Burr were sure to win the national election. Therefore, a plan was hatched to have the South Carolina electors withhold one vote from Burr to make sure Jefferson would be president and Burr would come in second, making him the vice president (remember, at that time, members of the Electoral College had to vote for two candidates). No one knows what went wrong, but all of the South Carolina electors ended up voting for *both* Jefferson and Burr meaning the tie vote was maintained, and that meant neither candidate had a majority. As stipulated in the Electoral College section of the Constitution, the decision about who would be president was sent to the House of Representatives.

One simple solution would have been for Burr to withdraw from consideration, but he refused.

When the election of the president goes to the House of Representatives, in order to be elected president, **a candidate has to get an absolute majority of the states** (not a majority of the representatives). That meant, nine of the sixteen states would have to come to an agreement about who they wanted to be president.

The **lame duck** Federalists in the House of Representatives did not have enough power to swing the election their way, but they did have enough votes to keep the Democratic-Republicans from electing their preferred candidates.

Ballot after ballot was taken with no clear winner. Days went by with no movement by either side.

At some point, the Federalists began to vote for Burr, apparently taking on an **anybody-but-Jefferson** attitude. It was clear, if this went on, nobody was ever going to win. **It was quite possible that there would be no president in 1800**. That presented a dire situation because the Constitution had no contingency for such an outcome (and still doesn't today).

After 34 ballots with neither side budging, everybody in Congress realized **the Electoral Collage system was a complete failure**. But because the process was mandated by the U.S. Constitution, Congress couldn't do anything about it. To change the Electoral College system, they would have had to pass a bill to amend the Constitution and get three-fourths of the states to ratify it. They knew the South would not give up the advantage they had in the Electoral College, so that was not a viable option.

Meanwhile, word about the stalemate in the House of Representatives was leaking out. People were upset about the whole flawed Electoral College system of electing a president. First, the people had not had any say in the election, and now their representatives in Congress seemed to be engaged in partisan squabbling that was going nowhere.

In Congress, there were rumors of armed bands of citizens marching on the capital to take things into their own hands. It was said they were coming to demand, by force of arms if need be, that Jefferson, the candidate most of them had voted for, be named president.

Finally, in response to what was clearly turning out to be dangerous situation, Jefferson approached the Federalist leaders and gave them assurances that he would not completely wipe out everything they had accomplished during the twelve years they had been in power. In response, in preparation for the 35th ballot, Federalist Party leader Alexander Hamilton (who strongly disliked Burr) allowed a few moderate Federalists to change their votes from Burr to Jefferson, and finally, Jefferson was elected president. Burr, having come in second, had to settle for the vice presidency.

It has often been said that the framers of the Constitution anticipated that no one candidate would get the required number of electoral votes so **the election of the president would generally be decided by the House of Representatives**. The problem was, they **hadn't considered the possibility that political parties would emerge**. They couldn't have realized that political parties would complicate the presidential election process by fighting with each other for advantage.

However, the framers of the Constitution did provide a mechanism for changing it through **an amendment process**. But they didn't want the Constitution they had so carefully crafted to be easy to change, so they stipulated that it would take agreement in Congress *and* agreement among three-fourths of the states to change it. They couldn't have realized how hard it would be to get that many states to agree on anything.

Chapter Four
Flaws in the Electoral College System

The decidedly messy **presidential election of 1800** initiated a debate in Congress about how to "fix" the Electoral College system. The debate was wide ranging and often contentious but despite the obvious flaws in the system, **the politicians of that era still did not want the decision about who would be president to be in the hands of the people. In the end, the only thing they changed was to stipulate that the electors** should make separate choices for president and vice-president.

Many of **today's politician still do not want the people to be able to vote to elect the president directly.** The reason is that whichever political party controls the smaller-population states still has much to gain by keeping the Electoral College system.

COMMENT

When the first few presidents were chosen, **only a few states held general elections**. The decision about who would be president was pretty much up to the political leaders in the states. Then they selected electors who would vote that way.

Although Americans now take the election of a president very seriously, voting for the president in an public election is not even mentioned in the Constitution. However, some states (not all) have passed laws that say the members of the state's slate of electors **have to** vote for the winner of that state's general presidential election. However, the most the state can do is levy a fine on an elector who disobeys that *suggestion.* (Some legal scholars say such laws are unconstitutional because there is nothing in the Electoral College section of the

U.S. Constitution that says an elector has to vote in any specified way.)

Although there is much ado about today's presidential elections, and untold amounts of money are spent on trying to get
Americans to vote for one candidate or another, the results of
that voting have no legal status.

No matter who the citizens of the country vote for, members of the Electoral College can vote for anybody they want
to. Over the years, many electors have ignored the popular
vote and done just that.

The most glaring problem with the Electoral College system is
that sometimes it does not agree with choice the voters made in
the general election.

So why haven't the people risen up to demand an end to the
Electoral College? Hard to say. It's probably just because we tend
to forget about things if they seem to be working "all right." Only
when things go wrong, do we get riled up and want to do something about it.

COMMENT

The presidential elections of 1796 and 1800, the young nation's first nationally contested elections, revealed **the flaws in
the Electoral College system**.

The most serious flaws are:

**1. There is nothing in the Electoral College section of the
Constitution about being guided by the popular vote.** In fact,
there is nothing in the Constitution at all about general elec-

tion by the people. It simply says "the states" will select the electors.

2. Under the Constitution, electors are not required to vote for the candidates chosen by the people. That means electors can, and sometimes do, vote for their own personal preference instead of voting for the candidate preferred by the political party that named them as electors (see the later section on "faithless electors").

3. The current Electoral College winner-take-all system may influence how people vote. Because of the winner-take-all system, if the pre-election polls show that most of the voters in a state are clearly planning to vote for one candidate, there is little point for the people in that state to vote for any presidential candidate.

4. A viable third-party candidate can change the outcome. In the presidential election of 2000, most people believe third-party candidate Ralph Nader took enough votes away from Al Gore in Florida to cost him the presidency even though he won the nationwide general election by more than half a million votes. Under the Electoral College system, it's surprising that hasn't happened more often.

5. A viable third-party candidate could send the decision about who becomes president to the House of Representatives. According to the U.S. Constitution, a candidate has to get an **absolute majority** of all electoral votes to win the presidency. In a close election, if a third-party candidate gets some Electoral College votes, it would make it hard for any candidate to get an absolute majority. In that case, the decision about who would be the president would go to the House of Representatives, and whichever party happens to be in the majority in the House at that time will undoubtedly determine which candidate gets to be president, no matter how the people voted. In the past, third-party candidates *have* gained some Electoral College votes, but those elections were not close. It seems likely that sooner or later, a strong third-party candidate will throw the election to the House of Representatives.

6. States with smaller populations have proportionally more electors than states with larger populations. Because even the smallest states are guaranteed under the Constitution to get at least three electoral votes, those states have a greater say in who will get to be president and vice president.

Because the design of the Electoral College gives more electoral voting power to the smaller-population states, a vote for president by a Wyoming resident counts about four times more than a vote by a California resident.

That advantage was critical in the presidential election of 2000. Although **Al Gore won the 2000 presidential general election by 543,895 votes,** the states with smaller populations, added together, had more Electoral College votes.

It was the fourth time in U.S. history in which the candidate that won the popular vote didn't get to be president.

As you might expect, after the drawn-out battle in the House of Representatives with Burr refusing to cooperate, Aaron Burr was no longer looked on as favorably by the Democratic-Republicans. As a result, he was given little to do during his four-year reign as vice president, and when Jefferson ran for reelection in 1804, he dumped Burr in favor of New York Governor **George Clinton**.

STORY

The presidential campaign of 1800 saw, for the first time, **inflammatory, personal attacks** on the good names of the candidates. Personal attacks were not taken as lightly back then as they are now, and as a result, they **often resulted in duels**.

After the 1800 election, a series of letters were circulated accusing Aaron Burr of various despicable acts.

After Jefferson replaced Burr with **Clinton** to be his running mate, Burr declared himself a candidate for governor of New York. Alexander Hamilton, the former Secretary of the Treasury, campaigned aggressively against Burr, and as a result, Burr was defeated in his quest to be the governor of New York.

The insults continued even after the election until eventually, **Burr challenged Hamilton to a duel.** Hamilton accepted, and on the morning of July 11, 1804, while Burr was still finishing out his term as vice president, the dueling parties were taken by boat to New Jersey (to avoid the anti-duel laws of New York state).

There is disagreement about exactly what happened because everyone present was instructed to turn away before shots were fired. The idea was that if they didn't directly see what happened, they couldn't be brought into court to testify about it.

What is known is that Burr killed Hamilton with a single shot from his pistol.

Burr, the vice-president of the United States, was never prosecuted for killing Hamilton.

Chapter Five
Presidential Politics Evolves

The Presidential Election of 1804

Although there was trouble brewing in Europe at the time of the presidential election of 1804, it was a period of relative peace in the United States. The American shipping trade had been further developed under President Jefferson, which resulted in an improved economy, and his successful negotiation and completion of the Louisiana Purchase was widely seen as a great achievement.

Therefore, Jefferson, with his new vice-presidential candidate, George Clinton, was elected over **Charles Cotesworth Pinckney**, a Federalist from South Carolina.

STORY

In 1803, President Thomas Jefferson initiated a deal with France to purchase a huge tract of land that became known as **the Louisiana Purchase**.

Jefferson was not sure at first whether or not he had the legal power to purchase land from a foreign government. However, he eventually decided it would be the best way to protect the port of New Orleans through which a great deal of the nation's farm produce passed.

After Spain transferred *some* of the territory west of the Mississippi to France, Jefferson undertook to buy land from France in and around New Orleans.

Napoleon knew that his ongoing conflicts with Britain would eventually lead to war, so he needed all the money he could get. Therefore, he proposed to sell **all** of France's land west of the Mississippi to the United States for the total sum of 15 million dollars (about 3 cents an acre).

There was resistance in Congress over the deal, but the Southern states favored it as long as Jefferson, a slave holder, agreed to allow the institution of slavery to expand into the new territory.

Eventually, the deal was made and the United States transferred three million in gold to France as a down payment and issued bonds for the other twelve million.

The U.S. assumed the new land stretched from the Gulf of Mexico in the south and into Canada to the north and all the way from the Mississippi River to the Rocky Mountains in the West. However, Spain disputed the sale and continued to claim it owned that land.

When Jefferson funded the Lewis and Clark expedition to map the new territory, Spain sent troops to try to stop them, but they could never find the Lewis and Clark party.

Following river routes and with the guidance of friendly Indians, Lewis and Clark eventually made it all the way to the West Coast near what is now Portland, Oregon.

With the threat from Spain still looming, Jefferson established forts in several places along the route to secure the new territory.

The new lands were to play a key role in three future conflicts, the Indian Wars, the War of 1812, and the Civil War.

The Presidential Election of 1808

By 1808, the nomination of presidential candidates was still in the hands of members of Congress. After President Jefferson decided to retire, a caucus of the Democratic-Republicans nominated Secretary of State James Madison of Virginia, with George Clinton as the vice-presidential nominee.

A caucus of the Federalists again nominated General Charles Cotesworth Pinckney of South Carolina, with former U.S. Senator **Rufus King** of New York as the vice-presidential nominee.

STORY

Although the nominations for president in 1808 featured the "usual suspects," men that had been involved in the founding of the new country, the election showed that the nation was evolving toward a desire for a broader selection of candidates. There was more dissonance in the selection of the candidates, and in the end, a great deal of "localism" in the Electoral College.

Virginia "insider," James Madison was selected by the Democratic-Republicans, but they selected a non-Virginian, New Yorker George Clinton, to be his vice-president. Clinton was not so sure he wanted to serve in a continuation of the Jeffersonian "Virginia dynasty." Nevertheless, he allowed them to put his name into nomination as the Democratic-Republican vice-presidential nominee.

There was also somewhat of a revolt in the Democratic-Republican caucus from the so-called "quids," men who supported Monroe rather than Madison and promoted a strict interpretation of the Constitution. They felt the Democratic-Republicans were moving away from the nation's founding principles.

Madison won in the Electoral College, 122 to Pinckney's 47. Clinton got the second most votes and was therefore to be Madison's vice-president, but he also got six votes for president.

The selection of Clinton as vice-president meant that the new president would have to work with an existing vice-president.

The Presidential Election of 1812

During the early part of the 19th century, **the Democratic-Republican party was as dominant** in U.S. politics as the Federalist had been in the first few presidential elections. This was because **the South voted as a block to make sure every new president continued to favor the existing system of slavery.** As a result, the Democratic-Republican presidential candidates were always **slave holders** from Virginia. With the support of *all* the Southern states, they always won easily.

In the election of 1812, Virginia plantation owner, **James Madison,** was nominated for reelection. He chose **Elbridge Gerry**, the former governor of Massachusetts as his running mate.

The Federalists, desperate for a win, supported a dissident Democratic-Republican, **DeWitt Clinton**.

The election campaign, as was becoming the norm, turned out to be mostly about the issue of slavery. But there was also a war going on. Early in the election campaign, the United States had once again declared war on Britain, a war that became known as **the War of 1812**.

The war was popular, and as a result, the people overwhelmingly voted to give Madison a second term (**Americans have a long history of reelecting presidents when a war is under way**).

STORY

The war of 1812, like all wars, changed the political landscape and influenced several of the presidential elections that were to follow. The war started as an outgrowth (some said as a sideshow) of **ongoing battles between two great military powers of that era, Britain and France**. Much of their war was being fought on the high seas, and when Britain tried to blockade France, trade ships from the United States sometimes got caught up in the conflict.

In the early 1800s **Napoleon Bonaparte was running roughshod over Europe**, but Br**itain ruled the seas**. Britain put together an alliance of countries against Bonaparte's France, and in the early months of 1812, they **began to capture American trade ships**. Britain claimed the trade ships were helping the French, if only to re-supply France with needed goods. The American trade ships were taken as the spoils of war, and **the captured sailors were forced to serve on British warships**.

In response, on the first day of June in 1812, **the United States shocked the world by declaring war on Britain**. It was a reaction not only to the taking of American ships, but also a reaction to a perceived violation of America's neutrality in the European conflict. President Madison declared Britain's actions were an affront to America's honor.

Although America's declaration of war on Britain surprised many people throughout the world, the U.S. had some ongoing unsettled issues with Britain that played a part in it. For one thing, Britain had been trying to thwart the American expansion into American western territories that the British wanted for themselves. They were arming the western Indians, trying to get them to organize against the United States.

In addition, there were many in **the U.S. government that hoped not only to expand into the West, but also into Canada**. Toward that end, one of the first American acts in the war was to invade Canada. American forces under General Hull, the governor of Michigan territory, **invaded Canada** north of Detroit. However, the attack was not well coordinated and **the British not only easily repelled it, but in response attacked Detroit. Within a month, General Hull was forced to surrender Detroit to the British.**

Several sea battles ensued, with American ships faring surprisingly well, but the land battles did not go so well. When De Witt Clinton, the governor of New York, **sent troops into Canada** near Niagara Falls, they were soon forced back and became trapped at the edge of the Niagara River with no way to cross back into the United States. Three hundred Americans were killed and nearly a thousand were taken prisoner.

Although the war wasn't going so well for the Americans, the people were mostly behind Madison. Although many Americans think their national anthem was written during the Revolutionary War, **the Star-Spangled Banner, was actually written during the war of 1812.** The song's lyrics came from a poem titled "Defence of Fort McHenry" written by a 35-year-old lawyer named Francis Scott Key. He wrote the poem soon after he witnessed the British Navy's 25-hour bombardment of Fort McHenry, a large fort built in 1798 to defend Baltimore Harbor. At the time, the poem was sung to the tune of a British song written for a men's social club in London. (With that tune more or less intact, **117 years later, in 1913, the song was declared to be the national anthem of the United States.**)

In the War of 1812, even pirates played a role. Realizing that the U.S. was outmatched in naval power, the U.S. government offered to commission any armed vessel that was willing to help, even pirate vessels.

The famous pirate, Jean Lafitte, had been operating several smuggling ships out of New Orleans and had only recently been forced to retreat to an out-of-the-way bay farther south.

A few months after the U.S. declared war on Britain, the British sent a delegation to try to recruit Lafitte to their side. They offered Lafitte and his men British citizenship and land in British areas of the western part of North America if they would fight against the Americans. Lafitte was a good enough tactician to see that the Americans held the land and therefore the advantage. He turned down the offer (and surprisingly didn't kill the envoys).

When **the British mounted an offensive against New Orleans**, Andrew Jackson brought troops to repel them.

The city was in dire straits and Jackson was outnumbered. He had only two ships and a few thousand unseasoned troops. When he learned Lafitte had many ships and seasoned fighting men, Jackson approached him with a deal: **if the pirates would help defend the city, Jackson promised them full pardons**. After the pirate agreed, Jackson managed to convince the Louisiana legislature to make the pardons official.

It is said that Lafitte's trained fighting men, and the pirates' knowledge of the area, were instrumental in the defense of the New Orleans. (By the way, just to make sure everyone knew he was still a pirate at heart, Lafitte went back to pirating after the war was over.)

After **Napoleon's infamous failure to invade and hold Russia** (he invaded Russia with 400,000 troops but came back with only 40,000), several countries united against France, and by 1814 Napoleon was defeated. Britain and France signed a peace treaty, and that put an end to the issues that had led to the War of 1812. The United States and Britain decided to call it a stalemate, and the two countries signed **the Treaty of Ghent** on the day before Christmas, 1814.

However, the treaty was signed in Europe and as a result, the news that the war was over had to come to America by ship. And even after the news of the treaty had reached the East Coast, given the lack of rapid communications during that era, especially in the West, **the news took over two months to reach all the troops that were still fighting**. The last major battle of the war, a British victory at the second Battle of Fort Bowyer at Mobile Bay, Alabama, took place on February 11, 1815.

Although the war was a stalemate with no territorial gains or losses, it did bring about **a feeling of national pride and unity**. And when the U.S. attempts to annex Canada ended, it also marked the beginning of the "**era of good feelings**" between the U.S. and Britain.

The Presidential Election of 1816

In **1816**, yet another member of the slave-holding "ruling class" of Virginia, **James Monroe**, won easily. He was the last U.S. President to have borne arms in the Revolutionary War.

STORY

At the beginning of 1815, there was a secret meeting of Federalist representatives from Connecticut, Rhode Island, Massachusetts, New Hampshire, and Vermont who were **tired of Virginia slave holders always being elected president** because of the bias in the design of the Electoral College. They were also unhappy with the prosecution of what they called "Madison's war."

There was much disagreement at the meeting, with some representatives even suggesting secession. The main unifying force was they all wanted amendments to the Constitution and changes to the Electoral College that would give them more of a voice in the country.

However, in the end, the Federalists didn't have much of a chance in the election. The people supported the war, and they didn't seem to care very much that the Southern slave holders were ruling the country.

The only real contention regarding the Electoral College was whether the electoral votes of the new state of Indiana should be counted. For some reason, Representative John W. Taylor of New York objected to including Indiana's electoral votes. He was voted down and the votes of Indiana *were* counted.

The Presidential Election of 1820

By **the election of 1820**, the Federalist party was no more. Democratic-Republican **James Monroe ran for reelection unopposed**. It would be the last time any candidate was to run for president unopposed.

After the War of 1812, politics in the early 1800s seemed relatively calm. There were ongoing troubles with the Indians as more and more western lands were developed, either pushing the Indians farther west or forcing them onto reservations.

STORY

In 1820, **the issue of slavery was dividing the people**: more and more people of the United States were saying slavery was not only inhuman, but it was also unconstitutional. America, they said, was supposed to be the land of the free, and yet slavery was still the law of the land in a time when most other countries were outlawing it.

France had officially abolished slavery (Napoleon did however enslave some of the citizens of countries he invaded.) Even **Russia and other eastern European countries had abolished slavery** many years before. **Denmark and Norway had abolished slavery**, and even declared the slave trade illegal. In 1807, the British not only abolished slavery, their ships began stopping slave ships and arresting their captains. It is estimat-ed that **the British anti-slave operation freed more than 150,000 captured Africans**. American's neighbors, **Canada and Mexico had either abolished slavery or were in the process of doing it district by district**.

The constant **contention over the issue of slavery contin-ued as the nation expanded westward**. The Southern states tried to enact laws that made slavery of African-Americans le-gal in any new western state that wanted to join the Union, but the Northern states fought against it. The **Missouri Compro-mise** of 1821 maintained the balance of slave states and free states, which meant slavery would not be as big an issue in the upcoming elections as many had feared.

Chapter Six
The Politics of Slavery

Dissonance over the issue of slavery had been brewing in the United States ever since the country declared its independence from Britain. By the early 1800s, it became the predominant issue in presidential politics.

Many Northerners were outraged at the very idea of slavery, saying it was contrary to the United States Bill of Rights. Those in favor of slavery pointed out that there was no specific mention of slavery in the U.S. Constitution. That was because **many of the framers of the Constitution, including George Washington, John Adams, Thomas Jefferson, and James Madison were slave owners**.

Whenever new states petitioned to join the United States, it brought the slavery issue into focus. The Southern slave states feared that if new states were allowed to join the Union as free states, the shift of power in Congress might lead to the eventual outlawing of slavery altogether. As a result, **the slave states used their disproportional power in the Senate to keep new states from joining the Union unless they agreed to allow slavery**.

The situation came to a head when Missouri wanted to join the United States. Missouri was the first state to be created out of lands of the Louisiana purchase. Most of the region's citizens had come from the South; therefore, there was an assumption that it would be a slave state. A House of Representatives committee approved Missouri's petition to become a state in 1819, but **James Tallmadge of New York added an amendment specifying Missouri had to be a free state**. Furthermore, his amendment stated that the new state would be prohibited from importing slaves and that all current slaves that had been born in the region would have to be freed when they reached the age of 25. The bill was passed by the House on February 17, 1819. Of course, **the Southern slave states used their disproportionate power in the Senate to vote it down**.

After much contentious debate, as so often happens in politics, a compromise was reached, and the bill was passed. The compromise was that **the northern part of Massachusetts would break off to become a new state (Maine)**, and it would be admitted to the Union as a free state, and at the same time, **Missouri would be admitted as a slave state**. That way, there would be twelve slave states represented in the Senate **which would make sure the twelve Northern free states couldn't pass any anti-slave legislation**. The law also included a stipulation that slavery would not be allowed in any territory north of latitude 36° 30' North (which marked the northern border of Missouri). The law became known as **the Missouri Compromise**.

As is typical of such compromises, neither side was happy about it. Thomas Jefferson said the division of the country created by **the Compromise Line** would eventually lead to the destruction of the Union. John Randolph, a Virginia slave owner himself, denounced the compromise and called Henry Clay, the Speaker of the House, "the great compromiser" (not a complimentary term). He sent plenty of other insults Clay's way, and not surprisingly, soon thereafter, the two met to fight a duel. Although shots reportedly were fired, the word that came back from the dueling ground was that the only injury was to Randolph's clothes (in other words, Clay did fire at Randolph, but it was a near miss).

Regardless of Randolph's stand on slavery, he felt all governing power should be in the hands of the states. He thought states ought to be free to accept or reject federal laws.

STORY

It is interesting to note that despite being a slave owner all his life, Randolph wrote a will that decreed all of his slaves should be freed upon his death. Known as **manumission**, the practice of specifying the freeing of slaves in a will was becoming more common as the debate about slavery heated up.

Randolph's will not only freed his slaves, it also **provided money to be used to resettle his slaves in the free state of Ohio**. After he died, three hundred and eighty three of Randolph's former slaves accepted the offer.

However, at that time, racism was as rampant in Ohio as it was most everywhere else in the country, so when they arrived, they were met by **mobs of angry white men with guns** who drove them farther on west. Sadly, the Ohio land that had been paid for with money from Randolph's will had already been sold off to white men, and **the sellers had run off with the money**. None of the Ohio law enforcement officials were willing to do anything about it, so all the "**Randolph slaves**" could do was move on.

Eventually, many of them were employed by Quakers that were sympathetic to their plight, and the rest either found employment doing odd jobs in the few Ohio counties that would accept them. Many of them moved on farther west and their fate is unknown.

Thomas Jefferson also specified in his will that some of his slaves be freed, but his was a very different story from that of Randolph.

Even as he served as president, it was rumored that Jefferson had been using one of his slaves as a mistress (slave owners using female slaves sexually was not all that uncommon during the slave era). **Modern DNA evidence revealed that a light-skinned slave, Sally Hemings, had bore six of his children**. All of the Jefferson-Hemings children were light-skinned, and although they were legally still slaves, three of them left the Jefferson plantation and lived as white in Northern states. Jefferson did not attempt to retrieve them, and **in his will, Jefferson freed all of the Hemings children**.

The Presidential Election of 1824

The presidential election of 1824 turned out to be contentious. It was to be the **first election in which the candidate that won the most votes--both popular and in the Electoral College--did not get to be president.**

As I noted earlier, after the demise of the Federalist party, the Democratic-Republican Party, dominated by Southern slave holders, pretty much had things their own way, not only in presidential elections, but also in running the country. In all the presidential elections since 1796, the winner had been a member of the Democratic-Republican Party. But by 1824, the people of the country were becoming disillusioned with the brand of "**insider politics**" that had become the norm. That disillusionment was soon to loosen the Democratic-Republican party's grip on political power.

Following the established precedent of serving only two terms, in 1824, **President Monroe chose not to run for reelection**. He said he was ready to retire to his estate at Monroe Hill near Charlottesville, Virginia (his estate is now part of the campus of the University of Virginia).

As a result, **the 1824 election season** began, just as it had for all prior elections since the demise of the Federalist Party, with a **Democratic-Republican Congressional nominating caucus** (known then as the "**King Caucus**") being held to decide who would be the next president and vice president. For president, they selected yet another Southern slave holder, **William Harris Crawford** of Georgia, but for vice president, they selected **Albert Gallatin** from the non-slave state of Pennsylvania.

STORY

The official **Democratic-Republican candidates, Crawford and Gallatin** were not well known at the time of their nomination. Nevertheless, both of them had been in and around politics for much of their adult lives.

In 1803, **Crawford was elected to the Georgia House of Representatives,** and in 1807 he was appointed to the U.S. Senate by the Georgia legislature (**at that time, U.S. senators were not elected by the people but were appointed by state legislatures**). In 1813, President James Madison had appointed Crawford to serve as minister to France. He served in that post until the end of the War of 1812, and when he returned from France, Madison appointed him Secretary of War. Later he was named Secretary of the Treasury. He remained in that position until, despite serious health problems, he was nominated to be a candidate for president.

Albert Gallatin's story is a more complex and interesting one. Born into a wealthy and influential family in Switzerland, he studied at the elite Academy of Geneva where he discovered the philosophy of Jean-Jacques Rousseau and Physiocracy (the belief that the wealth of nations is based on the land and agriculture).

In 1880, at age 19, he began hearing about the type of democracy that was being undertaken in the United States. Like many other young Europeans, he was fascinated with this new experiment in democratic government and soon set out to see it for himself.

In America, he tried various business ventures without much success, so he had to make his living teaching French. Eventually, he was able to use his family's influence to get a position at Harvard College. That didn't last long. He again set out to make his fortune in various businesses from farming to retailing to glass making. At one point, in response to the perceived threat from France, the Commonwealth of Pennsylvania called out to its militia and Gallatin signed a contract to make muskets for them. That didn't turn out to be very profitable either.

But **Gallatin had always had an interest in politics, and in 1793, he lobbied for an appointment to the U.S. Senate**, aligning himself with the Democratic-Republicans and against the Federalists.

He was appointed to the Senate, but the Federalists protested his appointment, saying he had not been a citizen of the United States for a long enough period to be a senator.

It went to a vote, and **the Federalists used their voting power to remove him from the Senate**. But he did not go without at fight, and it was his battle to stay in the Senate and his impassioned oratory that brought him some attention, especially from the anti-Federalist forces. (One outcome of his battle to stay in the Senate was that the proceedings of the Senate, for the first time, had to be made public.)

Back home in Pennsylvania, he played a role in **the Whiskey Rebellion**, a protest against a new tax on whiskey that grew violent. When **the government sent in the Army to put down the protest**, Gallatin used his notoriety and his skillful oratory to calm the situation.

As a result, **he was elected to House of Representatives in 1795 where he became an anti-Federalist leader of the Democratic-Republicans**. From then on, he held various positions in the government until 1824 when he was nominated to be a candidate for vice president by the Democratic-Republican congressional caucus.

With the people crying out for more open politics, some politicians in the Democratic-Republican party saw opportunity. Many decided against participating in the "king making" party caucus. To the great surprise of the party leaders, **only 66 of the party's 231 members showed up**. The caucus went ahead and nominated

Crawford and Gallatin, but the lack of party participation was a sign of things to come.

Soon after the "official" Democratic-Republican caucus had nominated Crawford and Gallatin, three other Democratic-Republicans, **John Quincy Adams**, **Henry Clay**, and **Andrew Jackson** defied the party leaders and made it known *they* wanted to be president.

STORY

The unofficial Democratic-Republican candidates, John Quincy Adams, Henry Clay, and Andrew Jackson were better known than Crawford and Gallatin. Adams was the son of the former president. Reportedly, he suffered from depression and was unsure of himself and not all that interested in politics. Nevertheless, he followed in his father's footsteps by serving as a foreign minister in several European countries.

Upon his return, he was still not sure he wanted to get involved in politics, but friends of his father pushed him in that direction. In 1802, he was elected to the Massachusetts State Senate.

That same year, he ran as the Federalist candidate for the United States House of Representatives, but he lost. Nevertheless, the Federalists soon got him appointed to the U.S. Senate where he served until 1808. As a senator, **he angered the Federalists who had appointed him by supporting the Louisiana Purchase which they were against**.

The Federalists, who controlled the Massachusetts legislature, decided to replace him. In response, **Adams became a Democrat-Republican**.

When James Madison, a Democratic-Republican, had been elected president, he appointed Adams as foreign minister to Russia. Adams was accompanied in Saint Petersburg by his wife Louisa, and it was said at the time she made up for his lack of charm in social situations. In fact, she soon became a favorite invitee at the tsar's parties.

By 1818, Adams was back in the U.S. serving as Secretary of State in the cabinet of Democratic-Republican President James Monroe.

With the election of 1824 drawing near, and it looking more and more like the election was going to be wide open, the New England Democratic-Republican party went looking for a "favorite son" candidate. Their choice fell to Adams, and eventually he was forced to accept their nomination.

Henry Clay was from a Virginian family who owned a large number of slaves. But Henry was not interested in the life of the plantation owner and instead decided to become a lawyer even though he had no formal education in the law. To learn about the law he secured an appointment as an assistant to the Virginia State Attorney where he learned about courtroom proceedings *and* about politics.

In 1797, he moved to Kentucky to practice law on his own. In Kentucky, everyone agreed he had a knack for politics and oratory, and in 1803, he was elected to the Kentucky General Assembly. It wasn't long before he was appointed by the Kentucky legislature to the U.S. Senate even though he was only 29 years old (the Constitution requires U.S. senators to be over the age of thirty). No one seemed to notice, or if they did, they didn't care.

In 1807, Clay returned to Kentucky where he was soon elected Speaker of the Kentucky House of Representatives.

However, his aggressive approach to lawmaking angered several members of the legislature, and he was involved in some scuffles on the floor of the House. One such scuffle resulted in **Clay challenging a legislator named Humphrey**

Marshall to a duel. The rules of the duel were that each man would get three shots. One of Clay's shots grazed Marshall's chest, and one of Marshall's shots hit Clay in the thigh. Both men survived and honor was served.

In 1810, the Kentucky state legislature again appointed Clay to the U.S. Senate. But one year later, he was elected to the U.S. House of Representatives.

Because of his reputation, he was elected Speaker of the House on the first day in office. Thereafter, he was re-elected five times to the House, and each time, he was reelected as Speaker of the House. It is important to note that Clay completely changed the role of the Speaker of the House from parliamentarian (merely a keeper of the rules) to political leader. He was the first U.S. Speaker of the House to appoint his allies to key committee chairmanships as a way of controlling what became law and what did not. He also used his position to support hostilities against Britain, which, in time, turned into the War of 1812.

By 1812, **Clay was becoming quite prosperous and owned a 600-acre tobacco and hemp plantation and 60 slaves of his own**.

In 1816, he became president of the **American Colonization Society, a group that wanted to send free blacks back to Africa**. Under Clay's leadership, the group founded a colony in Africa called Monrovia. **Clay said the god of nature had decreed against the amalgamation of the black and white races** as proven by the obvious differences of skin color and physical constitution. The main purpose of the group was to deport free blacks because they posed a threat to the practice of slavery, but some abolitionists from the North also got behind the effort.

As the election of 1824 loomed, it became clear that the Democratic-Republican caucus's nomination of Crawford and Gallatin was not receiving wide support. Clay made his bid for the presidency.

Andrew Jackson was the first candidate for president that could be described as an outsider. Although he was, like Clay, a Southerner who owned slaves, he was not part of the Southeast Coast group of political insiders. He was from Tennessee.

Little is known about Jackson's childhood except that his father had died in the Revolutionary War before he was born. His two brothers had also died in the Revolutionary War.

When Jackson was thirteen, he joined up with a local militia so he too could fight in the Revolutionary War. They made him a courier, but he was soon **captured by the British and held as a prisoner of war.** He was mistreated, almost starved to death, and contracted smallpox. It left him with a lifelong hatred of the British. Soon after his release, his mother died, leaving him **an orphan at the age of fourteen.**

After that, he was bounced around between relatives, had little education, and worked at various odd jobs. Eventually, he went to North Carolina to study law. Not all that much is known about his studies, or about his early law career, but he was said to have practiced law in the western part of North Carolina, the area that was to become the state of Tennessee.

When Tennessee became a state in 1796, he was **elected as its first representative in Congress.** Meanwhile, he was growing wealthy from investments and from his law practice. He bought up huge tracks of land in Tennessee, and **eventually accrued 150 slaves.**

He also became an active member of the Tennessee militia. During the War of 1812, several Indian tribes banded together, and with the aid of the British, attacked western towns. Jackson took his Tennessee militia into battle against them, and the Indians were repelled. Jackson's rank was raised to major general, and he started to get a national reputation as a capable military leader.

In 1814, when New Orleans came under British attack, Jackson took over command of the region's defense. Many others came to join the defense effort, including **Davy Crockett** and **Sam Houston**, and by the beginning of 1815, the British were routed.

During that conflict, Jackson became widely known as a tough and very strict officer. The word got out that his men called him "**Old Hickory**" (tough as old hickory wood), and the nickname stuck.

By the end of the War of 1812, Jackson was being described as a national hero. He received an official gold medal of thanks from the U.S. Congress, and more than a few political leaders began thinking of him as a potential political candidate. In 1823, the Tennessee legislature appointed him U.S. senator and encouraged him to run for president in the presidential election of 1824.

As the 1824 presidential election campaign progressed, it started to become clear that William Crawford, the Democratic-Republican party's official choice for president, was not fairing well. The campaigning had hardly begun when Crawford suffered a stroke that was said to have been brought on by an overdose of prescribed medication. He recovered well, but it hampered his ability to campaign and gave people doubts about his overall health.

It was only the first of many setbacks faced by the Democratic-Republican party leaders. Adams, the son of the nation's second president, who had formerly been a Federalist, was clearly gathering support from the old Federalists in the Northeast, and Jackson was beginning to look like the people's choice in the South and in the West.

Of the two candidates, the Democratic-Republican party leaders thought Jackson would be the easiest to discredit. They published many articles in Democratic-Republican newspapers that said Jackson had **no real national political experience,** that he was **nothing but a frontier backwoodsman**.

But that didn't work very well because it made the people think of Jackson as "one of them."

Then the Adams backers **said Jackson was a murderer**. They said they had proof that he had executed captured Indians without a trial and had even executed captured British troops. There may have been some truth to those charges, but many people saw those incidents as just part of war, and Andrew Jackson had been, after all, a military hero in Florida and in the War of 1812.

As a last resort, Jackson's political opponents said he had killed men in unfair duels, and that he was an adulterer living with another man's wife.

Although there was some truth to those charges, Jackson's support among the "common men" in the West and the South never wavered. In that era, although adultery was a serious matter and did hurt Jackson's reputation, duels were seen as matter of honor between gentlemen.

STORY

Although killing a man in a duel these days would certainly hurt a presidential candidate's chances of winning an election, it might well have been **a political advantage** in Jackson's time.

Jackson was rumored to have killed many men in duels, and it was a sign of the times that he never disputed the charge. His reputation of having great prowess with a pistol made a lot of the men of that era look up to him (and remember, at that time, only men could vote).

However, had the real truth about his dueling history been known at the time, it would have been considerably less flattering. While it was true that he was hot tempered and quick to challenge a man to a duel, the fact is his duels usually didn't take place. The problem was that he had a habit of challenging men to duels in the heat of the moment, only to find out later that his prospective opponent was a skillful and experienced duelist.

For example, at the tender age of 21, Jackson was trying to learn how to practice law. In one of his first court cases, an experienced lawyer ridiculed Jackson's judicial knowledge. Jackson immediately challenged the man to a duel. The duel was scheduled, but in the meantime, Jackson had learned more about the man's reputation as a duelist and had second thoughts. The details are lost to time, but the outcome on the field of honor was that both agreed to fire into the air.

Over the next several years, other duels were offered, but never took place. But then Jackson made an enemy of John Sevier, the governor of Tennessee. The story is that the two feuded for years until a duel was finally scheduled. However, before the day of the scheduled duel, they happened to meet on the trail. In a scene right out of one of that era's notorious Western "dime novels," Jackson dismounted and pulled out his pistol. Sevier dismounted and drew his sword. Quite a few insults were exchanged before they both got back on their horses and went on their way. The scheduled duel never happened.

The one duel that did happen, was indeed a deadly one. It was again a feud between lawyers, but it came to a head in a bar fight. After the fisticuffs, Jackson challenged a young lawyer named Charles Dickinson to a duel. The duel took place at Harrison's Mill, Kentucky. Unfortunately for Jackson, the young man turned out to be quite a good marksman, and when the command to fire was given, the young man shot Jackson square in the chest. Jackson managed to stay on his feet and shot Dickinson in the stomach, killing him. Jackson survived, but **he was to carry Dickinson's bullet in his chest for the rest of his life.**

The attacks on John Quincy Adams by Jackson's supporters were quite different. They said Adams was out of touch with the people. They called him an **Eastern elitist,** and they said he might even secretly be a royalist. They constantly brought up Adams former involvement with the Federalists.

Those kinds of attacks didn't erode Adams's support in the Northeast and in the urban areas of the country, but they did hurt him with the voters Jackson was reaching out to, the so-called "common man" (and there were a lot more of them).

Meanwhile, one of the best known candidate for president, Henry Clay, was getting left behind. Although he was a well-known politician, it was clear he was not popular among the people. He could only count on his home state of Kentucky, and maybe some additional support from the two neighboring states.

Jackson racked up victories in Alabama, Indiana, Mississippi, North Carolina, Pennsylvania, and Tennessee.

Adams won in the Northeast states, Connecticut, Maine, Massachusetts, New Hampshire, and Rhode Island

It meant the national sentiment was divided by region: Jackson was favored in the rural states by a large margin, but Adams was favored in the more populous states of the Northeast.

The only two states Crawford won were Delaware and Georgia. However, that doesn't mean Crawford was the people's choice in those two states. **Delaware and Georgia did not allow a popular vote. In those states, the electors were chosen by the legislature, and they were therefore Democratic-Republican party loyalists who did their duty and cast their Electoral College votes for whoever the party leaders told them to.**

The final Electoral College vote was Jackson 99, Adams 84, Crawford 41, Clay 37.

Since no candidate had the required absolute majority of 131 electoral votes, the selection of the president once again went to the U.S. House of Representatives. And as stated in the Twelfth Amendment, the House had to choose from the top three candidates.

Interestingly, a vice president *had been* elected in the Electoral College. John Calhoun of South Carolina won the majority of votes for vice president and was therefore elected to that office no matter which of the presidential candidates won.

STORY

Because **Henry Clay** had come in fourth in the Electoral College voting, he was eliminated from consideration. However, he was still the **Speaker of the House**, and that placed him in a position of great influence in the House.

At the time, Inauguration Day was in March. That meant the House should have acted quickly. But they didn't. First, there had to be the usual back room bargaining and arm-twisting. Some **representatives were putting the word out that their votes could be "bought" in exchange for a cabinet post.** or maybe even an important ambassador assignment.

Clay was the best at making such deals. He had been collecting political debts for many years, and now it was time to call them in. His main goal was to set himself up for the next presidential election. He knew Andrew Jackson, having won both the popular vote and the Electoral College vote, would be his main opposition in the next presidential election; therefore, **his goal was to manipulate the vote in the House to make sure Jackson didn't get to be president** this time.

In those days, the usual stepping stone to the presidency was the cabinet position of Secretary of State. Many suspected Clay might try to accomplish his goal by working a deal with Adams. The deal would be that if Clay could convince enough representatives to vote against Jackson, Adams would be elected president, and in exchange, Adams would select Clay as his Secretary of State. **Clay believed that would put him in line for the presidency next time**.

In actuality, **Clay disliked Adams, but he thought he would have a better chance against Adams than Jackson in the next election.**

As soon as the other representatives saw Clay meeting privately with Adams, they knew the deal was on.

Once the deal was made, it was Clay's job to get representatives to change their votes and go for Adams. It wasn't easy because few liked Adams. But **with threats and promises, Clay was able to pull it off**.

The House met to vote on February 9, 1825, and John Quincy Adams won the votes of 13 states, exactly the number needed to win the presidency.

Adams immediately named Clay as his Secretary of State.

Jackson and his supporters were furious. **They called the deal Clay and Adams had made a "corrupt bargain." The term stuck, and in the end, undid all of Clay's attempts to set himself up for the presidency in the next election.**

When the word of the House's vote and the "corrupt bargain" got out, the people who had voted for Jackson were outraged.

They saw him as the rightful president-elect, and they could not be consoled by the politicians telling them that it had all been done according to the rule of law as specified by the Constitution's section on the Electoral College.

Jackson came right out and said the whole thing was a travesty. He and his supporters asked what kind of system it was where the person who won both the popular vote *and* the Electoral College vote did not get to be president. He said the rights of the people had been bartered away, and **called for an immediate end to the Electoral College system** of electing the president. He demanded to know why the nation's most important office should not be elected *directly by the people.*

Although just about everybody agreed that the method of selecting a president was not fair, the smaller-population states were completely united in keeping the Electoral College system. In the first place, the two extra electoral votes each of the smaller states got gave them an advantage in determining who the president would be. And they didn't want to change the system of letting the House of Representatives decide close elections, because if the House decided the presidency, every state got one vote, no matter how large or small the state was. That disproportionate advantage pretty much guaranteed Jackson's demand for an end to the Electoral College system would be ignored by the smaller states. And because such a change would require an amendment to the Constitution and ratification by three-fourths of states, even Jackson knew changing it would never happen.

The dissatisfaction with the results of the election of 1824 led to a significant change in the American political landscape. Jackson declared that he would run again in 1828, and because of the unfairness of how the 1824 election had turned out, many predicted he would win this time.

The senator from New York, Martin Van Buren, saw the people's anger at the way Jackson had been denied the presidency through back-room dealings as an opportunity to enhance his own fortunes. In the 1824 election, he had been a supporter of Crawford, but when it became clear that the people wanted the "outsider" Jackson instead of the usual Washington insider, he switched his allegiance and declared it was time for a new Jacksonian democracy. He said it would be **a democracy of the common man** instead of a political monopoly by the eastern elites (although he himself might accurately have been described as being part of that cadre).

Van Buren and Jackson broke with the all-powerful Democratic-Republican party. (**Modern day Democrats now see that moment as the starting point of the Democratic party, and they claim Andrew Jackson as the party's founder**.)

Leading up to the 1828 presidential election, the so-called **Jacksonian movement** gradually grew in political strength. It was a coalition of farmers and low-wage Irish-Catholic laborers. It was strongest in the states with the largest populations, which in those days included Virginia, New York, and Pennsylvania. This new "**democratic**" party was "for the people" and quite vocally against the "rich and the powerful."

In line with that belief, **they fought to get rid of voting rules that said only men of property, or men who paid taxes, were allowed to vote**. They said all white men should be allowed to vote. It took many more years to accomplish that goal, but by 1850, *nearly* all the "property requirements" had been eliminated in the *majority* of the states.)

The Jacksonian Democrats also believed America had a "**manifest destiny**" to expand throughout the American West, possibly all the way to the Pacific coast. However, they were against the expansion of slavery into the West.

The Jacksonians were against unlimited expansion of centralized federal power, but they could not be called states' righters because they believed the power should be in the hands of the people, not in the hands of the rich and powerful who normally ran politics. They strongly believed **the Electoral College took power away from the people and put it into the hands of powerful politicians**. They were also against the idea that it was the rich and powerful who got to appoint the members of United States Senate. But the South was against direct election of either presidents or senators because **they were afraid the voters in larger states of the North would vote for men who might try to end slavery**.

The Jacksonian democrats favored a *laissez-faire* approach to economics; that is, they believed the federal government should not try to regulate businesses. They also believed in a "**hard money system**" in which only gold and silver could be considered true currency. They were suspicious of banks, and were against the idea of a government bank.

The Jacksonian Democrats were also in favor of the "**spoils system.**" The basic concept of the spoils system was that **to the victor shall go the spoils**; that is, a newly elected government official had the right to fire all of the previous administration's political appointees and bring in their own people.

COMMENT

The Jacksonian Democrats' innovation of **the spoils system is still in place today**. Whenever new presidents come into office, they get rid of a large percentage of the former administration's top-level employees. The newly elected leader mostly brings in party loyalists who helped win the election. The reasoning of the Jacksonian Democrats was that only through the adoption of the spoils system could an administration be held accountable for their failures. It's the "buck stops here" concept, meaning **the president makes all the personnel appointments; therefore he should be responsible for their failures**. However, although modern day presidents still use the spoils system to replace many of the nation's top government officials as soon as they are elected, they now seem less willing to take the blame when things go wrong.

The Presidential Election of 1828

As a result of the national outrage over the fact that Andrew Jackson did not get to be president despite winning the popular vote in 1824 pretty much assured him the win in 1828. He and his running mate, John C. Calhoun from South Carolina, won easily. It would mark the beginning of an era of "**Jacksonian democracy**" that tried to take political power out of the hands of the rich and powerful "elitists."

STORY

In response to Jackson's being elected president in 1828, Henry Clay and John Quincy Adams put together an oppositional coalition in Congress to fight against Jackson's new **Democratic Party**. Eventually, they took on the name "**Whigs**." (There was a Whig party in England that fought against the absolute rule of monarchy, and in America the term had been taken up as a reference to those who fought against tyranny.)

However, at first, the Whigs were unable to persuade the people that their plans for the nation were better than those of the Democrats. For one thing, **they were against the popular idea of westward expansion**, insisting that modernization of the still-undeveloped nation in the East was more important. **They felt Jackson and the Democrats were holding the nation back from modernization.**

The Whigs *did* find support among the professional classes, business owners, and the owners of large plantations, and the Whig's plans to modernize the cities and the nation's manufacturers struck a chord in the cities that depended on manufacturing for their existence.

The Democrats continued to describe the **Whigs as the party of the rich and powerful**, and that message resonated with the Irish-Catholic immigrants that had tended to settle in the eastern cities.

Some Protestant ministers, favoring the Whigs, tried to discredit the Irish-Catholics, telling their congregations that Jackson and his followers were immoral, and that a vote for the Democrats was a vote for immorality. **Protestant reformers railed against drinking and whoring, and they proposed a national prohibition on sales of alcohol that would put an end to what they saw as "the liquor problem" in America.**

Within a generation, the Whig Party was able to put up a candidate in nearly every election, and they gradually began to have more success.

The Whigs main agenda was to create an "**American system**" of rapid industrial growth and government support for manufacturers. **They proposed high tariffs against foreign imports that might compete with American manufactured products.** They were also in favor of government support of banking, and they felt the government should get involved in the expansion of the nation's infrastructure of roads and canals and railroads, anything that would make America more of a manufacturing country instead of an agrarian country.

The Whigs also felt America's educational system was in great need of modernization. They wanted the national government to get involved in creating a better public school system.

It soon became apparent that the main difference between the two political parties was that **the Whigs felt the national government should be stronger** and more involved in developing the future of the nation as a whole, while the Democrats felt such things should be left to the states.

The Presidential Election of 1832

The presidential election of 1832 saw the origination of national nominating conventions. The **Anti-Masonic Party**, the **National Republican Party**, and the **Democratic Party** all held conventions in Baltimore.

STORY

In 1832, most assumed that President Jackson would run for reelection along with his Vice-President, John C. Calhoun. But Jackson had a falling out with Calhoun over the issue of tariffs in Calhoun's home state of South Carolina. The highly protective Tariff of 1828 (nicknamed "the tariff of abominations" by South Carolina detractors) was designed to help American manufacturing win over European manufacturing, but many in the South blamed it for the gradual economic downturn the South had been suffering.

As a result of the disagreement, Jackson dumped Calhoun and replaced him with New Yorker, Martin Van Buren.

The Republicans nominated **Henry Clay**, a slave holder from Kentucky who had served both as a senator and in the House of Representatives. He had also served as Secretary of State under President John Quincy Adams.

Jackson, won the presidency easily, winning 219 of the 286 electoral votes cast. However, a number of other candidates also received electoral votes, mostly from their own states. They included **Hugh L. White**. a Whig from Tennessee who won 47 electoral votes, and Whig **Daniel Webster** who won 23 electoral votes. The electors from South Carolina, refused to vote for Jackson, and instead cast their 11 electoral votes for **John Floyd**, the governor of Virginia, who wasn't even a candidate.

The Whigs still managed to win some cites even though the

Democratic campaigns characterizing them as elites cost them a lot of votes among the poor.

After Jackson was reelected, **the outrage over the Electoral College was soon forgotten.**

New political parties were developed and new ideologies sprang up. For the next decade, the national political argument would be focused on slavery and about how involved the national government should be in people's lives.

The Presidential Election of 1836

In 1836, President Jackson supported his vice-president **Martin Van Buren** for the presidency. Kentucky Senator **Richard Mentor Johnson** was chosen as Van Buren's running mate.

STORY

The selection of Richard Mentor Johnson as the Democratic vice presidential candidate in 1836 was surprising to many because he was known to be having a sexual relationship with one of his female slaves. He was quite open about it. Although it was well known that some slave owners had sex with their slaves, it was not seen as appropriate to discuss it openly.

Johnson's first sexual relationship was with a slave named Julia Chinn. He described her as his common law wife and admitted that he was the father of her two daughters.

When Julia Chinn died in 1833, Johnson started a new relationship with another female slave, but she left him for another man. Johnson sent his men to capture her, sold her at auction, and took up with her sister.

In political circles, there was much talk about Johnson's history of sex with his slaves, and even more talk about his

---

unwillingness to keep quiet about it. As a result, when Van Buren ran for reelection in 1840, the Democratic party refused to endorse Johnson as Van Buren's running mate. Nevertheless, Van Buren stuck with him.

Van Buren was defeated in his bid for reelection, and Johnson went back to Kentucky where, in 1850, he was again elected to the Kentucky House of Representatives.

Johnson saw to it that both of Chinn's daughters were provided with an education and arranged for them both to marry white men. Nevertheless, when Johnson died, the local judge ruled that he left no legal children and divided Johnson's considerable holdings between his brothers.

The Whigs, knowing they would have little chance against Jackson's Democrats, came up with a unique strategy: they nominated several candidates. The hope was to take advantage of a "localism" bias in the Electoral College so that the various Whig candidates could collect enough electoral votes from their home districts to keep Van Buren from getting the 148 electoral votes he would need to win. That would throw the election into the House of Representatives. They nominated **William Harrison**, the popular former U.S. Senator from Ohio, **Daniel Webster**, a U.S. Senator from Massachusetts, **Willie Person Mangum**, a U.S. Senator from North Carolina, and **Hugh L. White**, a U.S. Senator from Tennessee.

The Whig plan almost worked. Van Buren won the election, but he only got 170 electoral votes, two votes more than the required number. Harrison came within a few thousand votes of winning Pennsylvania, which would have given him the state's 30 electoral votes which would have once again sent the decision about who would be president to the House of Representatives

The Presidential Election of 1840

In 1940, **President Van Buren** ran for reelection. However, an **economic panic in 1837** had hurt the U.S. economy and the people blamed it on **the restrictive economic policies of the Jacksonian Democrats**. As is common today, when the economy turns bad, the people vote against whatever political party is in power.

STORY

President Van Buren ran for reelection along with his controversial vice president, **Richard Mentor Johnson.** But his party **refused to go along with the nomination of Johnson** for fear that his sexual exploits with his slaves would be used against them in the general election. However, they couldn't agree on an alternative, and so they nominated no one, something that had never happened before.

The Whigs put up **William H. Harrison** from Ohio, and he chose **John Tyler**, a senator from Virginia to be his vice-president.

STORY

The nomination of Harrison brought the candidate's age into the discussion. He was 67 at the time he was nominated, and that was the oldest major party candidate up to then. Some questioned his ability to preside over the country at what was seen as an advanced age.

Nevertheless, Harrison was seen as a military hero for his role in victories against the Indians in the Northwest Indian War, and in the United States, military heroes have often been popular presidential candidates. Harrison's campaign mainly focused on the economic policies of the Democrats, and that worked. He was able to defeat Van Buren, overwhelming him in the Electoral College, 234 to 60.

However, Harrison died from pneumonia after only 32 days in office, and **Vice President Tyler** served out the rest of his term.

STORY

When **Harrison died after only 32 days in office**, there was no precedent about what to do. The question was, if a president dies in office, should a vice-president take over for a short time until a new president could be elected, or should he serve out the rest of the president's term? And if it is decided that the vice-president gets to serve out the remainder of the presidential term, **should he have all the power of a president, or only be seen as an "acting president."**

Tyler and the Whigs were determined to hold onto the presidency. **Tyler refused to sign any document that referring to him as an** "acting president." However, he was eventually convinced to go through the formal process of being sworn in as president.

Tyler moved into the White House and assumed full presidential powers. Just to make sure, the Whigs got both houses of Congress to adopt a resolution confirming that Tyler was the President of the United States.

That resolution served as the official mechanism for a vice president assuming the office after a president's death, **until the issue was clarified by the 25th Amendment in 1967.**

Tyler's time in the office of the presidency was not without controversy. Although he had been elected as a Whig, Tyler disagreed with many of their proposals, especially their position against the expansion of slavery, and **while he was still serving as president, he was thrown out of the Whig Party.**

The Presidential Election of 1844

The election of 1844 began with the odd circumstance that President Tyler was no longer a member of the party under which he had been elected. Instead of supporting the sitting president, the Whigs chose Henry Clay, a former Congressmen and senator from Kentucky.

Former president, Martin Van Buren, wanted to make another run for the office, but at the Democratic National Convention, he was rejected by the Southern Democrats because he would not pledge to annex Texas and thereby expand slavery into the West. Instead, they again chose a Southerner, James K. Polk, a former Congressman and Governor from Kentucky.

As a result, the issue of slavery soon became the predominate campaign issue.

STORY

In the early 1800s, the Mexican government was having a hard time enforcing their laws in Texas, especially their laws against slavery. They tried imposing stricter control over Texas, including military occupation, but that only encouraged rebellion. In 1835, the Mexican Army rode into Texas in an attempt to quash any attempts at self-government. Texans responded by declaring their independence from Mexico on March 2, 1836. The Texans, under Texas General Sam Houston, soon drove the Mexican army out of Texas. Nevertheless, the Mexican government still refused recognize Texan independence.

In 1844, President Tyler, hoping to make a run for reelection as an independent, declared himself to be the pro-slavery candidate. He pressed the issue by signing a treaty with Texas and he submitted a proposal for the annexation of Texas to the Senate. His plan was to ally with Southern Democrats who would present the North with an ultimatum: support Texas annexation and allow slavery there or risk the chance that the entire South might choose to leave the Union.

When the public found out the Senate was considering such a bill, they saw it as yet another attempt to spread the institution of slavery to the West. Public support of the bill threatened to become a liability to both of the other candidates, so they opposed it. Both Polk and Clay were from Southern slave-holding families, so behind the scenes, they too were in favor of the annexation of Texas as a slave state. Once Tyler had assurances of their support, he dropped out of the race.

In a fairly close election, Polk won over Clay, and that ensured statehood for Texas and the spread of slavery into the Western territories.

Mexico refused to accept the loss of Texas and it led **the Mexican-American War**.

STORY

Unlike the War of 1812, the American people *were not* **solidly behind the Mexican-American War**. Democratic president Polk encouraged **the annexation of Texas** as part of his plan to expand the United States all the way to the Pacific Ocean even though such a plan was almost sure to result in a war with Mexico. Anti-slavery groups, hoping to stop the spread of slavery into the West, were against the annexation of Texas.

One of the main reasons the Texans had declared their independence from Mexico was that the Mexican government had tried to enforce its government policy forbidding the practice of slavery. As soon as the declaration of Texan independence was official, **many of the larger Texas landholders began bringing in slaves from the American Sout**h to use in their farming and ranching enterprises, and by **1845, slavery was a well-established practice in Texas**.

At that time, most of the territories petitioning for statehood were in the North and the Southern states feared there would soon be enough non-slave states to outvote them in Congress. They worried it could mean the end of slavery in the United States.

Mexico had warned President Polk that if Texas was granted statehood, it would definitely lead to war. President Polk sent representatives to Mexico City to try to forestall hostilities, even offering Mexico huge amounts of money as compensation. But Mexico would not negotiate. They felt reclaiming what they saw as the theft of a piece of their country was a matter of national honor.

After the failure of negotiations, **President Polk sent troops to establish a fort on the banks of the Rio Grande river. In response, Mexico sent 2,000 cavalry troops to the area.** Accidentally, they ran into a small U.S. Army patrol, and they killed 16 U.S. soldiers.

In response, President Polk declared, "Mexico has passed the boundary of the United States, has invaded our territory and shed American blood upon American soil." **He demanded Congress grant a declaration of war against Mexico**. After a short, but bitter, debate, they did so with the unanimous support of the Southern Democrats.

Americans were divided over the war. Many in the North felt it was a war designed to spread slavery to the West. But others, knowing that Mexico also controlled California, thought **it might be a chance to grab California as well. There was much talk about "manifest destiny," the belief that the United States should extend from "sea to shining sea."**

The Whigs, including Abraham Lincoln, lobbied against the war. Nevertheless, preparations for battle went on unabated. President Polk soon sent troops into Mexico under the command of **General Zachary Taylor**, and **ordered naval forces to the Mexican coast in support**.

As General Taylor drove deeper into Mexico, Mexican General Santa Ana brought troops north from Mexico City to meet him. After extended fighting, Santa Ana was forced to retreat.

President Polk also sent a second army under General Winfield Scott to invade Mexico by sea. Santa Ana's army rallied to meet that advance, but was again routed.

Scott pushed on deeper into Mexico and soon captured Mexico City. Faced with the possible loss of even more territory, **Mexico had no choice but to surrender**. On February 2, 1848, Mexico signed **the Treaty of Guadalupe Hidalgo**, agreeing to the Texas boundaries specified by the United States.

At the same time, **U.S. forces invaded California, and within a year, they controlled California from San Diego to San Francisco**. On January 13, 1847, the **Treaty of Cahuenga**, signifying the surrender of California, was signed near what is now Los Angeles.

Despite the relatively easy victory over Mexico, the people of the United States were still divided over the war and over the issue of slavery being expanded into the new Western territories.

It is worth noting here that **President Ulysses S. Grant, who fought in Mexico under General Taylor, said in his later memoirs that the Civil War was largely the outgrowth of the Mexican-American war.**

The Presidential Election of 1848

In 1848, the nation was becoming more and more divided over the issue of slavery, which led to the creation of a new political party, the **Free Soil Party** which put up anti-slavery candidates at both the local and national level.

STORY

The Free Soil Party focused on one issue, slavery. After the annexation of Texas had spread slavery to the American West, there was a general assumption that even more states would eventually join the union in the West. The Free Soil Party was determined to keep them from being slave states.

In 1848, the Free Soil party nominated former president, Martin Van Buren, to be their presidential candidate. He ran under the motto, "'Free Soil, Free Speech, Free Labor, and Free Men." **They maintained that slavery was not only fundamentally undemocratic, it was holding the nation back.**

At the New York State Democratic convention, a large number of the delegates walked out because the Democratic party wouldn't take an anti-slavery position. **Many of them joined the Free Soil Party.**

After President Polk decided against running for reelection due to health problems, the Democrats nominated **Lewis Cass**, the former Governor of the Michigan Territory who had been President Jackson's Secretary of War. (In that position, he had implemented the Indian Removal Act of 1830.) **He said he believed it should be up to the people of a territory to decide whether or not they would permit slavery**. That satisfied the Southern Democrats.

Zachary Taylor, a Virginia slave owner, was nominated by the Whig Party. Taylor's position on the issue of slavery was unclear, but he was seen as a war hero, having defeated the Mexican Army in the Mexican-American War, and the voters of the United States had long favored military heroes.

Taylor defeated **Lewis Cass** in yet another close election, with each candidate carrying 15 states. **If Cass had been able to carry New York, the Electoral College vote would have ended in a tie and the decision about who was to be president would have again been sent to the House of Representatives**.

The Presidential Election of 1852

In **the election of 1852**, there was **constant arguing about how to deal with the issue of slavery** at the Democratic presidential nominating convention. When they finally did get around to the nominations, there were four strong candidates and therefore the voting got nowhere. Finally, **Franklin Pierce**, who was not one of the four main candidates, was put up as a compromise candidate and he was eventually selected as the party's nominee. Pierce was from the small state of New Hampshire, a non-slave state. However, he was known to favor allowing slavery to be practiced in the new western states. His main attribute, as far as the Democrats were concerned, was that **he had fought in the Mexican-American War** and had been so valued as a leader of men that he had risen to the rank of brigadier general of volunteers.

The Whigs nominating convention also had to deal with disagreement over the slavery issue. In the end, the party leaders decided to support the **Compromise of 1850,** which was a compromise that forced Texas to surrendered its claim to New Mexico, and allowed California to come in as a free state. However, the South added language to the compromise that **allowed new states to decide for themselves whether to allow slavery** or not. That threatened to overturn the prior **Missouri Compromise** of 1821 which made slavery illegal north of the **Compromise Line** (any territory north of latitude 36° 30' North, which marked the northern border of Missouri). The South was also able to insert a **Fugitive Slave Act** into the compromise, which made it illegal for slaves to run away to the north and specified that if they did, the North had to return them to their rightful owners.

After much contention, the Whigs finally nominated **Winfield Scott, another Virginian from a slave-holding family**. He had made his name as a general in the Mexican-American war. Although his family still owned many slaves, he made it known that **he was against expanding slavery into the West.**

The issue of slavery was to play a big part in the presidential election of 1852. People were note sure of the Whig position on slavery. Scott was a slave owner, but he said he was against expanding slavery into the new Western states. Because Scott's stated position on slavery was not in line with the wishes of the Southern states, he did not get the solid support from Southern voters he expected, and as a result, **Pierce, a relative unknown, won the election.**

STORY

Most people thought **General Winfield Scott** would be elected president simply because he was **a military hero** in the Mexican-American War and in the Indian Wars.

However, the Mexican-American War was not fully supported by most Americans because of the slavery issue in Texas. And there were rumors that his **"victories" over the In-**

dians included almost-unbelievable **cruelty to non-combatant Native Americans.**

Although **most Americans supported the idea of moving the Indians off their land and onto reservations,** the citizens of the East did not support excessive cruelty while doing it. News about the terrible treatment of the Indians leaked out, diminishing Scott's reputation as a military hero.

However, in Scott's defense, it should be pointed out that he was just carrying out policies that had been around for a long time. **A policy of "civilizing" American Indians had been in place since the presidency of George Washington.** Under that policy, **Indian agents were assigned to make the Indians give up their nomadic hunting and gathering ways and settle down to farming.** They Indian tribes were also encouraged to break up the communal lands and assign property ownership to individual Indian families. The problem was, as soon as that was done, the land could be sold by those families, and through various means, some legal and some not so legal, **much of what had been Indian lands ended up in the hands of white settlers.**

Many Indian tribes, including the Cherokee, Chickasaw, Choctaw, Creek, and Seminole, resisted resettlement, so Congress passed the **Indian Removal Act.** President Jackson signed it into law at the beginning of the summer of 1830. The act deemed that the tribes would have to resettle in unclaimed land far to the west, into what is now Oklahoma, The area was henceforth deemed to be "Indian lands."

By law, communal Indian lands were considered sovereign. That meant they were not under the control of the United States, and therefore could only be acquired by the United States through treaties. However, pursuant to the Indian Removal Act, **the Indians were put into a position of either** signing treaties that would give them *some* payment for their lands and the right to settle in new land in the West, or face the prospect of being forcibly removed and getting nothing. Many signed, but many others refused to leave their ancestral lands. Some used the services of sympathetic lawyers to try to fight the act, but they had little success. **A key 1823 Supreme Court decision stated that Indians could only *occupy* land within the United States; they could not legally hold title to those lands.**

In 1838, General Scott was sent to forcibly move the Indians off their lands and into holding camps. General Scott wanted to use regular troops to do the job, hoping they would treat the Indians more humanely than the locals, but none were available, so he had to use the local militia. **Almost all of the 7,000 militiamen that participated were local citizens who were glad to get rid of the Indians so they could take over their lands.**

By the time it was over, the newspapers were proudly reporting that Scott's troops had **captured or killed every Indian in Alabama, Georgia, North Carolina, and Tennessee.** Those that were captured were sent to concentration camps near the U.S. Indian Agency that was near Cleveland, Tennessee. Eventually, they were sent West.

In the dead of winter of 1838, most of the remaining Native Americans, including almost all of the 15,000 Indians that were part of the Cherokee nation, were **forced to walk one thousand miles west to the new reservations**. Most had little warm clothing and some were barefoot. Many had contracted smallpox while being held in the concentration camps, and as a result, untold thousands died on the trail. It became known as the **Trail of Tears**.

The Presidential Election of 1856

By the time the election of 1856 came around, the Whig Party had been torn apart by the issue of slavery, and a new party, **the Republican Party**, emerged specifically to fight the spread of slavery to new states entering the Union.

The **Kansas Nebraska Act** of 1854 had created the new territories of Kansas and Nebraska, but the South had again used its unfair voting advantage in Congress to force language to be inserted into the law to allow the new states to determine for themselves whether or not to allow slavery.

Once again, they ignored the previous compromise, known as **the Missouri Compromise,** which made slavery illegal north of Missouri.

President Pierce's handling of the contention over slavery in Kansas proved to be his undoing. His party, sensing defeat at the polls, refused to grant his request to be nominated for a second term. Instead, they nominated **John C. Fremont**, another Mexican-American war hero from the new state of California.

STORY

The **Kansas Nebraska Act** created immediate **contention over the issue of slavery in the new states**, especially in Kansas. Slave holders in Missouri flooded across the border into Kansas and created a territorial legislature in a town near the Missouri border. **One of their first acts was to pass a law making Kansas a slave state.**

In response, a "**free soil**" group set up an opposing legislature in Topeka, Kansas. They declared the slave holder's legislation invalid.

The "free soil" advocates opposed what they called "**slave power**." Slave power was the idea that the Southern slave states had so much inordinate power in Congress and in electing the president, that they could make any new state a slave state.

Tensions escalated when an armed group of pro-slavery men attacked the free-state town of Lawrence, Kansas to destroy the anti-slavery newspaper offices. They burned buildings and stole everything they could get their hands on.

Senator Charles Sumner of Massachusetts denounced the attacks in Kansas, and in response, Preston Smith Brooks, a congressman from South Carolina came into the Senate chambers and attacked Sumner with a cane. The senators who were present tried to stop the attack, but some of the Southern representatives pulled out pistols and held them back to let the attack go on. **Sumner was beaten so badly he was bedridden for years and was unable to return to the Senate**.

Soon, **John Brown, a well-known anti-slavery advocate**, went to Kansas and entered the fray. One of his first acts was to lead an attack on a pro-slavery settlement at Pottawatomie Creek where he and his supporters killed five men.

As the tensions escalated, **Congress passed a resolution declaring the pro-slavery legislature illegal in Kansas** and the resolutions they had passed as improperly done.

But **President Pierce ignored the congressional resolution and continued to recognize the pro-slavery legislature**. Then he outraged the North by sending federal troops to break up the anti-slavery legislature.

Emboldened by the support of the president, **Missouri pro-slavery men formed an army and marched into Kansas**.

In what was to become known as the time of **Bleeding Kansas**, battles between the pro-slavery forces and the anti-slavery forces continued for years, foreshadowing the terrible Civil War that was to come.

In opposition to **John C. Fremont**, the Whig's candidate in the 1856 election, the Democrats nominated Senator **James Buchanan** from Pennsylvania. Buchanan won the election, however, the relatively unknown Fremont had managed to carry 33% of the popular vote, which is remarkable given that he got **no votes at all in the South**. This established the Republican Party as a viable political force in the United States.

Chapter Seven

The Election of Lincoln and a Country in Crisis

The Presidential Election of 1860

The presidential election of 1860 was the most contentious election in the history of the nation. It **led directly to the Civil War**.

Throughout the history of the United States, **the South had tried to maintain enough of a voting advantage in Congress** to block new free states from joining the Union.

Most other nations had already outlawed slavery, so the South knew that if they allowed a majority of even one free state to exist in Congress, the voting power of the North would make it likely that sooner or later Congress would vote to outlaw slavery.

The South's control of Congress and the Electoral College went all the way back to the founding of the nation when they had refused to join the Union unless they got extra power in both Congress and the election of presidents. Eight of the original thirteen states, Delaware, New Jersey, Georgia, New York, Maryland, South Carolina, Virginia, and North Carolina had slaves, and they always voted as a block.

However, as the nation grew in the mid-1800s, more free states joined the Union. Up until then, **the South had managed to use their veto power in Congress to maintain the balance between slave states and free states**. By 1848, there were fifteen slave states, Delaware, Georgia, Maryland, South Carolina, Virginia, North Carolina, Kentucky, Tennessee, Louisiana, Mississippi, Alabama, Missouri, Arkansas, Florida, and Texas, and fifteen free states, New Jersey, Pennsylvania, Connecticut, Massachusetts, New Hampshire, New York, Rhode Island, Vermont, Ohio, Indiana, Illinois, Maine, Michigan, Iowa, and Wisconsin. But as a result of the Mexican-American War, in 1850, **California was brought in as a free state, and that upset the balance**.

Soon, other western states petitioned to join the Union, and the Kansas Nebraska Act of 1854 made it possible that these new states might become slave states. The Republican Party was formed to fight against that possibility.

In 1856, to make their point, the Republicans had nominated **John C. Fremont** for president simply because he was from the new free state of California.

When two more western states, **Minnesota and Oregon, joined the Union** in 1858 and 1859, they chose not to become slave states.

For the South, the handwriting was on the wall. They had lost their voting advantage in both the Senate and in the Electoral College, and it was clear that sooner or later, the Northern states would elect a president that would try to abolish slavery.

That was the situation leading into the presidential election of 1860. **It was clear that slavery would be the main issue in the election**, and it was sending the American political process into chaos. New political movements were springing up as special-interest groups fought to gain control over both local and national political interests.

The Democrats held their 1860 presidential nominating convention in Charleston, South Carolina, which assured that there would be plenty of agitation from the local pro-slavery groups.

Senator Stephen A. Douglas was from the free state of Illinois, but he had been a key proponent of the Kansas Nebraska Act which allowed states to decide for themselves whether to allow slavery or not.

Many in the Democratic party thought he would make a good compromise candidate for president. Douglas had made a name for himself as a capable orator in his campaign against **Abraham Lincoln** for an Illinois Senate seat. (In that election, Lincoln had narrowly won the popular vote, but the state legislature instead chose the incumbent, Douglas.)

However, the Democratic Party was deeply divided. The **Supreme Court's Dred Scott decision** of 1857 had shocked the nation by declaring that once a person had been a slave, they could not be an American citizen, even if freed.

The Democratic party leaders knew that the nation's voters would be paying as much attention to the party's stance on slavery as to what candidate they nominated. Many Southern hard-liners insisted that the Democratic party should openly take a pro-slavery stance and try to elect a president that would fight for legislation to make slavery legal in all states. But **now that the South had lost their advantage in the Electoral College, the party leaders knew that would all but guarantee a loss in the upcoming election**.

By the time balloting began, six major candidates had been put forward for the Democratic nomination. In the first ballot, Douglas led, but by not enough to be the nominee. There were just too many staunch pro-slavery delegates against him. The balloting went on and on with much pro-slavery agitation, until finally, after 57 ballots, the delegates voted to adjourn the convention and meet again later in a Northern city.

When the Democrats met again in Baltimore, two months later, there was even more contention about whether the troublesome pro-slavery delegates from the South should be admitted. In the heated debate that resulted, all of the Southern delegates walked out, thus assuring Douglas's nomination. As a compromise, **Senator Benjamin Fitzpatrick** of Alabama was nominated for vice president, but he refused to run with Douglas. He was replaced by former **Senator Herschel V. Johnson of Georgia**.

The Southern delegates who had walked out held their own convention and nominated **John C. Breckinridge** from Kentucky for president and **Joseph Lane,** from North Carolina, for vice president.

STORY

The Supreme Court's Dred Scott decision of 1857 caused an uproar throughout the North. The court had been asked to decide if Dred Scott, a slave who had been taken by his master to the free state of Illinois, was now free due to his having lived there for an expended period of time. Scott had been legally married while in Illinois, even though slaves were not supposed to have any legal rights, not even the right to marry. The court, in a seven to two decision, shocked the anti-slave forces by stating that slaves were not legal citizens of the United States and therefore had no legal right to appeal to the court. The majority members of the Supreme Court went on to state that **slaves were private property even if they were taken to a free state**. They said a slave could not be taken away from his or her owner without due process.

Unexpectedly, **the court's decision triggered the economic panic of 1857** when investors and businesses got worried about the implications of the decision.

The 1860 Republican presidential nominating convention was held in Chicago a month after the debacle of the Democrat's multiple conventions.

The favorite candidate going into the Republican convention was former **New York Governor William H. Seward**, and he led after the first two ballots. But when he failed to rally any more delegates to his side, **a local Illinois dark horse, Abraham Lincoln, was put forward.** Lincoln had gained some national notoriety as a calm and effective orator in his series of debates with **Stephen Douglas** during their race for an Illinois Senate seat, and there were a lot of pro-Lincoln agitators in attendance at the convention. With some aggressive tactics on the convention floor, and some clever back-room bargaining by Lincoln's supporters, Lincoln was able to squeak out the nomination.

Of special note was the Republican Party's written platform: it stated that **slavery would not be allowed to spread any further**.

Besides the Republican, Lincoln, the voters were presented with ballots that included three others, Democrat **Stephen Douglas**, Southern Democrat **John Breckenridge**, and **John Bell**, representing the Constitutional Union Party.

The result was that the Southern votes were split between Breckenridge, Bell, and Douglas, **leading to a relatively easy victory for Lincoln**.

When Lincoln was elected, most Southerners assumed he would try to abolish slavery. **Seven Southern states, South Carolina, Mississippi, Florida, Alabama, Georgia, Louisiana, and Texas, seceded from the Union.**

When hostilities commenced with the Confederate forces attacking Fort Sumter in South Carolina on April 12, 1861, **four additional states, Virginia, Arkansas, North Carolina, and Tennessee joined the Confederacy**.

COMMENT

The causes and effects of the American Civil War are beyond the scope of a book about how U.S. presidents are elected. Thousands of other books have discussed the Civil War, and its causes and consequences have been covered in great detail.

But I should point out that it was the biased Electoral College system that gave the Southern state extra votes in the U.S. Senate, plus the extra votes the South got in the House of Representatives **by counting millions of slaves as part of their population**, that kept the South in the Union as long as they were. **The South's extra voting power in the Electoral College resulted in ten of the first twelve presidents being Southern slave holders, and each of those presidents made sure slavery continued to be the law of the land.**

> Even after Northerners began to be elected president, the South was able to use their voting power to keep a balance between slave states and free states. **The Civil War South was able to make the United States the last major country in the world to abolish slavery.**

As soon as the Civil War started, President Lincoln took a hands-on approach. He personally supervised the North's war strategy and selected the generals to fight it. And when he was disappointed with the performances of his generals, he replaced them. Eventually, Lincoln selected General **Ulysses S. Grant,** a military leader who was having great success in the West, to be his top general.

Lincoln knew he was going to have to try to hold the nation together throughout a war that was pitting friends and family against each other, but **he was determined to end slavery**.

During his first term in office, after much debate and consternation, Lincoln used his position as commander-in-chief and the war powers granted to him by the Constitution to announce an **Emancipation Proclamation** which declared slaves to be free. He urged Congress to pass an amendment to the Constitution outlawing slavery.

He also appointed five judges to the Supreme Court, all of them well known for their anti-slavery positions. But he did not want the nation to be forever divided, so long before the war ended, he was already proposing plans for the reconstruction of the South.

The Presidential Election of 1864

Despite the terrible loss of human life in the war, Lincoln was again nominated by the Republicans for reelection in 1864.

However, Lincoln was unhappy with his vice president, **Hannibal Hamlin**, so he replaced him with **Andrew Johnson**. It was a decision that was to have a profound effect on Johnson's life and on the post-war nation.

The Democrats put up General **George B. McClellan**, the general Lincoln had demoted early in the war.

McClellen won only a few states, and because there was no Southern vote, Lincoln easily won reelection.

STORY

In the days after Lincoln's reelection, the war dragged on into yet another spring. However, Lincoln was sure the war would soon be over. The Confederate Army was exhausted and in retreat, but the Southern leadership was still not ready to give in.

The Union Army marched deeper into the Southern states, freeing millions of slaves as they went. At Lincoln's request, some of the slaves were recruited into black regiments of the Union Army.

Extended Union Army forays into the South, such as Sherman's infamous **March to the Sea,** destroyed much of the South's ability to continue the war.

Lee understood that continuing to fight would only result in more pointless bloodshed, so he finally **surrendered his army to General Grant at Appomattox**, Virginia on April 9, 1865.

As the nation continued to celebrate the end of a long and terrible war, the news came that Lincoln had been assassinated. The assassin was a well-known actor in and around the nation's capital, **John Wilkes Booth.** Only later was it learned that Booth was a spy being supported by the Confederate secret service and by Canadian anti-union forces.

Lincoln's vice president, **Andrew Johnson**, was sworn in as president the next morning, and for the next four years, he oversaw the rebuilding of the nation. He was known as a compromiser who repeatedly vetoed Congressional bills that were designed to punish the South or to give more rights to the freed slaves.

When Congress passed the bill to create the Fourteenth Amendment to provide civil rights to all U.S. citizens, including freed slaves, **he vetoed it**.

Congress quickly overrode Johnson's veto, and there was **a move to impeach him**, but the vote in the House of Representatives to remove Johnson from office failed by one vote.

Chapter Eight
Democrats Versus Republicans

The Presidential Election of 1868

The presidential election of 1868 took place during the post-war reconstruction period.

Johnson ran for reelection, but his Republican Party didn't want him because they saw him as being too soft on the South. Instead, they nominated Civil War hero, **General Ulysses S. Grant.** They nominated Indiana Congressman, **Schuyler Colfax**, to be his running mate.

President Johnson then sought support from the Democrats, but they didn't want him either. Instead, they nominated **Horatio Seymour**, the former governor of New York. **Francis Blair**, a Congressman from Missouri who had also served as a general in the war, was named as his running mate.

STORY

After the war, Congress passed several Reconstruction Amendments, including the Fourteenth Amendment which gave full rights to all citizens of the nation, including former slaves. None of the breakaway Southern states would be allowed to participate in the election until they ratified the amendment. By the time the election took place, Mississippi, Texas, and Virginia had not done so and were therefore left out of the election process.

Another aspect of the new reconstruction laws was that the vote of the Electoral College should be "based on" the vote of the people.

As a result, most states put in place some kind of system to do that. However, in Florida, the state legislature still cast the electoral votes.

While Grant favored full citizenship and full civil right for the freed slaves, the Democrats held fast to the "states rights" position which meant that issue could be decided state by state.

Grant easily won both the general election and the Electoral College vote. However Seymour surprised everyone by **winning his home state of New York.** An accusation of voter fraud in New York was put forth and a Congressional investigation was initiated, but in the end, no action was taken.

It was said **if all of the Southern states had been allowed to vote, the outcome of the election might have been quite different**.

The Presidential Election of 1872

In 1872, the Republicans nominated President Ulysses S. Grant for re-election. However, because Colfax had been implicated in a scandal, they were no longer willing to accept him as the vice-president. Instead, they nominated Senator Henry Wilson of Massachusetts.

STORY

During the presidential election of 1872, new political parties sprung up. A group of Republicans split off from the main party and formed the **Liberal Republican Party**. They nominated New York publisher **Horace Greeley** as their presidential candidate and Missouri Governor **Benjamin Brown** as vice-president.

Another Republican-leaning group formed the **Labor Reform Party**, and they nominated **David Davis**, a Supreme Court Justice from Illinois who had been placed on the court by President Lincoln. However, he refused the honor, so they turned to **Charles O'Conor**, a well-known New York lawyer.

He also refused, but the Labor Reform Party decided to go ahead and put his name on the ballot anyway. It was a mistake that was to spell the end of the Labor Reform Party.

The Democrats didn't know what to do. They wanted to defeat Grant and try to overcome some of the sanctions that had been put in place against the South. But knowing they had little chance, they did a surprising thing—**they nominated the same two men the Liberal Republicans had nominated,** Horace Greeley and Benjamin Brown.

Grant easily won reelection, but **five other men also received votes in the Electoral College.** Horace Greeley, came in second in the popular vote, but died before the Electoral College met. Despite his not being alive, three electors voted for him anyhow.

STORY

In the election of 1872, there were accusations off widespread voter fraud designed to keep African-American voters away from the polling places. The electoral votes from five Southern states were questioned, and **the electoral votes of Arkansas and Louisiana were rejected due to clear evidence of voter fraud and intimidation of African-American voters.**

The Southern states all voted against the Republicans, the "party of Lincoln."

The Presidential Election of 1876

The election of 1876 was one of the most controversial in the history of the United States.

For president, the Republicans nominated **Rutherford B. Hayes**, the former governor of Ohio. He chose as his vice president, **William Wheeler**, a U.S. Congressman from New York.

Hayes was a compromise candidate, selected after many ballots at the Republican nominating convention failed to produce a clear winner.

The Democrats nominated Governor **Samuel J. Tilden** of New York, and **Thomas A. Hendricks**, governor of Indiana, to be his vice-presidential nominee. Tilden had gained national recognition for finally managing to send New York's corrupt **Boss Tweed** to prison.

STORY

Politics during the eighteenth century was a rough and tumble business. Although some may say politics in our current era is mostly run by the rich, it was clearly so in New York in the mid 1800s.

William Tweed, known as "**Boss Tweed**," was one of the largest landowners in the state of New York, and he was a director of railroads and banks. He was elected to Congress in 1852, and later served in the New York state Senate.

After that, **he got himself appointed to various city positions in which he could dispense political favors -- for a price**. By controlling New York City boards and commissions, he was able to gain great influence over local politics, and even more influence over how public money was spent. Over time, he was able to create a political machine that controlled much of New York's politics. **He became known as the "Grand Sachem" of Tammany Hall.**

The end of his "reign" came when **Governor Tilden worked with local prosecutors to convict him of stealing millions of dollars of public money** through various schemes. The prosecution said he paid "workers" huge payments for mostly nonexistent city building projects just to get kickbacks.

They gave examples such as the **plasterer who had been paid over a hundred thousand dollars for a day's work and a carpenter who had been paid over three hundred thousand dollars for supposedly doing woodwork carpentry in a building that turned out not to have any woodwork in it** (at that time, the average urban New England worker made about $300 **per year**).

Tweed was imprisoned, and a million dollar bail was set. He had no trouble raising that much money and was therefore released.

Unbelievably, while all this was going on, Tweed was re-elected to the state senate.

Soon, he was arrested again, and this time the bail was raised to eight million dollars, an astounding amount of money in that era. Again, he had no trouble raising it.

But it was clear his empire was falling apart. His associates were also being arrested, and some of them were being convicted despite Tweed's attempts to subvert the legal process.

Tweed was finally convicted of corruption and graft and given a prison sentence of twelve years. But when **the local jailers allowed him out for a "home visit," he escaped and fled to Spain.** He was eventually caught there and put on an American warship to be brought back to the United States.

Now apparently out of money and desperate to get out of prison, he said he would tell prosecutors all about how his corruption system worked if they would release him. The agreement that was reached resulted in the prosecution of many members of Tweed's inner ring.

After confessing, Tweed was ready to get out of prison, so he could to try to reestablish his empire. **But Governor Tilden refused to let him go. Tweed was held in a local New York City jail until his death in 1878.**

Everyone knew the election of 1876 was going to be close. The Democrats were resurgent, especially in the South, and with the retirement of General Grant, they felt they had a good chance to take the presidency back from the Republicans. The Democrats tried to paint the Republicans as involved in graft and political manipulation, and contrasted them with Tilden who had a reputation as a reformer.

The Republicans main approach to the campaign was to remind the people that it was the Democrats that had caused the Civil War through their support of slavery.

STORY

The Democrats referred to this tactic of associating them with the Civil War as "**waving the bloody shirt**." They pointed out that not every Democrat had been a rebel, and they reminded the voters that both Tilden and his running mate Hendricks were Northerners. They called for "a return to normalcy, which would mean **an end to the repressive rules of reconstruction. It was a message designed to appeal to a war-exhausted country.**

During the election, all over the South, Southern paramilitary groups such as the **Red Shirts** and the **White League** disrupted Republican rallies. They **used violence and intimidation to try to stop Republicans, and especially blacks, from voting**.

When the results of the popular vote were in, Tilden, the choice of the Southern states, had apparently won by 252,666 votes, the closest national vote in history.

However, there were cries of fraud with regard to the counting of votes in the South. The Republicans claimed their voters in Florida had either not been allowed to vote or had been tricked into voting for the wrong candidate by deceptively designed ballots. They cited **numerous instances of voter intimidation and fraud in Florida,** pointing out that documents certifying the election there had been signed by the state attorney-general, a Democratic, and by the Florida governor, also a Democrat (as we shall see in a later chapter, Al Gore's supporters were later to make similar accusations regarding the 2000 election in Florida).

Reports of voter intimidation and ballot fraud were also raised in Louisiana, and South Carolina. One of the Democratic tricks in the South was to print a picture of Abraham Lincoln on the Democratic ballot to try to get illiterate voters to select that one.

In addition, because the Constitution did not stipulate that Electoral College electors *had to* vote for the popular vote winner, there was no assurance that Southern Democratic electors would be willing to cast their votes for the anti-slavery Republicans.

When the ballots of the Electoral College voters were counted, it appeared that Hayes had won by one vote. But neither candidate had the requisite 185 electoral votes that were required for a majority. It appeared that once again the selection of the president would take place in the House of Representatives, and at that time, the House was controlled by the Republicans.

STORY

Because of the many accusations of voter fraud in the South, Congress created **a special commission** to review the results. All that did was lead to more **contention about who should be appointed to the special commission.** In the end, the Democrats (who controlled the Senate because of the two senators given to each Southern state) were allowed to appoint five members, and the Republicans (who controlled the population-based House of Representatives) were also allowed to appoint five. Four Supreme Court justices were added to the commission, two with Republican leanings, and two with Democratic leanings. Those four Supreme Court justices were allowed to select one more justice to serve on the commission, and they chose **Justice David Davis** who they saw as politically independent. Hoping to gain a deciding vote on the commission, the Democrats who controlled the Illinois senate immediately appointed Davis to fill their vacant U.S. Senate seat. The four justices then selected **Justice Joseph P. Bradley** who was supposed to be another impartial member of the court.

In January of 1877, the special Congressional commission met to examine the results of the Electoral College votes from Florida, Louisiana, Oregon, and South Carolina. If the commission hoped for easy answers, they were disappointed: those states each presented **two conflicting sets of Electoral College results**, one from the Republicans and one from the Democrats.

After much debate, the Congressional members of the commission voted right along party lines. That meant the vote was a tie. The decision was up to Justice Bradley. He voted with the Republicans, making the decision 8-7 in favor of giving the disputed Electoral College votes to Hayes. **That gave Hayes a 185-184 Electoral College victory**.

The election of 1876 is **the only election in the history of the United States in which a candidate received an absolute majority of the popular vote and did not get to be president** (although Al Gore won the popular vote in the 2000 election by 543,895 votes, because a third-party candidate also received votes, Gore did not win an absolute majority).

It is not clear under what authority Congress made their decision about the winner of the 1876 election. **There is nothing in the Electoral College section of the Constitution that there is any way the winner of the Electoral College vote can be denied the presidency.**

After it was all over, the people of the South thought the election had been stolen from Tilden by the North. The people of the North felt it was the right decision because they were sure that large numbers of former slaves in the South had not been allowed to vote. They were sure that in such a close election, if they had they been allowed to vote, they would have easily carried the election for Hayes.

The Presidential Election of 1880

In 1880, the incumbent president Rutherford B. Hayes did not seek reelection. That left the race wide open. For the Republicans, Tilden, their candidate from the previous election was seen as the favorite. But the Republican National Convention was very divided, with U.S. Senator **James G. Blaine** and Treasury Secretary **John Sherman**, among others, vying for the nomination. A surprise candidate was **Ulysses S. Grant** who had decided to seek an unprecedented third term. In the first ballot, Grant almost won: he got the most votes, but didn't have a majority. Blaine had come in second, and many other ballots followed, but neither Grant nor Blaine could get a majority. Finally, a compromise candidate, **James A. Garfield**, a U.S. Congressman from Ohio was put forward, and he was able to get enough votes to win the nomination. Chester A. Arthur, a party regular from New York won the nomination for vice-president.

When the Democrats held their national convention, Tilden was assumed to be the favorite. But he was not sure he was willing to undergo yet another grueling election campaign.

Among the many other candidates, **Major General Winfield Scott Hancock** from Pennsylvania and U.S. Senator from Delaware, **Thomas F. Bayard**, were seen as the favorites.

On the second ballot, Hancock was nominated and William Hayden English, a former U.S. Congressman from Indiana, was nominated for vice president.

STORY

As the presidential election of 1880 approached, the Democrats, rallied around the concept that the election of 1876 had been stolen from them by Northerners. In fact, in the years leading up to the election, the Democrats in the House of Representatives spent much of their time trying to prove it. By the time the new election rolled around, they had no new evidence, but they were still convinced of it, and that turned out to be their main argument in favor of their presidential candidate in 1880.

As in the previous president election, new political parties sprang up. The **Greenback Party** favored safety regulations in factories, an eight-hour work day, and an end to child labor. They nominated **James B. Weaver**, a U.S. Congressman from Iowa who had been a general in the Civil War.

A new Prohibition Party entered the fray, with the avowed purpose of ending the sale of alcoholic beverages. They nominated **Neal Dow**, a Civil War general from Maine.

With the North and the South still divided politically, the idea emerged, for the first time, that "**swing states**" (states that tended to swing back and forth in which party they supported) could determine the outcome, and that turned out to be true.

In the general election, the vote was extremely close. Republican **Garfield** got 4,453,337 votes to Democrat **Hancock**'s 4,444,267 votes. **With a tiny national margin of only 9,070 votes, you would expect the Electoral College to end in a tie**, but because of the strange winner-take-all system which had by then been accepted by almost every state, Garfield won in the Electoral College, 214 to 155.

Garfield, the Republican, had won all the Northern states, and Hancock, the Democrat, had won all the Southern states. However, now that there were more Northern states in the Union, they had enough Electoral College votes to give Garfield the victory.

Interestingly, if only a few thousand voters in a handful of Northern states had voted for Hancock, he would have won both the popular vote and the Electoral College vote.

STORY

During his first year in office, Garfield was assassinated by a mentally ill man who had failed to get a job in the Garfield administration. Vice president, **Chester A. Arthur** served out the remainder of his term.

Despite the fact that he was a Republican Party regular who had grown rich off of patronage jobs, **President Arthur soon became known as a reformer**. He signed **the Pendleton Act** into law and strongly enforced its provisions.

The Pendleton Act created the United States Civil Service Commission and attempted to undo the spoils system in which government positions were given out based on political affiliation rather than on merit.

Today, Arthur is one of the least known of all our past presidents.

The Presidential Election of 1884

As the 1884 presidential election season began, there were questions as to whether President Arthur would run for reelection. There was also speculation that Lincoln's son, Robert Todd Lincoln, would run. He had been serving as the U.S. Secretary of War. Another possible candidate was Civil War general William Tecumseh Sherman, but he soon made it clear that he was not interested. Robert Todd Lincoln also declined.

By the time the Republican National Convention started, **President Arthur also declined to run for reelection due to health problems** (he had been keeping his health problems secret for a long time). As a result, several prominent Republicans came forward to seek the nomination. The two leading figures were U.S. Congressman from Maine, **James G. Blaine** and Vermont Senator **George F. Edmunds**. After several ballots, Blaine was nominated and chose Illinois Senator **John A. Logan** to be his vice-presidential nominee.

By the time the Democratic National Convention started, there was a clear front-runner, **New York Governor Grover Cleveland**. As the balloting began, several other candidates names were put in, but it only took two ballots to nominate. Cleveland. He selected **Thomas A. Hendricks**, a former governor and senator from Indiana as his vice-president.

STORY

Alternative political parties were again involved in the presidential election. The **Greenback Party** nominated candidates, as did the **Prohibition Party**.

In addition, two new parties emerged, the **Anti-Monopoly Party** and the **Equal Rights Party**.

The Anti-Monopoly Party focused on one issue, being against the emergence of huge monopolistic corporations.

The Equal Rights Party was formed to bring voting rights to women in the United States. They held a national convention in San Francisco and nominated **Belva Ann Lockwood**, an attorney from Washington, D.C., for president. In the general election, even though women couldn't vote for her, it is estimated that she received over four thousand votes.

Cleveland won to become the first Democratic president since before the Civil War. He won by a very narrow 57,579-vote margin, and the Electoral College vote was also close, 219 to 182. **He did it by winning the South**, of course, and by winning Indiana, New Jersey, and most importantly New York. **He won the popular vote in New York by only 1,149 votes**, thereby gaining all of New York's 36 electoral votes. Had those 1,149 votes gone the other way, **Blaine would have been elected the nation's 20th president in the Electoral College.**

The Presidential Election of 1888

The 1888 presidential election campaign began with the Democrats nominating President Cleveland for reelection. However, his vice-president, Thomas A. Hendricks, had died in office, and a replacement had to be found. They chose former U.S. Senator **Allen G. Thurman** of Ohio.

The Republican national convention did not go as smoothly. The presumed nominee, **James G. Blaine**, a former U.S. Congressman and Secretary of State from Maine, withdrew in an attempt to promote harmony within the party.

Nevertheless, it still took eight ballots to secure the nomination for Senator **Benjamin Harrison** of Indiana.

In the end, part of the reason Harrison was nominated was because he was from Indiana which, at the time, was considered to be a key swing state.

Levi P. Morton, a former U.S. Congressman from New York was chosen to be his vice-presidential nominee.

STORY

Once again, the **Prohibition Party**, the **Equal Rights Party**, and the **Greenback Party** also nominated presidential candidates.

In addition, a number of new political parties were formed.

The **Industrial Reform Party** sought an increased money supply. They also supported women's right to vote.

The **American Party** opposed immigrants and members of the Catholic faith, who they saw as possibly being more loyal to the Pope than to the United States.

Two labor parties also nominated candidates, the **Union Labor Party** and the **United Labor Party**.

Once again, in 1888, it was the strange workings of the Electoral College and not the will of the people that determined which of the candidates would be president. Democrat **Grover Cleveland won the popular vote, but** Republican **Benjamin Harrison got more Electoral College votes** and was therefore elected president.

STORY

In the 1888 popular vote, Cleveland got 5,538,163 votes to Harrison's 5,443,633—Cleveland had won the election by 94,530 votes.

But Cleveland was not to be the next president because **Harrison won the Electoral College vote by squeaking out narrow popular vote margins in states with a lot of Electoral College votes.** He won Illinois with its 22 electoral votes,

Michigan with its 13 electoral votes, and Missouri with its 16 electoral votes. He won the people's vote in each of those states, but by very slim margins. Nevertheless, all three of those states were winner-take-all states.

Harrison's win in New York, with its 36 electoral votes, was the key to his victory in the Electoral College. He got only 14,373 more popular votes than Cleveland, out of 1,319,748 votes cast, but he got all of New York's electoral votes. Therefore, **for the second presidential election in a row, a few voters in one state determined who would get to be president, and this time it *was not* the candidate who won the popular vote.**

Unlike the election of 1824 when there was national outrage over the fact that Andrew Jackson did not get to be president despite winning the popular vote, there was little public outrage this time. The reason the people of the North didn't complain about the election's outcome was because it was common knowledge that hundreds of thousands of former slaves had been kept away from the polling places in the South. It was reasoned that those voters would have voted for Harrison if they had been given the opportunity, and so he would have won the popular vote as well.

Nevertheless, the outcome of the election made it clear that close elections would continue to reveal the flaws of the Electoral College system.

The Presidential Election of 1892

By the time the election of 1892 rolled around, many in the Republican Party were unhappy with President Harrison.

At the 1892 Republican National Convention, there was a

dump-Harrison movement. In fact, many believed Harrison didn't want to serve another term.

Once again, even before the Republican convention got started, **James Blaine's name was being put forward**. Not wanting Blaine to win, motivated Harrison to more actively seek reelection, and as a result, he was quickly nominated for another term as president.

Most expected the incumbent Vice President, Levi Morton, would also be re-nominated, but Harrison wanted a different vice-president because he suspected Morton had secretly been supporting Blaine. Instead, Harrison chose **Whitelaw Reid** of New York to be his vice-president, mainly because he was a fellow graduate of Miami University in Ohio. Reid had formerly served as U.S. Ambassador to France, and at the time of his nomination, he was the editor of the New York Tribune.

The election results again demonstrated that **voters don't like it when the candidate they chose through popular election does not get to be president. They voted against the incumbent Benjamin Harrison and returned Grover Cleveland to the presidency**. He was the only person to be elected to a second term as president, non-consecutively.

Although the South was still solidly in the Democratic camp, **six new Northern states, Idaho, North Dakota, South Dakota, Montana, Washington, and Wyoming voted for the first time** in a presidential election, and they mostly supported the Republicans. That made all the difference.

In the presidential election of 1892, third parties again put forward candidates. In addition to the Prohibition Party and the various labor parties, a new party, the **People's Party** emerged. It was mainly made up of farmers, and they allied in purpose and in principle with the labor parties against the capitalists. Some of the populist parties actively included women in their affairs.

STORY

After the Civil War, women were allowed to vote (on some matters) in the state of Wyoming, and soon thereafter, in the Utah and Washington territories. (The men of the Wyoming may have had more personal reasons for trying to draw more women to their state; at the time, there were about 6,000 men living in Wyoming and only about 1,000 women.)

However, **Women's suffrage** in the whole United States did not come easily. There had been no serious movement in the United States to allow women to vote until 1848 when Gerrit Smith, a candidate for president, made it part of his Liberty Party's platform. However, at that time, the idea didn't get much traction.

By the mid 1850s, there was still no concerted effort on the part of the all-male political establishment to allow women to vote. However, women were starting to get some legal rights. In some states, a woman could file for divorce, and a few states passed laws that said working women didn't have to turn over their wages to their husbands.

Some states, especially Southern and rural states, were unwilling to give women *any* legal rights. A famous legal case in North Carolina made the point. A woman had appealed to change the state law so a woman would be allowed to file for divorce if she had been badly beaten by her husband. The state Supreme Court turned down her appeal in 1862, stating, "The law gives the husband power to use such a degree of force necessary to make the wife behave and know her place."

After the Civil War, there was some talk of Women's suffrage, but it took female activists like **Susan B. Anthony** to bring the issue to the public's attention. She and others like **Elizabeth Cady Stanton** organized women's rights gatherings and wrote books about the lack of women's legal rights in the

U.S. Their books were intended to be read by women, but were also read by men. Some men voiced approval, but others tried to ban the books, saying for a women to have rights would be against the will of nature.

There was considerable resistance, even among women's groups. Many women felt the suffragettes shouldn't be trying to change traditional women's roles.

Movements were formed to fight against the very idea of women gaining *any* legal rights, let alone the right to vote. One prominent organization was the **National Organization Against Women's Suffrage,** and it counted many women as members.

In 1869, Susan B. Anthony and Elizabeth Cady Stanton formed the **National Woman Suffrage Association (NWSA).** They lobbied for women's rights and proposed an amendment to the Constitution giving women the right to vote in all elections.

In 1890, several women's rights organizations came together to form the **National American Woman Suffrage Association** which was headed by **Carrie Chapman Catt.**

After Wyoming gave women the right to vote, lobbying efforts by Susan B. Anthony and others encouraged some of the other Western states to follow suit, apparently in hopes of attracting more women to the still untamed and almost all male Western territories.

Utah territory was one of the first Western states to allow women the vote, but it was not activist women who were behind the effort; it was activist men who were trying to stamp out the practice of polygamy. A group of men known as **Godbeites** left the Latter Day Saints (Mormon) church and took up the fight against the church-condoned practice of men having multiple wives. They hoped women, if given the right to vote, would be freed from the male dominance officially sanctioned by the Mormon Church and would vote to end polygamy.

The practice of men having multiple wives was part of the Mormon religion, but the church's leader, Brigham Young, got behind the women's suffrage movement effort in hopes it would help change the image of Utah women as oppressed, and maybe even sidetrack anti-polygamy legislation that was working its way through Congress. With Brigham Young's support, there was no resistance to the idea, and in 1869, the territorial legislature passed an act giving women the vote (but not the right to run for office).

Paradoxically, the U.S. Congress overrode the new Utah act by passing the **Edmunds-Tucker Anti-polygamy Act**, which specifically banned voting by women in Utah. The movement to stamp out polygamy in Utah was gaining momentum across the nation, and it was becoming a major issue in every presidential election. There was even a call to send U.S. Army troops to Utah to put a stop to the practice.

In 1890, the Mormon Church leaders declared that the church would no longer sanction the practice of polygamy. With that controversy out of the way, Utah was granted statehood in 1896 and **the right of Utah women to vote was written into the new state's constitution**.

In 1865, Republicans proposed the **Fourteenth Amendment** to the Constitution that would give the vote to the millions of newly-freed black **men, but not women**.

It was not until 1915 that Congress passed the **Nineteenth Amendment** to the Constitution which prohibited the states from denying the right to vote based on sex.

Even at that late date, with the country becoming more and more industrialized and all of the lower 48 states now part of the Union, only some Western states and a few Midwestern states had granted women the right to vote. **Until 1915, women were specifically barred from voting** even in local elections in all of the East Coast states and most of the Southern states.

The Presidential Election of 1896

As the presidential election of 1896 began, the nation was still recovering from the panic of 1893, a nationwide economic depression that had started with a run on the U.S. gold reserves. Many banks closed and many businesses failed. As a result, the election campaign mainly focused on economic issues.

One contentious issue was about whether the U.S. should remain on **the gold standard**, and the Democratic party was split over the issue of whether the U.S. should stay on the gold standard or not.

After much contention, the Democrats nominated **William Jennings Bryan** who was against the gold standard and in favor of liberalizing the nation's banking standards.

Famous as an orator, Bryan used the Democratic National Convention as a forum to deliver a powerful speech that became known as the "Cross of Gold" speech. It accused big business of profiting on the backs of factory workers and farmers that had been hurt by the economic depression and the closing of banks. He called for an end to the gold standard, and government relief efforts for the poor.

After the conclusion of his speech, the delegates hoisted Bryan to their shoulders and carried him around the convention hall.

Bryan won the nomination, the youngest presidential nominee in American history, only one year older than the constitutional minimum of 35.

To serve as his vice-president (and to help get the votes of the conservatives) the Democrats nominated **Arthur Sewall**, a New England industrialist.

The Republicans nominated **William McKinley** who had

served in the U.S. House of Representatives from Ohio, and as that state's governor.

The election of 1896 was also one of the first elections in which campaign money played an important role. **The Republican campaign outspent the Democratic campaign by sixteen to one**.

With little money to mount an effective national advertising campaign, Bryan took to the railroads and went on a nationwide **whistle-stop campaign**. Up to that time, **it was seen as unseemly for presidential candidates to actively go out and campaign for themselves,** and the novelty of seeing a presidential candidate in person drew large crowds to Bryan's campaign stops. Outside of the large Eastern cities, few had ever had the chance to listen to the powerful oratory of a skillful speaker.

In the end, money won out, but the election was fairly close because the South again voted solidly for the Democrat, as did a few of the Western states. McKinley won by only about 600,000 votes out of almost 14 million votes cast.

STORY

The presidential election of 1896 campaign is considered significant in that it signaled a change in American politics in which new coalitions were the key to winning elections. There was a new alignment of voters, with the voters in the cities responding to issues that were in marked contrast to the issues favored by voters in rural areas of the country.

As part of the new political alignments, new political parties appeared.

The **Gold Democratic Party** was formed in response the Bryan's anti-gold speech and his nomination by the Democrats. They saw themselves as the only legitimate heirs to Jeffersonian principles.

The **Populist Party** agreed with Bryan's attack on big business and was mainly supported by farmers.

Presidential candidates were again put forward by the **Prohibition Party**, but like the rest of the country, they were split over economic issues. A "broad-gauge" group called for woman suffrage and generous pensions for war veterans, arbitration of international disputes, and other measures. A "narrow-gauge" group limited their platform to calling for the prohibition of liquor.

The Presidential Election of 1900

The first presidential election of the new century in 1900 turned out to be a rematch of the 1896 election, McKinley versus Bryan. This time, William McKinley chose New York's governor, **Theodore Roosevelt**, as his running mate. Although Roosevelt didn't want to give up his powerful position as the governor of the nation's most populous state just to be vice president, he finally relented. (It was a decision that was to have significant ramifications for him and for the country.)

Although **Bryan again carried the South**, which was still solidly voting against any representative of "the party of Lincoln," McKinley won by carrying more of the Western states in addition to the North.

STORY

In light of recent assassinations of public figures by anarchists in Europe, there was extra security in place for McKinley's planned visit to the Pan-American Exposition in Buffalo, New York during the fall of 1901. While in Buffalo, McKinley stayed at Milburn House, the expansive home of the Exposition's president, **John G. Milburn.**

On his first day at the exposition, McKinley spoke to a huge crowd of some 50,000 people and there was no trouble.

However, the next day, at the request of Milburn, he again visited the exposition to help build the gate receipts This time, instead of giving a speech, he planned to meet the public. That gave a man named **Leon Czolgosz** an opportunity to get close to the president. Czolgosz was a peripheral member of some American anarchists groups, and he believed the design of the government of the United States was perpetuating social injustice against poor people like himself. He was aware that an anarchist had killed King Umberto I of Italy and that the killer said he had done it for the sake of the common man. Czolgosz decided to do the same thing.

At a large ornate building named the Temple of Music, space was cleared to make room for a line of people who would get to meet the president and shake his hand. McKinley was a skilled hand-shaker who had developed a practiced technique of gripping peoples' hands firmly and guiding them past him. That way, he could greet a lot of people and shake a lot of hands.

Czolgosz procured a pistol and got himself into the greeting line. He waited patiently for his turn to shake hands with the president, and when he got close, he quickly pulled out his pistol and shot McKinley twice in the stomach.

As Czolgosz shouted, "I done my duty," the crowd immediately attacked him, but McKinley told them to stop.

Even as McKinley was guided to a chair, he tried to tell his staff that he was not seriously injured. Mostly, he was worried about how his ill wife would take the news.

The president was taken to an local infirmary where a local doctor probed the president's stomach wound, but could not find a bullet.

McKinley was taken to Milburn's home where he seemed to recover somewhat, and doctors assured the public that the president was going to be fine.

After news of the shooting went out by telegraph, members of the cabinet rushed to Buffalo and vice-president Roosevelt hurried back from a camping trip in the Adirondack Mountains.

A large crowd stayed near the Buffalo police headquarters threatening to lynch Czolgosz.

Unfortunately, the doctors were wrong about their rosy prognosis. The president's condition soon began to deteriorate due to the gangrene that was growing around the bullet that was still lodged in his intestines. Thomas Edison sent a newly-invented X-ray machine to Buffalo to try to determine the location of the bullet inside the president, but the attending doctors would not allow its use. Within a few weeks, McKinley died, and Roosevelt was sworn in as the new president.

Czolgosz was quickly put on trial for the murder. He was found guilty and sentenced to death. He was executed by electric chair only a month later.

The Presidential Election of 1904

At the Republican National Convention of 1904, **Theodore Roosevelt**, who had assumed the office of president upon the death of president William McKinley, easily won the nomination on the first ballot. Republican conservatives, feeling Roosevelt might be too liberal to get elected, pressured him to accept Indiana Senator **Charles W. Fairbanks** of Indiana as his vice-presidential candidate. Roosevelt would have rather had a more progressive vice-president, but he went along with the "old guard" to avoid a floor fight.

Because Roosevelt had already served most of McKinley's term in office, he promised, if elected, he would not run for another term. The Democratic National Convention was much more contentious.

STORY

The Democratic National Convention of 1904 foreshadowed what twentieth-century politics was going to be like.

When the delegates were unable to talk former president Grover Cleveland into running again, they turned away from the presumed favorite, William Jennings Bryan, and instead put forward the name of a relative unknown, Judge **Alton B. Parker,** who had been out of politics for twenty years.

Bryan, still a force in the Democratic Party, strongly opposed Parker because he had been one of the "Gold Democrats" who had opposed Bryan in 1896. He said Parker was "a tool of Wall Street," pointing out that Parker had been one of the New York Court of Appeals judges who had declared the eight-hour work day law unconstitutional. Bryan went so far as to suggested that if Parker was nominated, he would encourage Democrats not to vote for him.

Bryan said the delegates should go for New York publisher **William Randolph Hearst**. (Hearst's newspapers had endorsed Bryan in his bid for the presidency.) Hearst's newspapers were known to be on the side of labor and against the monopolies of big business.

The Democratic delegates were so worried that a labor candidate like Hearst might take over the Party, they all rallied behind Parker.

However, the strife of the convention was not over. Parker was upset that the Democratic platform didn't include anything about the monetary issue. He said the platform would have to include support of the gold standard or he would not accept the nomination.

It was a bold move, and it worked. The Democratic platform also called for reduced government spending, an end to big business monopolies, an eight-hour work day, and oddly, the extermination of polygamy. It also called out the Roosevelt administration as "spasmodic, erratic, sensational, spectacular, and arbitrary," something more likely to be seen in today's party platforms.

After the Democrats had nominated Parker for president, they nominated former Senator **Henry G. Davis** of West Virginia for vice-president, hoping he could deliver the vote in his home state (he didn't). Davis was 80 years old (the oldest major-party candidate ever nominated for national office).

The relatively unknown Parker had little chance against the popular president, Roosevelt. **He was only able to carry the South, which continued to vote against the Republicans no matter who they put up**. In essence, **they were still voting against Lincoln**. In Florida, Louisiana, Mississippi, and South Carolina, Roosevelt was only able to get a few thousand votes despite his overwhelming popularity everywhere else in the country.

The Presidential Election of 1908

The 1908 president campaign began with the popular Republican incumbent president, **Theodore Roosevelt**, staying true to his pledge not to run for another term. Although that could have led to a wide-open race for the Republican nomination, it was not to be: Roosevelt made it clear that he wanted his Secretary of War and good friend, **William H. Taft**, to be the Party's nominee. At the

Republican National Convention, with Roosevelt's endorsement, Taft easily won the nomination.

STORY

In 1904, the Democrat Party in Florida had held a primary election to elect delegates to their national convention.

In 1908, **the Republican Party decided to also hold primaries**. Four states participated, California, Ohio, Pennsylvania, and Wisconsin. It resulted in a larger than normal number of candidates being presented at the Republican National Convention, many of them local favorites from the four states.

Despite the large number of potential candidates brought forward by the primary election method, the Party leaders still held sway, nominating their man, **William H. Taft.**

The Democratic National Convention was held in Denver, Colorado. It was the first time the national convention of a major party was held in a Western city.

At the convention, Populists, labor parties, and even socialist parties tried to make their voice heard.

However, in the end, it was again the great orator, William Jennings Bryan, who prevailed.

Bryan chose U.S. Senator from Indiana, **John W. Kern**, as his running mate (Indiana was still considered to be a swing state, and once again, it dictated the selection of a vice-presidential candidate).

STORY

Although William Randolph Hearst had lost his bid for the presidency in 1904, he was not the type to give up. In 1908, rebuffed by the Democrats, Hearst decided to create a new party, **the Independence Party**, and attract votes from populist voters. When his new party didn't get much attention, Hearst withdrew.

Nevertheless, he took an active role at the convention to influence the party's platform and in the general election to try to keep William Jennings Bryan from being elected.

Although Bryan was by then a very experienced presidential campaigner, his campaign was under funded. He was only able to carry the South and a few of the Western states.

Taft was elected by a comfortable margin.

The Presidential Election of 1912

The presidential election season of 1912 began with the threat of war in Europe. However, that threat was not to play a large role in the election. Instead, the nation's attention was fixed on the domestic issues of monetary supply, the gold standard, and labor versus big business.

STORY

By 1912, **some states had adopted the primary elections approach to choosing delegates** to send to the Republican National Convention. But the primaries were to yield a surprising result.

Even though President Theodore Roosevelt had originally endorsed William Howard Taft to be his successor, **Roosevelt had begun to feel that Taft was moving the party away from Populist principles.** Roosevelt took the surprising step of challenging Taft and announcing that he would once again seek the office of president. As a result, Roosevelt won most of the primaries. Taft only won Massachusetts; he even lost his home state of Ohio.

At the Republican National Convention, **both Roosevelt and Taft worked behind the scenes to sway delegates**, and when it seemed that Taft was going to be victorious, Roosevelt cried foul. He said that **he had proof that a number of state delegations had been illegally taken over by Taft forces, and he refused to participate in the convention any longer.**

After Taft won the nomination and selected his incumbent vice-president, **James S. Sherman**, Roosevelt started his own progressive political party. It was eventually nicknamed the "Bull Moose Party."

With the splitting off of Roosevelt from the Republican Party, the Democrats felt they had a good chance to oust the incumbent president. However, they struggled to select a candidate.

U.S. Congressman **James "Champ" Clark** from Missouri was serving as the U.S. Speaker of the House, and many felt he would be the Democratic nominee. **At the Democratic National Convention, Clark did receive the most votes on the first ballot, but he didn't get the two-thirds majority that was required to win the nomination**. Part of the reason why he didn't get the required number of votes, was because **he didn't have the support of William Jennings Bryan** who was still considered to be one of the movers and shakers of the Democratic Party. Bryan favored New Jersey Governor **Woodrow Wilson**. This led to neither candidate getting enough votes to win.

When ballot after ballot failed to yield a winner, **Thomas R. Marshall**, the Governor of Indiana, ordered his state's delegates to switch their allegiance to Wilson, and finally, after 46 ballots, Wilson was nominated. Of course, he selected Marshall to be his running mate.

STORY

Another political party, **the Socialist Party of America**, became better known during the president election of 1912. The
party had been growing in stature after it managed to pull together coalitions of trade unionists along with other populist
groups such as factory workers, immigrants, and farmers.
They declared themselves "at war" with capitalism with its
subjugation of workers. They nominated **Eugene V. Debs**, a
former U.S. Congressman from Indiana, along with **Emil Sei-
del**, the mayor of Milwaukee, to be his running mate.

With the split in the Republican Party and the emergence of the
Socialist Party, the presidential campaign of 1912 created a situation that made the unseating of an incumbent president more and
more likely.

Although Roosevelt and Taft received more votes in the general election than Wilson, together they won only 96 Electoral College votes. Wilson received 453 Electoral College votes and was
therefore elected the nation's 28th president. **It was the worst defeat in U.S. history of an incumbent president.**

Chapter Nine
The Politics of War

The Presidential Election of 1916

The **presidential election of 1916** took place against the backdrop of an ongoing bloody war in Europe. Wilson ran for reelection as a **Democrat** on a platform of **keeping the U.S. out of the war**. It was a popular position in 1916.

The **Republicans** put up Supreme Court Justice **Charles Evans Hughes**. He received the support of former president, Theodore Roosevelt.

The **Socialists** again put up a candidate, **A. L. Benson**, and although the socialist ideas were gaining some popularity in the country, there was little chance he would be able to win any Electoral College votes.

The popular vote was close, with 9,126,868 votes going to Wilson and 8,548,728 votes going for Hughes.

The Electoral College vote was also close, but Wilson, helped by the fact that women were now allowed to vote in some 30 states, was able to prevail 277 to 254. **His 23 vote majority in the Electoral College meant it would have taken only one or two states to swing the Electoral College in the other direction.** In many states outside of the South, the vote was very close.

STORY

Despite the ongoing war in Europe, after the election of 1916, most **Americans wanted the United States to maintain its neutrality**.

However, part of Germany's war effort was to use their fleet of U-boats (submarines) to attack and sink any ship that might be bringing supplies to England.

At that time, the United States was very dependent on its trade with England and other European countries that were allied with Britain. When the U.S. tried to maintain that trade despite the war, the **German U-boats began to sink U.S. ships,** and **President Wilson threatened retaliation.**

At about the same time, American officials learned **Germany was trying to use the memory of the Mexican-American war to get Mexico to join Germany's war effort.**

When that information was published by several U.S. newspapers, Americans were outraged. Although Wilson had promised in his campaign for the presidency to keep the United States out of the war in Europe, he now went before Congress to ask for a declaration of war against Germany.

Many Americans still wanted to stay out of the war, but **throughout history, few members of Congress have dared to vote against going to war if a president requests it.** On April 6, 1917, the Senate voted 82 to 6 to declare war on Germany. The House followed suit and voted 373 to 50 to allow the United States to enter **World War One** against the Germans.

The Presidential Election of 1920

By 1920, President Wilson had not only failed to keep the United States out of the "European War," he had also failed to rally the country behind his hope for a united League of Nations. He decided against running for reelection. As a result, the Republicans felt they had a good chance of regaining the White House.

However, The Nineteenth Amendment giving women the vote had been ratified earlier that year, and the Republicans were worried about how to get the women's vote. Some women had been allowed to vote in the presidential election of 1916, and they had mostly voted Democratic.

STORY

The presidential election of 1920 was the first to be held after the ratification of the Nineteenth Amendment. Therefore, it would therefore be the first presidential election in which women would be voting in all 48 states.

In the 1916 presidential election, about 30 states had permitted women to participate. Most political analysts believed the women would simply vote the way their husbands did, and the post-election analysis in 1916 showed that to be true in most Midwestern and Eastern states. But it was not true in the West; many women in the West had voted for the Democrat Wilson, even if their husbands voted Republican. When women were asked why they voted for Wilson, they said because "He kept us out of war." This distinction was especially notable in California where 400,000 women had voted. They mostly voted Democratic, even though the National Woman's Party had endorsed the Republican candidate.

However, in 1920, after Wilson had failed to keep the U.S. out of the European war, most women turned against the Democrats and voted Republican.

In the South, however, the dominate issue was not war, but was instead white supremacy. That meant the white women in the South mostly voted Democratic, and few women of color were allowed to vote.

Leading up to the **presidential election of 1920,** there was much turmoil in the country. Not only was the country war-weary, but also **labor unions were gaining considerable power**. They had begun using **strikes** as a tactic for improving wages and working conditions. Racial issues were also becoming more of a problem. Strife over labor issues led to race riots in several parts of the country. **One race riot that pitted blacks and whites**

against each other in East St. Louis resulted in the deaths of more than one hundred African-Americans. Another riot erupted in Chicago when **Irish groups fought African-Americans** that were attempting to get jobs at the Chicago stockyards.

Because the previous several elections had been close, **both of the leading political parties tried to pick candidates from states with the most Electoral College votes**. At that time, Ohio had 24 electoral votes, and as it turned out, both parties ended up picking candidates from that state.

The Democrats nominated Ohio Governor **James M. Cox**, and the Republicans chose Ohio Senator **Warren G. Harding**. Both had influence because **both were newspaper publishers** in an era when newspapers were becoming powerful political tools.

The Socialist again put up **Eugene V. Debs**, and although he was unable to win any Electoral College votes, he was able to capture almost a million popular votes.

The race between Harding and Cox did not turn out to be as close as everyone thought it would be. Harding won Ohio easily, and he also won most of the other large states. Cox, the Democrat, carried all of the Southern states, of course, but it was not enough to win.

Warren G. Harding won the Electoral College vote and became the 29th president.

In 1923, Harding died in office and his vice president, **Calvin Coolidge**, the former governor of Massachusetts, served out the last year of his term.

The Presidential Election of 1924

In 1924, it was a given that **incumbent president Coolidge** would be nominated by the Republicans. However, things were not so clear on the Democratic side. Harding's Secretary of the Interior, **Albert Bacon Fall**, had been convicted of receiving bribes from the oil companies in the so-called **Teapot Dome scandal**. However, **there was no proof that Coolidge had any knowledge of it**. Therefore, the Democrats would have to find a candidate that could successfully go up against him. At the Democratic National Convention, it took much back-room deal making and many ballots to finally select a candidate.

STORY

Going into the 1924 Democratic National Convention in New York City, there was much optimism. It was hoped that the voters would associate the Republicans with the Teapot Dome scandal. However, as more information about the scandal came out, it soon became clear that Democrats had also been involved.

Going into the convention, it seemed as if **William Gibbs McAdoo,** a lawyer from California and the son-in-law of former president Wilson, was the overwhelming favorite due to his support from labor.

However, it was soon leaned that **McAdoo also had a lawyer-client relationship with one of the central players in the Teapot Dome scandal. Also, McAdoo was supported by the Ku Klux Klan, and he was not willing to come out and say he did not welcome their support.** Even though the Democrats were the party of the South and the Klan was active in trying to keep African-American voters away from the polling places, there was growing distaste for the Klan's violent methods.

William Jennings Bryan was still a key player in the party, and when some said the Democrats should come out against the Ku Klux Klan, **he suggested avoiding the issue altogether so as to not lose the votes of the rural South.**

McAdoo came into the convention with a lot of delegate support he had gained in the primaries, and in the first ballot, most of the votes either went to McAdoo or New York Governor Al Smith, But neither was able to get the required two-

---

thirds majority. **Smith failed to get any votes from the Southern delegates because he was a Catholic.**

In ballot after ballot, the votes swung back and forth between McAdoo and Smith, and the **observers in the galleries were getting more and more rowdy.**

Many began to complain about New York rowdyism. William Jennings Bryan at one time suggested the convention should be halted and moved to another city.

After the sixtieth ballot, the delegates began to look for a compromise candidate. Indiana Senator **Samuel Ralston** was one name put forward, and **he had the full support of the Ku Klux Klan.** But like the other candidates, he couldn't get enough support to win.

Finally, on the one hundred and third ballot, the delegates settled on another compromise candidate, U.S. Congressman **John W. Davis** from West Virginia.

The delegates then nominated the **Charles W. Bryan**, governor of Nebraska and brother of William Jennings Bryan, to be their vice-presidential candidate.

A third-party candidate, **Robert M. La Follette**, a **Progressive** from Wisconsin also ran. **He was to become the most successful third-party candidate in the modern era.** He won 4,831,706 votes and carried his home state of Wisconsin with its 13 Electoral College votes.

However, **this time, the election was not close enough for the presence of a third-party candidate to throw the decision into the House of Representatives.**

Although Davis, the Democrat, once again carried the entire South (of course), he won no other electoral votes.

Coolidge won the Electoral College with a large majority.

The Presidential Election of 1928

In the presidential election of 1928, Coolidge chose not to run for reelection, and the Republicans nominated **Herbert Hoover** from California. He had been the nation's Commerce Secretary under president Harding.

The Democrats nominated Governor **Al Smith** from New York. Smith was a Catholic which meant the Ku Klux Klan would not support him, and that would cost him a lot of Southern votes. Also, there was widespread concern among Protestants that, if elected, he might take orders from the Pope.

Despite Smith's religion, he was still a Democrat going up against a Republican, so he won all of the South except for Florida. After 68 years, the South was still voting *against* the Republicans, the party that had elected the hated Abraham Lincoln, even if it meant voting for a Catholic.

STORY

Religion has rarely played a role in presidential elections because nearly every candidate has been a Protestant. After Al Smith lost badly in 1928, **neither the Democrats nor the Republicans dared nominate another Catholic until Democratic Senator John Kennedy was nominated in 1960** (he won in a very close election, despite much discussion about his religion).

Hoover easily won the presidential election of 1928 by one of the largest pluralities in modern presidential election history.

The Presidential Election of 1932

The **presidential election of 1932** took place in the middle of **the Great Depression**. The Republicans put **Herbert Hoover** up for reelection and Kansas Senator **Charles Curtis** for vice-president. However, with the economy being in such bad shape, few believed the Republicans would be able to hold onto the presidency.

The Democrats nominated **Franklin D. Roosevelt**, the wealthy governor of New York. He chose **John Nance Garner IV from Texas** as his running mate.

STORY

During the campaign, there was some talk about Roosevelt's health being an issue. **Roosevelt had contracted polio in 1921 and the infection left him permanently paralyzed from the waist down.** At that time, polio (poliomyelitis) was a common childhood disease and outbreaks of the disease were all too common during the summer months, especially in large cities.

Roosevelt learned to get around a bit with the help of leg braces and canes. At home he used a wheelchair, but he was careful to never be seen by the public in that wheelchair. The most famous pictures of him, such as in the back seat of his convertible, or on the deck of the USS Quincy at the end of WWII, always showed him sitting down.

Hoover's chances looked grim from the start. It was the first and only election (until 2016) in which many leading members of the Republican Party refused to support the party's nominee. Hoover only won the Northeastern states, Connecticut, Delaware, Maine, New Hampshire, Pennsylvania, and Vermont, and even in those states his margin of victory was very slim.

The election was a landslide for Roosevelt who became the first Democratic presidential candidate to win since Wilson had won in 1916. Roosevelt won the South, of course (the Democrats had been winning the South since the election of Republican Abraham Lincoln in 1860), but he also won the Midwest and the

West which marked quite a change in national voting patterns (only four years before, Republican Hoover had won every single Midwestern and Western state).

The Presidential Election of 1936

With the depression still going on, **Roosevelt** ran for reelection in **1936**. His running mate was again John Garner.

The Republicans nominated **Alf Landon**, the governor of Kansas.

STORY

The Great Depression influenced several presidential elections. The poor economy was the main reason Hoover was overwhelmingly rejected by the voters in 1932.

Roosevelt's voter "mandate" meant he was able to enact many radically new "New Deal" programs. (However, some of his programs were later declared unconstitutional.)

Although there were some fundamental problems in the U.S. economy before 1929, the depression is usually thought to have begun on "**Black Tuesday**," October 29, 1929. That day the U.S. stock market dropped dramatically. **The downturn had actually begun the week before** when stock market instability had scared some investors, and many of them chose to get out of the market. Then on "Black Tuesday," even more investors sold out. That day, a huge number of shares were traded, and stocks fell an average of twelve percent.

William C. Durant and **the Rockefeller family** saw the fall in stock prices as an opportunity to buy at historically low prices, so they stepped in and bought stocks in large quantities. That helped convince some investors that the market was safe. But after a bit of recovery, the market began to fall again.

Although investors like **John D. Rockefeller** tried to talk about a stock market comeback, the problem was that many ordinary citizens had begun to invest in the market, and many had lost money in the downturn. At that time, **in order to attract investors, stock brokers were in the habit of lending small investors money to buy stock**s, so it was not just stock speculators that were wiped out. Many people reacted to the economic downturn by spending less. That started **a cycle of business slowdown and job layoffs, which led to even less spending.**

It didn't help that the Midwestern plains states were suffering from an extended drought that eventually led to what was referred to as the "**dust bowl**" (the drying out and blowing away of rich agricultural soil).

President Hoover's response to the economic slowdown was to try to pressure businesses to keep workers employed and to keep wages high. That didn't work very well because the businesses were under too much pressure from decreasing sales. Hoover did lower some taxes, but at first he was opposed to the government getting involved in job programs or putting money into the economy in any other way. Instead, **he believed churches and private charities should take up the challenge.** As for government back-to-work programs, he said that was up to local and state governments.

When the depression worsened, Hoover *did* begin to institute some large-scale government job-creation programs. The huge Hoover Dam project on the Colorado River is one example.

For the Democrats, there was some concern that Roosevelt might lose the South in 1936 because **Southern Republicans had started calling him as a socialist**. They claimed his "**New Deal**" policies, including Social Security and unemployment relief, were taking the United States down the road toward socialism.

But Roosevelt needn't have worried about losing the South. In the Southern states where African-Americans were systematically kept from voting, **the Republican candidate hardly got any votes at all.** For example, in Mississippi, Landon got only 4,443 votes, and in South Carolina he only got 1,646 votes. It was clear that **even 76 years after Lincoln's election, the South was still voting *against* Lincoln and the Republicans, even if it meant voting for a very liberal (and some said *Socialist*) candidate.**

Roosevelt carried every state except Maine and Vermont. His Electoral College win was an overwhelming 523 to 8.

The Presidential Election of 1940

By the time the presidential election of 1940 came around, the economy was improving and all attention was on the ongoing World War II in Europe. The country was divided as to whether the U.S. should go to the aid of England and France to try to stop Hitler's German aggression.

John Garner, Roosevelt's vice president, **assumed Roosevelt would stick to tradition and not run for a third term**, so he decided to make a run for the presidency on the Democratic ticket. He was much more conservative than Roosevelt and disagreed with much of the New Deal agenda. As a result, he had much wider support in the South and in the conservative rural states.

However, President Roosevelt **decided to break with tradition and run for a third term**. He chose his Secretary of Commerce, **Henry Wallace** from Iowa to be his Vice President.

When the Republicans were unable to agree on a candidate, a surprising dark horse named **Wendell Willkie** came forward. He was an industrialist from Indiana who had never been much involved in politics.

Throughout the election, the Republicans focused on Roosevelt's perceived failure to end the depression and his willingness to get the United States involved in the ongoing war in Europe.

Roosevelt responded by saying it was his New Deal programs that were ending the Great Depression, and **he said he had no intention of getting involved in the European war**.

Again, there was talk that Roosevelt was too liberal, and that meant he would lose the conservative South. In 1940, it did seem possible that a Republican could win the South because a "conservative coalition" had emerged in Congress that brought together conservative Southern Democrats with conservative Republicans. By election time, they had already been successful at defeating *some* of Roosevelt's liberal New Deal policies. Many thought the two groups would work together to defeat Roosevelt in the upcoming presidential election.

STORY

Nationally, there was little notice that during the second Roosevelt administration there had been a dramatic shift in how African-Americans were voting in presidential elections. In the North, Midwest, and West, African-Americans had been voting Republican since the election of Abraham Lincoln. However, in the South, even as late as 1932, many African-Americans were still either being kept away from the polling places or being discouraged through the use of poll taxes and literacy tests (**The 24th Amendment, which prohibited poll taxes wasn't passed until 1964**.)

In the 1930s, **the Ku Klux Klan was still a powerful political force in the South**, especially in rural areas. The Klan always supported Democratic candidates, and they used intimidation and/or violence to keep African-Americans from going to the polling places to vote Republican.

However, by the time the 1934 election was underway, many African-Americans had seen the benefits of Roosevelt's New Deal policies and were starting to shift their loyalties away from the Republicans. It was the beginning of **a strange coalition of Southern Whites and Southern Blacks that helped to keep Roosevelt in power for four terms of office.**

As it turned out, there was no shift away from the Democrats in the South: white Southern voters were still unwilling to vote for the hated "Lincoln-Republicans," no matter how liberal Roosevelt was.

The East also went for Roosevelt, except once again, conservative Maine and Vermont voted against him.

The Presidential Election of 1944

By the time the presidential election of 1944 came around, the nation was at war. Germany's ally, **the Japanese, had attacked the U.S. naval base at Pearl Harbor in Hawaii** and it immediately drew the United States into **World War Two.**

As the fall election approached, the entire country was focused on winning what was turning out to be a very difficult war.

Nearly every family had somebody involved "over there," and casualties were high. Most of the families in America dreaded the arrival of the telegraph delivery boy, sure that any news from Europe would be bad news about their loved one.

In addition, **nearly every family in the country was either working on something related to the war effort, or suffering restrictions because of it.** Although the war was taking place far away, there was a feeling that if the Germans and the Japanese were not stopped they would soon arrive on our shores. As a result, the people were probably less involved in the election of 1944 than any previous election.

For the 1944 presidential election, the **Republicans** put up **Thomas E. Dewey**, the governor of New York. He chose **John Bricker**, the Governor of Ohio, as his running mate.

It was no surprise when **Roosevelt ran for reelection in 1944,** this time with **Harry S. Truman** as his vice president. With the U.S. in the middle of a war, most assumed Roosevelt would be re-elected.

Dewey campaigned hard against Roosevelt, saying four terms for a president was too many. Some accused the president of trying to become a king. Others continued to **try to paint him as a socialist**, pointing out that some of his New Deal programs had been declared unconstitutional, and others had been overturned in Congress (mostly through the efforts of the conservative coalition).

COMMENT

When Franklin D. Roosevelt ran for a third term it was unprecedented in U.S. presidential election history. The Republicans pointed out the fact that George Washington had declined to run for a third term as president. They said President Washington's decision indicated the founding fathers wanted to limit the time a president could serve.

Based on that reasoning, they introduced a measure to amend the Constitution to limit the number of terms a person could hold the presidency. It was passed and the result was **the Twenty-Second Amendment which limited any one individual's term of presidency to two terms**. It was ratified by three-fourths of the states on February 27, 1951.

By the time the election campaign was underway, the economy was improving, helping Roosevelt's chances. In addition, U.S. troops had landed on the beaches of Normandy on June 6, 1944, and although American casualties were heavy, **the invasion of Europe was being seen as a success**.

By the end of August, U.S. troops were in Paris, and there had also been a string of successful battles against Japan in the Pacific. By election day, U.S. troops were at the Germany border.

The military successes of that summer were enough to convince most U.S. citizens that Roosevelt was running the war properly.

Roosevelt was reelected for a fourth term, again winning all of the Southern states. However, much of the conservative Midwest voted against Roosevelt, and Dewey, the Republican candidate, actually got quite a few votes in some of the Southern states. The conservative versus liberal message was beginning to gain some traction in the South. For example, although Roosevelt won North Carolina, Dewey managed to get 263,155 votes. In West Virginia, where Roosevelt had won easily in 1940, Dewey got 322,819 votes.

However, in South Carolina, Republican Dewey only got 4,610 votes. In Mississippi, he only got 11,601 votes.

Nationwide, the popular vote was fairly close, 25,612,916 for Roosevelt and 22,017,929 for Dewey. But the Electoral College vote was not close at all. It came out 432 for Roosevelt and only 99 for Dewey.

Roosevelt died after only a few months into his fourth term. His vice president, **Harry Truman,** was sworn in as president, and he presided over the last few months of the war, including the atomic bomb attacks on Japan.

STORY

World War Two did not play as much of a role in U.S. presidential politics as you might think. Although the war did influence the voting that took place prior to the election of 1940 when Wendell Willkie accused Roosevelt of trying to get the U.S involved in what people saw as "a European war," Roosevelt's promise to keep the country out of the war defused Willkie's attack.

But when Japan attacked the American naval base at Pearl Harbor, nearly all Americans supported Roosevelt when he went on the radio to tell the country he was asking Congress for a declaration of war on Japan. **His "day of infamy" speech** was a rallying cry for the U.S. to enter the war on the side of the allies. He issued a presidential order that said any government agency that was in any way related to the war effort would report directly him. **He ordered many corporations to modify their manufacturing lines to make war materials** and established a goal of producing 10,000 new fighter airplanes per year. **He also ordered an emergency shipbuilding program to quickly build ships** to carry troops and war materials.

The **Selective Service Act** was passed with Roosevelt's help, and when the U.S. declared war on Japan and Germany, all men in the United States between the ages of 16 and 65 were required to register for the draft.

Millions of young men were drafted into the Army and millions more voluntarily signed up to serve in one of the military branches.

It is a little known fact that the Selective Service Act even provided a role for those who were, for reasons of religion or personal belief, unwilling to fight in wars. It said they would not be required to undergo combat training but would instead undergo training for noncombatant support roles.

The Presidential Election of 1948

In 1948, Truman ran for reelection. He was nominated by the Democrats, and he chose Senator **Alben Barkley** as his running mate.

The Republicans again nominated **Thomas Dewey** and his running mate, **Earl Warren**, the Governor of California.

Henry A. Wallace, Roosevelt's former vice president, was also on the ballot as a **Progressive Party** candidate.

Despite the national joy that the war was finally over, Truman was not all that popular. There was trouble brewing in Asia, and elsewhere, as an aftermath of the war, and there was some **unease about the fact that Truman had ordered atomic bombs dropped on innocent Japanese civilians when many thought the war was all but over anyhow.**

There was also concern about what was going on in Europe. The division of Berlin between the Eastern and Western powers was still unsettled, and Russia's blockade of Berlin was an **indication of the cold war that would develop between Russia and the United States.**

STORY

The election of 1948 was the first in which the Democratic stranglehold on the South began to loosen. Four terms of a liberal president had not deterred Southern voters from voting against the Republicans, the hated party of Lincoln. But when the Democrats began to talk about civil rights for Southern Blacks, many in the South saw unwanted change coming

At the Democratic national nominating convention, Truman promised that if he was elected, he would introduce **civil rights legislation.** Hearing that, the **Southern Democratic delegates all got up and walked out.** They held their own convention in Birmingham, Alabama and **nominated Senator Strom Thurmond** from South Carolina as a States' Right Democrat.

Thurmond ran on a segregationist platform and managed to squeak out wins in Alabama and Louisiana. He also won his home state of South Carolina, and he won Mississippi overwhelmingly.

With the loss of some of the South, the first results showed the election was very close. Truman had also lost some of the Midwest, but he won the Northeast and the West coast.

Some newspapers came out the morning after the election with mistaken banner headlines declaring "**Dewey Wins**," but when the long process of counting the ballots was finally finished, Truman had won after all with 24,179,347 nationwide popular votes over Dewey's 21,991,292 votes.

The final Electoral College vote was Truman 303, Dewey 189, and Thurmond 39.

Thurmond's wins in the South **marked the first time in the modern era that a third-party candidate had won a significant number of electoral votes**. Had only a few states in the rest of the country gone for Dewey, **it would have meant that no candidate would have reached the required majority**, and that would have thrown the decision about who would be president into the House of Representatives.

Chapter Ten
Postwar and Cold War Politics

The Presidential Election of 1952

In 1952, the Republicans finally managed to convince **World War Two hero, General Dwight D. Eisenhower**, to run for president. They had tried to convince him to run in 1948, but he had refused. This time they told him it was his duty to the country, and he finally accepted.

Because the **Cold War** with Russia was bound to be one of the main election issues, Eisenhower chose noted anti-communist, **Richard Nixon,** from California, as his running mate.

The Democrats were in a quandary because **Truman, the incumbent, had decided not to run**. By 1952, primary elections to select a party's candidate were becoming the norm and in the Democratic primaries, Governor **Adlai Stevenson II** of Illinois was showing well. He was nominated at the 1952 Democratic national presidential nominating convention in Chicago. In **an attempt to recapture the Southern vote**, he selected **John Jackson Sparkman from Alabama** as his running mate.

There was little doubt about the popularity of General Eisenhower, but some of his opinions were very controversial. He was a strong believer in the United Nations, and thought that organization could better control the expansion of nuclear weapons than the United States could.

Those kinds of non-nationalistic opinions were strongly opposed by **Republican Senator Joseph McCarthy** who was beating the drums of nationalism and stirring up anti-communist "witch hunts" through the use of his congressional committee that was finding anti-American communist spies under every rock. He said there were "commies" everywhere, including, he said, within the entertainment industry and even deep inside the U.S. government.

Two years before, the **Korean War** had flared up as a result of the postwar division of that country. The conflict was showing signs of expanding into a showdown with China, and maybe even Russia.

Having just been involved in a horrific world war, this time the **people of the United States were not so enthusiastic about getting involved in yet another war**.

By 1952, **Russia had developed its own atomic bomb**, and Joseph Stalin, the Russian Premier was making threatening comments toward the U.S.

In the face of such threats, what the United States needed was a hero. Eisenhower, the famous Army general, fit that bill. **He was elected by a large majority in the Electoral College, 442 to 89, to be the first Republican in the White House in 20 years.**

As usual, the South mostly went to the Democrats. Stevenson won most of the Southern states by large majorities. However, for the first time in many years, a few Southern states, Florida, Tennessee, and Virginia, went for the Republican candidate, although by narrow majorities in each case.

After 92 years, cracks in the anti-Lincoln, anti-Republican Southern attitude were beginning to show.

STORY

The **Korean War** was one of the Asian conflicts that flared up after World War Two over **who would control a country after the Japanese were forced to withdraw.**

Without consulting the Koreans, the allies decided to divide the country north and south. In 1950, armed conflict broke out between the divided sections.

As the conflict escalated, the North Koreans were supported by the People's Republic of China and Russia (the Union of Soviet Socialist Republics), while the South Koreans were being supported by the United States. It was to become **the first** armed conflict of the so-called "cold war" that pitted the U.S. against what was seen as a communist agenda to control the post-war world. From the U.S. point of view, the "war" was mostly against Russia, but there was also talk about a threat from communist China.

With the support of the U.S. military, the South Koreans invaded the North, only to be pushed back when the Chinese army came to the aid of the North Koreans.

In 1953, an uneasy stalemate was reached along the 38th parallel that divided the country north and south.

A **Demilitarized Zone** along that line still maintains the stalemate to this day. Democratic South Korea has developed a thriving economy based on manufacturing and export, while North Korea has retreated into a secretive communist dictatorship which has, reportedly, pushed most of its citizens into poverty.

Nevertheless, many South Koreans still hope for eventual unification.

The Presidential Election of 1956

In 1956, Eisenhower again ran against **Adlai Stevenson,** and for the first time, **political television advertising played a significant role.** Much of the TV advertising was aimed at women voters.

The cold war was still going on, but Senator McCarthy had been discredited, leaving most Americans less worried about communist infiltration here at home.

Nevertheless, despite the country being in a period of peace and prosperity, the U.S. military was **actively pursuing development of even more powerful nuclear weapons** in response to a perceived threat from Russia.

Meanwhile, Russia was doing the same. The proliferation of

nuclear weapons continued until it actually became a policy known as **mutual assured destruction,** which many hoped would keep either side from being the first to use such weapons.

With the Korean War becoming only a memory, and the U.S. economy doing well, most thought Eisenhower was assured of another term.

STORY

Despite the traditional strength of the Democratic Party in the South, some voters there were beginning to rebel against what they saw as Northern liberalism taking control of the country.

The main issue in the South was civil rights; they worried that Northerners, if elected, might pass new legislation that would break down the established Southern policy of strict segregation and give African-Americans more civil rights.

In the 1956 election, some Southern Democratic leaders broke with the national Democratic Party and tried to manipulate the Electoral College outcome by getting a slate of "**unpledged**" electors onto the ballot. (**An unpledged elector has not pledged to support any particular candidate for President.**) By voting for unpledged electors, voters could register their displeasure with either candidate.

In Alabama, the unpledged electors got 20,150 votes. In Louisiana, they got 44,520 votes. In Mississippi, they got 42,266 votes (seventeen percent of the total vote), and in South Carolina, they got 88,509 votes (almost thirty percent of the total vote). It was clear voting patterns were changing in the South. Although the unpledged electors were unable to win any states, it was a sign of things to come.

In the end, the Republican Eisenhower was soundly beaten by Stevenson in the traditionally anti-Lincoln, anti-Republican states of Mississippi and South Carolina. But he won every state outside of the South, and he managed to pick up a few of the border states that he had lost in the previous election, squeaking out wins in Kentucky and West Virginia.

The Presidential Election of 1960

In 1960, Eisenhower's vice president, Californian **Richard Nixon**, was nominated by the Republicans to run against the Democratic nominee, **John F. Kennedy, the young senator from Massachusetts**.

From the beginning, everyone knew it was going to be a close election. The economy was not doing all that well, and **the Russian launch of the world's first satellite, Sputnik**, gave Americans the feeling that the U.S. was falling behind Russia. It was a notable milestone in "**the cold war**" that would dominate politics for decades.

There was even talk that the election would end up in the House of Representatives because there was a movement underway in the South to take votes away from Kennedy because he was seen as a Catholic liberal who might introduce legislation that would outlaw segregation and end discrimination against African-Americans.

Nixon, despite having served as vice president under the fairly liberal Eisenhower, was known to be conservative and anti-communist.

People began to speculate that the Democratic Party's hold on the South was about to end. If that happened, it would dramatically change all future American presidential elections.

STORY

The **1960 election introduced televised debates.** Many wondered if they would change how people voted, and if it could overcome the influence of local party machinery. **Some thought the election would be won or lost by how well the candidates came across on the small screen,** and that turned out to be at least partly true. Analysis of the four televised debates revealed an interesting fact: **those who heard the debates on the radio thought Nixon did very well, but those who watched the debates on television thought he did very poorly** against the calm and polished (and handsome) Kennedy. **It was becoming clear that television was going to be the way people learned about the candidates.**

The first televised debate was watched by an estimated 77 million people. **At the time, that was over sixty percent of the adult population in the U.S.**

Four prime-time debates, in which journalists asked the candidates to respond to questions, were shown on TV in September and October, the period in which it was thought independents would still be making up their minds.

Kennedy was well prepared for the debates. He looked directly at the camera and spoke not to the journalists in the hall, but to the TV audience. Nixon, on the other hand, seemed to be having a private dialogue with the journalist who had asked the question.

The overall appearance of the candidates was much discussed in the post-debate analysis. Kennedy, who was considerably younger than Nixon, seemed athletic and at ease. Nixon, who was recovering from the flu, seemed unsteady and uncomfortable. He refused to wear make-up, which made him look pale and drawn as compared to the tanned Kennedy.

Despite the attention the post-debate analysts paid to Kennedy's appearance, it was undoubtedly the way he dealt with the medium of television overall was probably even more important: **he talked directly to the TV audience, and he kept his answers short and to the point.**

In the 1960 presidential campaign, **television advertising was also becoming more important.** Kennedy was one of the first to use television clips in his ads. He used an excerpt from one of President Eisenhower's press conferences in which a reporter had asked what contribution Vice President Nixon had made to his two terms in office. Eisenhower joked that if he could be given a week, he might think of something. It got a good laugh from the assembled reporters, but in the campaign, Nixon had been making much of his experience in government.

By 1960, Alaska and Hawaii had been admitted to the Union, and the citizens of the two newest states would finally be able to participate in a presidential election. However, with only six electoral votes between them, they didn't get much attention from the candidates.

The real election battleground was in the South. To help him win the Southern States, Kennedy chose **Texan Lyndon B. Johnson** as his running mate.

Despite much negative talk about Kennedy being a Catholic, **most Southerners were still voting against the "Lincoln Republicans."**

For that reason, Kennedy was able to win the predominantly Protestant Southern states of Georgia, Louisiana, North Carolina, and South Carolina.

But the growing anti-liberal movement in the South cost him Florida, Kentucky, Tennessee, and Virginia. In Mississippi,

Southern conservatives again put up a slate of unpledged electors as a protest against voting for either candidate. In that state, **the unpledged electors received more votes than either Nixon or Kennedy, winning Mississippi's eight electoral votes.** In Alabama, Nixon received more votes than Kennedy, but **the majority of the state's voters voted for the six unpledged conservative electors** who, it was clear, were not going to cast their Electoral College votes for either Kennedy or Nixon.

When the Electoral College met to cast their ballots, all of the unpledged electors cast their votes for segregationists, Harry F. Byrd and Strom Thurmond.

Nevertheless, **Kennedy managed to win enough Electoral College votes to be elected president. The final Electoral College vote was Kennedy 303, Nixon 219, and Harry Byrd 15.**

COMMENT

As in most close elections, there were **accusations of voter fraud in favor of Kennedy, especially in Mayor Daley's Chicago, and in Johnson's home state of Texas.** Investigators later found that in some counties in Texas, more votes were cast for the Kennedy-Johnson ticket than there were voters in that county.

As soon as Kennedy was elected, he instituted new domestic programs and set about to change the nation's foreign policy. At home, he reinvigorated the space program and promised a balanced budget.

STORY

The Republicans often said Kennedy was soft on communism, but in the spring of 1961, **he authorized a plan to try to overthrow the communist government of Cuba**. The CIA and the U.S. military landed 1500 former Cubans near the **Bay of Pigs** on the remote south side of the island of Cuba. They had been trained by the U.S. military in guerrilla tactics and were supposed to rally the people against Fidel Castro's government.

However, the Cuban military soon killed or rounded up all of the guerrillas, and **the U.S. was forced to pay a ransom to get the survivors back**.

Then, in October of 1962, **CIA U-2 spy planes photographed missile sites being built by Russian technicians in Cuba**. It was possible the missiles could be used in a future nuclear attack on the United States.

It was **the greatest crisis of Kennedy's administration**. The military wanted to immediately bomb the missile sites, but Kennedy was afraid that would lead to a direct confrontation with Russia, with the potential that it could escalate into nuclear war.

Kennedy decided on **a naval blockade of Cuba** until the missiles were removed.

Tension with Russia mounted until a deal was secretly struck. Russia's Premier, Nikita Khrushchev, agreed to dismantle the missile sites in Cuba if the U.S. would dismantle its missile sites in Turkey and promise never to invade Cuba. Kennedy agreed.

The **"Cuban Missile Crisis"** as it came to be known, **quieted Republican criticism of Kennedy as being soft on communism** and considerably enhanced Kennedy's approval rating.

In November of 1963, President Kennedy was on a visit to Dallas. He was riding in the back seat of a convertible limousine when **he was shot and killed by Lee Harvey Oswald,** a former Marine marksman who had positioned himself above the street in a 6th floor window of a nearby building.

Lyndon Johnson was immediately sworn in as president to serve out the last year of the presidency before the election of 1964.

Chapter Eleven
The Politics of War and Antiwar

The Presidential Election of 1964

In 1964, sitting president **Lyndon Johnson** was nominated for reelection by the **Democrats**. Johnson's only serious competition in the primaries came from **Alabama's governor George Wallace** who had come to national prominence when he **stood in the doorway of the University of Alabama** to block the entrance of black students. The event was covered on live TV.

Wallace's name appeared on that ballot in three of the sixteen states that were holding Democratic presidential primaries that year, Wisconsin, Indiana, and Maryland. **Running on a segregationist platform, Wallace won a surprising number of votes in those states.**

STORY

George Wallace's infamous "**stand in the schoolhouse door**" came about after the United States Supreme Court handed down a decision that state taxpayer-supported universities could not legally refuse to admit students because of their race. Most states complied to one degree or another, but the University of Alabama, with the support of the state's governor and other leading politicians, **found ways to reject a student application if they found out the student had *any* African-American heritage**.

When the University of Alabama refused to accept the applications of three fully-qualified African-American students, the students went to court. A federal judge ordered them to be admitted.

When the three student arrived on the opening day of classes, Governor Wallace was there in the doorway with local police to block their entrance. He had made sure there would be plenty of news media present to record the confrontation, and the national TV networks carried the event live for all the nation to watch.

Knowing ahead of time what was going to happen, President Kennedy federalized the Alabama National Guard and ordered them to make sure the students were admitted, by force if necessary.

The students were admitted, but **it gained Wallace a big following throughout the South and that emboldened him to later make a run for the presidency of the United States.**

Despite Wallace's presence in the race, at the Democratic national nominating convention, Johnson won easily. He chose U.S. Senator **Hubert Humphrey** from Minnesota as his running mate.

The Republicans nominated **Barry Goldwater**, a conservative from Arizona. He chose Congressman **William E. Miller** from New York as his running mate.

In 1964, the candidates primarily used television to get their message across to the public, and **television "attack" ads began to evolve.**

Johnson's ads used skillfully done movie-like scenarios to portray what might happen if Goldwater was elected. The infamous **"Daisy Girl" ad** showed an innocent-looking little girl picking petals from a daisy in a field of flowers. As she counted the flower's petals, the screen morphed into a missile launch countdown followed by a dramatic nuclear explosion. The ads were in response to **Goldwater's statement that nuclear weapons might have to be used in some circumstances**. Although the ad didn't come right out and accuse Goldwater of being an advocate of nuclear war, it effectively made the point that Goldwater's militaristic opinions could lead the country in that dangerous direction.

Paradoxically, Johnson was already secretly getting the country more deeply involved in the cold war against the communists. As the election campaign progressed, U.S. forces were beginning to engage enemy forces in Vietnam. President Johnson was fully aware of the worsening situation there, but he didn't want a new war to be at the forefront of the American public's attention with the election coming up, so he kept it quiet.

Johnson won most of the nation in a landslide, but Goldwater carried Alabama, Georgia, Louisiana, Mississippi, and South Carolina. It was the first time a Republican had carried that much of the deep South, and it **marked the end of a one hundred year dominance of Democrats in the region**. That change in voting preferences was to have a profound effect on every presidential election from then on.

STORY

By the time Johnson won the election in the fall of 1964, **U.S. forces were secretly becoming more engaged in combat in Vietnam**.

Years before, President Eisenhower had told President Kennedy that he believed the U.S. would end up having to send troops to Vietnam. After soviet Premier Nikita Khrushchev said Russia would support the North Vietnamese communists, Eisenhower predicted Vietnam would be the next hot spot in the escalating "cold war."

In 1961, Johnson, as vice president, had visited President Diem in South Vietnam and hailed him as the "Winston Churchill of Asia."

Soon after that visit, skirmishes with troops from North Vietnam began. In response, President Kennedy sent a few hundred Green Beret '"advisors" to South Vietnam to help train the South Vietnamese Army.

When more attacks on South Vietnam came from the north, Vietnamese President Diem requested more military aid from Kennedy. In response, Kennedy sent General Maxwell Taylor to Vietnam to access the situation. Taylor came back alarmed at what he had seen. He told Kennedy that if Vietnam fell into the hands of the communists, all of Southeast Asia could eventually fall.

The Pentagon advised Kennedy's Defense Secretary Robert McNamara that a massive show of force was needed in Vietnam. McNamara concurred and suggested to Kennedy that the U.S. should send at least 20,000 troops there. Kennedy decided against it, and to this day there is discussion about **whether the U.S. would have gotten so deeply involved in Vietnam had Kennedy not been assassinated**.

Kennedy *did* continue to send advisors to Vietnam (eventually more than 16,000), and he also sent helicopter units. In the fall of 1961, he guaranteed President Diem that the United States would help Vietnam "preserve its independence."

In 1962, a reporter had asked President Kennedy if any Americans in Vietnam were engaged in the fighting there. The president said no, but in fact, they were. U.S. pilots were participating in bombing runs using U.S. aircraft, and in some of the attacks, civilians were being killed, leading to more and more ill will among the locals toward the American presence.

Defense Secretary McNamara visited South Vietnam during the summer of 1962 and **came back to tell President Kennedy that the South Vietnamese war against the northern invaders was going well** because of U.S. help.

Soon after that visit, the first U.S. Special Forces base was secretly established at Khe Sanh.

When Buddhist rioters in South Vietnam took to the streets in Saigon to protest a government crackdown on religion, they were fired on by South Vietnamese troops. **Several Buddhist monks publicly burned themselves to death as an act of protest,** and the worldwide publicity from those acts brought Vietnam to the attention of American citizens for the first time. Some citizen groups began asking what we were doing over there, and reports began to circulate that the U.S. was supporting a corrupt government in Vietnam.

Soon, a coup was mounted against President Diem, resulting in the assassination of Diem and his brother. Later evidence suggested that the CIA had at least tacitly supported the coup.

By the time Kennedy was assassinated in November 24, 1963, the situation in Vietnam had become very unstable. **Viet Cong guerrillas were occupying more and more of the countryside.**

As soon as President Johnson was sworn in, he took over management of the war. At press conferences, **he began making strong statements that the U.S. would not allow the communists to take Vietnam.**

At first, President Johnson made sure most of **the U.S. involvement in the Vietnam War was being done covertly.** Secret U.S. bombing raids, using U.S. airplanes and "volunteer" American pilots, were attacking Viet Cong bases both in Vietnam and in Laos.

Defense Secretary McNamara began making more and more public statements indicating that the U.S. would support the new Vietnamese military government. He said, **"We'll stay for as long as it takes."**

After that, America was committed. Johnson believed the reputation of the U.S. (and his personal reputation) was on the line.

But when word leaked out that our "support" of the South Vietnamese was already **costing the U.S. more than two million dollars a day**, more people began to ask if it was such a good idea to be committing those kinds of resources in a tiny and relatively unknown country halfway around the world.

Johnson continued to try to keep the war low profile, mainly because **he knew he didn't have the support in Congress for another Asian war so soon after the debacle in Korea**.

He mostly used the CIA to conduct secret operations out of Saigon, and he used U.S. Navy warships to harass North Vietnamese installations along the coast.

Meanwhile, in Vietnam, the increasing success of the Viet Cong was causing political instability. **In one year, South Vietnam saw five different governments come into power**.

In the summer of 1964, President Johnson was preoccupied with running for election. He named Lt. Gen William C. Westmoreland to oversee operations in Vietnam.

Senator Barry Goldwater, Johnson's very conservative Republican opponent in the election, tried to use the lack of more aggressive action in Vietnam to paint Johnson as soft on communism.

At the beginning of August, only a few months before the presidential election was to take place, the "**Gulf of Tonkin Incident**" took place. It involved U.S. warships that were supporting South Vietnamese speed boats that were staging attacks on North Vietnamese coastal installations. North Vietnamese torpedo boats came out to respond and were shelled by the USS Maddox, a Sumner-class destroyer. It was reported that at least one of the torpedo boats fired back, and that one 14.5 mm round hit the destroyer. The round didn't cause any serious damage on the Maddox, and no one was injured. Later that same day, a second attack was reported.

As minor as the incident was, it was nevertheless the excuse Johnson had been looking for to show he was not soft on communism. He went on the radio to describe **two attacks by North Vietnamese vessels against U.S. Navy ships "on the high seas,"** and that the U.S. could not allow such things. In his speech, he did not indicate that the U.S. was already involved in Vietnam in any way other than in a supporting role. The implication of his speech was that the North Vietnamese had launched an unprovoked attack on a U.S. ship that was just minding its own business out in international waters, and therefore, the U.S. had to respond in Vietnam.

The truth, as we later learned, was that **neither Johnson nor McNamara were sure there really had been an attack**, and later the captain of one of the ships involved said the second attack might have actually been a false radar image.

There was some resistance in Congress to getting involved in Vietnam, but after some deliberation, they passed the **Tonkin Gulf Resolution** which authorized President Johnson to use "conventional" military force in Southeast Asia if necessary. Significantly, it was not a formal declaration of war by Congress. The "Vietnam War" was never actually designated as a war; it was termed a **"police action."** Looking back, "police action" is an odd euphemism for a conflict that is estimated to have **cost the lives of 266,000 Army of the Republic of Vietnam soldiers, 1,100,000 North Vietnamese Army and Viet Cong soldiers, 58,272 American soldiers, and 843,000 Vietnamese civilians**. In addition, **303,644 American soldiers were wounded in action** -- not counting those that suffered from **post-traumatic stress disorder (PTSD)** as a result of what they experienced in Vietnam.

As the U.S. involvement in Vietnam escalated, there were some protests against it back home in the U.S. Later, as the news media began showing footage of Americans fighting and dying over there, the protests increased. **Eventually, some of the antiwar protests attracted as many as half a million people.**

The **Viet Cong's Tet offensive** in January of 1968 further undermined U.S. support for the war. Popular CBS anchorman Walter Cronkite went on TV to say that in his opinion the U.S. was mired in a stalemate in Vietnam. He was one of the first public figures to suggest that the U.S. might actually lose a war.

On March 31, 1968, **President Johnson went on live television to announce that he would not seek reelection,** saying, "There is division in the American house now."

His 1964 campaign promise of creating a "great society" had been ruined when his focus turned to combating communism. It caused him to escalate a pointless war in Vietnam that ended in complete failure. By the end of his presidency, there was no great society, only a divided nation that was deeply involved in a war that was costing the country untold amounts of money and many thousands of American lives.

The Presidential Election of 1968

In 1968, **Johnson's decision not to run for reelection meant the race for the presidency was wide open.**

Richard Nixon, Eisenhower's former vice president threw his hat into the ring. His two main rivals were Michigan Governor **George W. Romney** and California Governor **Ronald Reagan**.

Everyone knew the election would be a referendum on the Vietnam War, and there were clear choices between the candidates. Nixon and Reagan were both saying America had to be tough on communism, and that Vietnam was a key test of America's resolve. Romney had voted for the **Tonkin Gulf Resolution,** and he had been an early supporter of the war. But now he said Vietnam was a mistake. **He said he had been "brainwashed" by the military into supporting the Vietnam War**. That remark cost him a lot of votes in the Republican primaries.

Both Nixon and Reagan knew the Democrats were likely to run somebody who would make ending the Vietnam War a priority. In order to make the election about fighting communism, **Nixon and Reagan tried to show they would be tougher on communism, and that they would win the war in Vietnam**. Much of Nixon's oratory was to rail against the anti-war protesters that he characterized as un-American supporters of worldwide communism.

By the end of the Republican primaries, it was clear Republican voters were responding to Nixon's pro-war, anti-communist message.

There were a few antiwar protests at the **Republican national presidential nominating convention**, but most of the Republicans in attendance were in favor of continuing what they saw as a fight against communist aggression.

Nixon was nominated, and as part of the new Republican "**Southern strategy**," he selected **Maryland Governor Spiro Agnew** as his running mate.

The **Democratic national presidential nominating convention** was anything but peaceful. Held in Chicago, it attracted many **thousands of antiwar protesters who gathered outside the convention center**. Mayor Richard Daley brought in 23,000 police and National Guardsmen to control the situation, and **many of the protesters were beaten and arrested**. Unfortunately for the Democrats, all this was shown on live TV, disrupting the coverage of the convention and making the Democrats, or at least the Chicago police, seem unnecessarily cruel. The **Walker Report**, a federal investigation of what happened, characterized it as "a police riot." The report blamed Mayor Richard J. Daley for what it called "unrestrained and indiscriminate police violence."

The **assassinations of the leading Democratic presidential candidate, Senator Robert F. Kennedy, and civil rights leader,**

Martin Luther King, were on everybody's mind, and because of the ongoing Vietnam war, the convention was very divisive. **Hubert Humphrey**, Johnson's vice president had won the most votes in the Democratic primaries, but after Robert Kennedy was assassinated, Minnesota Senator **Eugene McCarthy** began to get a lot of votes in the primaries as an antiwar candidate.

Despite the divisive nature of the convention, Humphrey easily won the vote for nomination. Surprisingly, instead of doing the usual Democratic thing and picking a Southerner as his running mate, he picked **Edmund Muskie**, a senator from Maine.

The 1968 presidential election took place in an atmosphere of ongoing antiwar protests. Although Nixon worked hard to get Southern votes by appealing to conservatives, the segregationist **Alabama Governor George Wallace** managed to get himself on the ballot in the Southern states as the presidential nominee of the **American Independent Party**. He chose the militaristic Air Force **General Curtis LeMay** as his running mate.

Wallace's main election strategy was to try to get enough Electoral College votes in Southern states to send the decision to the U.S. House of Representatives. He aggressively campaigned against the anti-segregation policies of Johnson. He also pledged an immediate withdrawal of U.S. troops from Vietnam, but he made sure nobody thought he supported the antiwar protesters. Far from it; he said he was simply against the waste of money and lives in a pointless war in faraway Asia (which, of course, was exactly what most of the antiwar protesters were saying).

During the election, Wallace's running mate **Curtis LeMay got a lot of attention by saying he did not fear using nuclear weapons in the fight against communism**. He was widely quoted when he said the U.S. had the capability to **bomb Vietnam "back into the stone age."**

In the general election, Nixon's "Southern strategy" failed to win many Southern states, mainly because of the strong showing of third-party candidate, George Wallace. But Nixon was able to get enough votes in the Midwest and West to win the election, even squeaking out a win in his home state of California.

The national popular vote was one of the closest ever, with 43.42% of the popular vote going to Nixon and 42.72% going to Humphrey. 31,783,783 votes were cast for Nixon, 31,271,839 went to Humphrey, and 9,901,118 went to Wallace. In the Electoral College, Nixon won 301 votes to Humphrey's 191.

Nixon's seemingly contradictory message of being *for* the war but promising to *end* the war (with honor), had resonated with the American people.

Many observers felt Humphrey had lost a lot of votes because he didn't try hard enough to dissociate himself from Johnson's failed Vietnam policy. In addition, he had failed to follow through with the Democrat's "Southern strategy" to win votes in the South by supporting some of their demands.

With two Northerners running on the Democratic ticket, **Wallace was able to get 46 Electoral College votes in the South**.

His strategy of getting enough electoral votes to deny either Nixon or Humphrey the majority and send the decision to the House of Representatives failed, but it would have worked if Humphrey could have accumulated more votes in the West and in the South. If Humphrey would have toned down his talk about civil rights legislation, and if he would have selected a running mate from the South, he might have been able to win the more moderate states like Georgia, where he lost to Nixon by only 45,671 votes (Wallace got 535,550 votes there). **If Humphrey could had won even a few of the Southern states the Democrats had traditionally won, he would have won the presidency**.

Wallace's role as a spoiler showed that **a third-party candidate could have a dramatic effect on the outcome of the presidential race**. As we shall see when we look at the presidential election of 2000, a third-party candidate can even deny the presidency to the popular vote winner.

STORY

It didn't take Nixon long to grab hold of the same "**Vietnam tar baby**" that had ruined Johnson's presidency. By the time Nixon entered the White House, **over 500,000 troops were stationed in Vietnam and American soldiers were dying at the rate of 1200 a month**. With the antiwar protests mounting and public opinion turning against the war, many expected Nixon to de-escalate U.S. involvement there. But he didn't. In fact, he escalated it.

The new Secretary of State, Henry Kissinger had convinced Nixon that the war was not "winnable" in the traditional sense, but **Nixon knew withdrawal would be political suicide**. He had been elected to "win" the war in Vietnam and to win it "with honor." That meant military victory in Vietnam was mandatory.

Nixon and Kissinger came up with a two part strategy: they would build up South Vietnam's military and get them to take over more of the actual combat. At the same time, Nixon would order an increase in the intensity of the war in hopes it would bring the North Vietnamese to the bargaining table.

Nixon ordered increased bombing of North Vietnam, including civilian areas. And he **ordered U.S. troops into the neighboring neutral countries** of Cambodia and Laos.

Meanwhile, at home, **Nixon tried to paint anti-war groups as supporters of communism**. Even as the antiwar protests grew, **he tried to appeal to the "silent majority," the majority of Americans he said were quietly supporting what he was doing in Vietnam**. He tried to paint anyone who disagreed with him as radical communist sympathizers. **He also railed against the "liberal media,"** saying most of their stories about him were mere attempts to discredit him.

Meanwhile, **the antiwar protests increased**. In response to the protests at Kent State University in Ohio, the governor of Ohio, James Rhodes, **sent in the National Guard with live ammunition** in their rifles. On Monday, May 4, 1970, **members of the National Guard fired into a crowd of students. Thirteen students were hit, and four died**. Some of the students who were killed were shot intentionally as they tried to run away, but other students were killed some distance away as they were walking to their classes.

When the details of the killings at Kent State were reported, many American Universities were shut down in sympathy.

Even though a presidential commission harshly criticized the guardsmen, concluding that "the indiscriminate firing of rifles into a crowd of students and the deaths that followed were unnecessary, unwarranted, and inexcusable," the killings dramatically increased the popularity of Governor Rhodes in Ohio and helped rejuvenate his flagging campaign for reelection. It was a clear indication of how divided the country had become during Nixon's presidency.

Nixon's more aggressive approach to the war in Vietnam was somewhat discredited in 1970 when news leaked out that **the Army had been covering up massacres of Vietnamese civilians. It was learned that the military had successfully hushed up a U.S. Army massacre of 504 Vietnamese women, children, and old men in a village called My Lai**. The massacre had taken place in the spring of 1968 and had been systematically covered up by the Army brass at all levels of command. Later **interviews with some of the soldiers present at the massacre said they had been under orders to kill everybody in the village as part of a new "search and destroy" approach to the war**. They said the mission was not an unusual one and that **such things had been going on for some time**.

They said that at My Lai, in addition to the murders, **rapes and torturing had also taken place, and that there was some mutilation of the civilian's bodies in revenge** for American soldiers that had been killed or wounded over the preceding months.

Although the details of the mission were well known (several officers where on the ground during the massacre, and Colonel Oran K. Henderson, the brigade commander who had ordered the attack, observed it all from a helicopter hovering over the village), no action had been taken against the soldiers involved. On the contrary, everyone involved had been told to keep quiet about it.

Years later, in November of 1970, **a military trial brought criminal charges against 26 American soldiers who had been involved in the My Lai massacre.** By the time the trial was over, **all of the charges had been dropped.** Only one officer, Second Lieutenant William Calley, a platoon leader, was found guilty. He was convicted of the premeditated murder of 22 Vietnamese civilians, even though he said he was only following direct orders that had been given to him by his superiors.

He was given a life sentence, but the next day, **President Richard Nixon canceled the sentence and ordered Calley to be held under house arrest at Fort Benning.**

While today we might think the news that soldiers in Vietnam had been torturing and raping civilians, and killing Vietnamese women and children would lead to public outrage, **many in the U.S. rallied to the defense of the soldiers who had participated in the massacre.** It was an indication of how divided the country was at that time. **Some people were upset to learn there was an Army policy to cover up such occurrences, but at that time, it didn't seem to damage either the**

Army's credibility or Nixon's. approach to the war. Indiana's governor asked that all **state flags to be flown at half-staff in support of Calley** and his men. **The governors of Utah and Mississippi came out publicly in support of Calley**, and against his sentencing. The state legislatures of Arkansas, Kansas, Texas, New Jersey, and South Carolina **voted to request clemency for Calley.** Alabama's governor **George Wallace visited Calley to express his support,** and he formally requested that Nixon pardon Calley.

Calley stayed in his personal quarters at Fort Benning for three and a half years until President Nixon quietly arranged a pardon for him.

The Presidential Election of 1972

In 1972, it was clear that once again, the election was going to take place while the war in Vietnam dragged on.

In the Republican primaries, Nixon's only serious competition came from **Congressman Pete McCloskey** of California who ran as an antiwar candidate. At the Republican national convention presidential nominating convention, Nixon won easily.

The Democratic race was wide open with fifteen men and two women declaring their candidacy.

The 1972 election also saw the emergence of several third-party candidates vying for the presidency. Conservative U.S. Congressman **John G. Schmitz**, a member of the ultra-conservative **John Birch Society**, ran as a representative of the **American Party** which George Wallace had run on in 1968. Schmitz got onto the ballot in 32 states and received 1,099,482 votes, but he won no Electoral College votes.

Linda Jenness was nominated by the **Socialist Workers Party**, with Andrew Pulley as her running-mate.

Benjamin Spock was nominated by the **People's Party**.

1972 was the first time the **Libertarian Party** fielded a candidate. They nominated **John Hospers**, but he was only able to get on the presidential ballot in Colorado and Washington (each state has their own rules about how to get on the presidential ballot, and Colorado and Washington are among the easiest.) Hospers received only 3,573 votes, but he did get one Electoral College vote in Virginia from a "**faithless elector**."

COMMENT

The term "**faithless elector**" refers to a member of a state's Electoral College who does not vote for the presidential candidate who won the state's popular vote. As stated very specifically in the U.S. Constitution, **members of the Electoral College are not required to vote for the candidate that wins the popular vote**.

It might seem surprising that the framers of the Constitution of this nation *did not even suggest* that members of the Electoral College should vote for the winner of the popular vote, but the fact is, **there was no popular vote**. The electors were given the freedom to vote for anyone they wanted to in case **the people wanted "the wrong person"** to be their president By freeing members of the Electoral College to vote for anyone they chose to, *even if that person was not a candidate*, they **assured that political leaders in the states would have the final say about who got to be president**.

Faithless electors have never overturned an election, but over the years, there have been many who tried. Below is a brief description of each incident.

In 1796, Samuel Miles, an Federalist elector from Pennsylvania, refused to vote for the winner of the popular vote, Federalist candidate **John Adams**. Instead, he voted for **Thomas Jefferson**, the Democratic-Republican candidate. The Electoral College voting was so close, that had only a few more Federal-

---

ist electors done the same thing, it would have changed the outcome of the election.

In 1808, six Democratic-Republican electors refused to support **James Madison**, their party's candidate for president, and instead, voted for **George Clinton**, the Democratic-Republican candidate for vice president.

In 1812, three Federalist electors refused to vote for the Federalist vice presidential candidate **Jared Ingersoll**. Instead, they voted for **Elbridge Gerry**, the vice presidential candidate from the opposing Democratic-Republican Party.

In 1820, James Monroe would have received all of the Electoral College votes if **William Plummer, the governor of New Hampshire** and a Democratic-Republican elector hadn't decided at the last minute to cast his vote for his friend, **John Quincy Adams** even though Adams was not a candidate in that election. Supposedly, Plummer was protesting against the "wasteful extravagance" of the Monroe Administration and **he used his Electoral College vote to bring attention to that issue**. He also voted against **Daniel D. Tompkins**, Monroe's vice presidential choice, saying the man did "not have the weight of character which that office requires."

In 1828, seven of the nine electors from Georgia refused to vote for **Andrew Jackson**'s choice for vice president, **John Calhoun**. Instead, they voted for **William Smith**, a senator from South Carolina who was a vocal opponent of Calhoun. (In 1837, President Andrew Jackson nominated Smith to the Supreme Court, but he declined the honor.)

1832 saw the largest rebellion of electors in history. Thirty-two electors from Pennsylvania and Maryland refused to vote for the presidential candidate that had won the popular vote. Two Republican Party electors from Maryland **refused to vote for anyone** rather than cast their votes for **Henry Clay,**

the candidate who had won their state. **In Pennsylvania, all 30 electors refused to vote for vice presidential candidate, Martin Van Buren**, even though he had won the popular vote. Instead, they voted for **William Wilkins**, the senator from their home state of Pennsylvania (Andrew Jackson and Martin Van Buren won anyhow).

1836 saw something happen in the Electoral College that changed the outcome of the 1836 election and could have set a precedent that would change all future presidential elections: **some electors refused to vote for the candidate that won the popular vote just because they didn't like his personal behavior.** Twenty-three Democratic electors from Virginia refused to cast their votes for the winning Democratic vice president, Richard M. Johnson of Kentucky, because **they had learned he was involved in a sexual relationship with an African-American woman.** Johnson caused much consternation when he openly admitted he was the father of one of his slave's children. Furthermore, after that slave woman died, he took up sexual relationships with other female slaves, and he was not shy about telling everybody about it.

With the loss of those 23 votes, there was no majority in the Electoral College, and as specified in the U.S. Constitution, the decision about who would be vice president was sent to the U.S. Senate. In the Senate, with little debate, the senators voted strictly along party lines to name Johnson vice president.

An unusual situation occurred in **1872. Sixty-three of the sixty-six Democratic electors** who were from states Horace Greeley had won voted for somebody else because Greeley had died between the time the election was held and when the Electoral College met. **That was something the founding father hadn't considered when they created the Electoral College system.** Seventeen of the Greeley electors chose to cast no vote at all, but the other 46 electors voted for whoever they liked. They voted for four different candidates for president, and eight different candidates for vice president. **Three of the electors followed what they saw as their duty and voted for the dead man.** These votes were later disallowed by Congress, but it is not clear under what authority they disallowed the votes for Greeley because there is no provision in the Electoral College section of the Constitution specifying how such a situation should be dealt with.

As described earlier, the **presidential election of 1876** was the only election in which **Samuel J. Tilden, the candidate that won both the popular vote and the Electoral College vote did not get to be president.** A special Congressional commission, created after considerable contention, voted strictly along party lines to **invalidate many of the Electoral College votes from the South** due to perceived voter fraud. The commission declared the Republican, Rutherford B. Hayes, the Electoral College winner(by only one vote). Again, it is not clear under what authority they disallowed the Electoral College votes for Tilden. The Electoral College section of the Constitution does not mention any possible circumstance in which the winner of the Electoral College vote can be denied the presidency.

In 1896, four electors, unhappy with their winning vice presidential candidate, **Thomas E. Watson**, switched their votes to a different vice presidential candidate, **Arthur Sewall** from Maine.

In 1948, Preston Parks, a Southern Democratic elector from Tennessee, refused to cast his vote for the Democratic winner, Harry S. Truman. Instead, he cast his vote for Strom Thurmond, the segregationist States' Rights candidate. It was a remarkable moment in Electoral College history because **it**

showed that an elector could go so far as to vote for the opponent of the winner of the popular vote if the elector had a personal disagreement with the policies of the winner. Strom Thurmond ended up getting 39 Electoral College votes, all from Southern electors.

In 1956, a Southern Democratic elector, W.F. Turner from Alabama, voted for his friend, Walter Burgwyn Jones, a U.S. congressman from Alabama (who was not a candidate of any party). The elector didn't like Adlai Stevenson, the winner of the popular vote in Alabama, so he simply refused to vote for him.

In 1960, one elector planned a revolt that showed the danger of letting a few selected individuals decide who the nation's president would be. Republican elector, Henry D. Irwin, from Oklahoma, refused to vote for Richard Nixon, the candidate that had won his state. He simply said he "could not stomach" Nixon. And he went further: he tried to get all the other electors to reject both Nixon and Kennedy and vote instead for two of the most conservative members of the Senate, Harry Byrd of Virginia and Barry Goldwater of Arizona. He secretly tried to arrange a revolt among the Southern electors, but in the end, the other electors were not willing to go along with his plan (fourteen *unpledged* electors from Mississippi and Alabama *did* cast their presidential votes for Harry Byrd). Although Irwin's plan failed, it did show what could happen if enough of the Electoral College members decided to get together and elect their own preferred candidate. If that ever happens, according to the wording of the Electoral College section of the Constitution, there is nothing anyone will be able to do about it.

In 1968, Republican elector, Dr. Lloyd W. Bailey of North Carolina, refused to vote for Richard Nixon. Instead, he voted for George Wallace. Dr. Bailey pointed out (accurately) that the U.S. Constitution said nothing about him having to vote for the candidate who won his state. He also pointed out (accurately) that George Wallace had won his home district and that before the winner-take-all system had been instituted he would have been obliged to vote for Wallace.

In **1972, Republican elector Roger L. MacBride from Virginia** refused to cast his electoral vote for Richard Nixon, and instead voted for John Hospers, the Libertarian Presidential candidate. He also voted for the Libertarian vice presidential candidate, **Toni Nathan, making her the first woman ever to receive an Electoral vote.**

In **1976, Republican elector Mike Padden, a lawyer from Washington** refused to vote for the winner of his state, Gerald Ford, and instead voted for Ronald Reagan (who was not a candidate at that time).

In **1988, Democratic elector Margaret Leach from West Virginia** was shocked when she learned members of the Electoral College were not required to vote for the candidates they were pledged to. She decided to draw attention to this ridiculous situation by switching her votes for president and vice president. She cast her vote for Bentsen for president and Dukakis for vice president, and she tried to get the other electors to do the same in order to show the citizens of the United States what was possible with the nonsensical Electoral College system in place. But she was unable to convince any of the others to do what she had done.

In **2000, Democratic elector Barbara Lett-Simmons from the District of Columbia** refused to cast any vote at all. She intended it as a protest against the lack of Congressional representation for the citizens of Washington, DC.

Today, 29 states and the District of Columbia have passed laws that impose penalties on electors who do not cast heir vote for the presidential candidate that wins the popular vote in their state. That means there are **21 states that today still do not even attempt to exert any kind of legal control over how their electors vote**.

It is still not clear if laws that attempt to control how a member of the Electoral College votes are constitutional. Most historians believe the wording of the Electoral College section of the Constitution is no accident; **the founding fathers wanted to be sure the electors *did* have a free rein to vote for anyone they wanted to.**

As the 1972 presidential election neared, it was clear that if Nixon was to win reelection, he was going to have to show progress was being made in Vietnam. The public's perception of the war in Vietnam was constantly growing less favorable. They were ready for the war to be over.

As a result, Nixon's campaign message was twofold: first, he tried to convince the American public that the war was going well; second, he had to convince them that his strategy was working to the degree that the war would soon be over, meaning we would be able to get out of the Vietnam mess with some semblance of honor.

Peace talks were still going on in Paris, and just before the election, **Henry Kissinger returned to the United States and went before the press to announce that "peace is at hand."**

Nixon's message was also positive. He said the U.S. had never lost a war, and "we are not going to lose this one."

Nixon's plan worked. Although the public was fed up with the war in Vietnam, and there were stories being printed in the newspapers about a secret group of "dirty trick's" anti-Democrat operatives that were said to be connected to the White House, Nixon still had plenty of support in the country (the silent majority?). He won the Electoral College vote of every state except Massachusetts.

However, the popular vote was close in some states. For example, Michigan cast 1,961,721 votes for Nixon and 1,459,435 votes for McGovern, and in Wisconsin Nixon only won by 179,256 votes.

When Nixon won the South in 1972, it was **the first time in U.S. history a Republican had won every single Southern state**. After 132 years, it appeared **the South had finally forgiven the Republicans for electing Lincoln.**

It was clear that with the Republicans finally gaining the upper hand in the South, they would have a much greater chance of winning the presidency in future elections, and that was the way it turned out. **Four out of the next five presidents (all except for Ronald Reagan, the very conservative candidate from California), were Southerners**. Jimmy Carter was from Georgia, George H. W. Bush was from Texas, Bill Clinton was from Arkansas, and George W. Bush was from Texas.

STORY

The **Paris Peace Accords** were signed in January of 1973. Nixon had ordered intense bombing of civilian areas of North Vietnam in order to force North Vietnam to the peace table, but a much more important concession was that America was ready to leave Vietnam to the Vietnamese. **The country would remain divided. The U.S. would train and equip the South Vietnamese Army, but the U.S. military would leave the country**.

Although the peace accords ended America's involvement in the war, it didn't end the war. Nixon ordered a "Vietnamization" of the war, a program of training and equipping the Army of the Republic of Viet Nam (ARVN) to be sure they could hold South Vietnam without the presence of U.S. troops.

The Vietnamization program was a complete failure. When the North Vietnamese again invaded the south, the South Vietnamese military was unable to hold them back.

President Nixon had said publicly that if the North Vietnamese invaded South Vietnam again, the United States would again intervene. But when his Secretary of Defense, James R. Schlesinger, stated that he was **ready to recommend resumption of the U.S. bombing of North Vietnam, the U.S. Senate quickly passed the Case-Church Amendment to prohibit any more direct U.S. involvement in Vietnam**.

It could be said that the U.S. role in the Vietnam war began with secret CIA involvement, and ended when the CIA left. Near the end of April, 1975, the last CIA station personnel in Saigon were airlifted off of the roof of the American Embassy by helicopters belonging to Air America, a small airline secretly owned by the CIA.

Chapter Twelve
Secret Presidential Power

As Nixon was winning the presidency in 1972, Americans were just starting to hear about a secret group that had been arrested for breaking into the Democratic National Committee's offices. The group, that was to become known as the **White House plumbers,** claimed to be investigating leaks and other security matters, but diligent newspaper reporters eventually found out that the group was tied to President Nixon's reelection committee. The cover-up that followed, eventually led to Nixon's resignation.

STORY

On the night of June 17, 1972, a group **broke into the Democratic National Committee (DNC) headquarters in the Watergate building in Washington, D.C.** They looked for information about Democratic strategy, and they placed wiretaps in the DNC offices. A security guard noticed tape on a door that was being used to keep the door from locking. He called the police, and five men, Bernard Barker, Virgilio González, Eugenio Martínez, James McCord, and Frank Sturgis, were caught inside the Democratic National Committee offices and arrested.

As soon as Nixon found out about the arrests, he and his Attorney General John Mitchell began a frantic cover-up to keep the American public from finding out what was really behind the break-in.

Nixon's **presidential counsel, John Dean**, spearheaded the cover-up effort, and at first, Nixon was confident they would be able to distance themselves from it.

But two reporters from the **Washington Post** newspaper, **Bob Woodward and Carl Bernstein**, kept digging and eventually managed to contact an informant who gave them information implicating the president. The two reporters refused to name their informant. They said the informant was known only by the code name, "**Deep Throat**" (many years later the informant was revealed to be **Federal Bureau of Investigation Associate Director Mark Felt**). Woodward and Bernstein were able to trace money that had been paid to the Watergate burglars. **It turned out to be money that had been donated to the president's reelection effort**. Piece by piece, Woodward, Bernstein, and other reporters ferreted out more information about the White House plumbers group. Eventually, all five Watergate burglars were **tied directly or indirectly to Nixon's reelection committee**. On October 10, 1972, **a month before the election**, Woodward and Bernstein reported that fact in **a front page story in the Washington Post**. But people either didn't believe the story, or they didn't care. The polls still showed Nixon had plenty of support.

Only one week before the 1972 election, it was revealed that **Attorney General John Mitchell had controlled a secret Republican fund** used to finance intelligence-gathering against the Democrats. Although there were suspicions that Nixon himself was involved, the election results showed the Republicans were still solidly behind him.

Despite intense efforts on Nixon's part to cover up the whole mess, information continued to leak out.

In March of 1973, five **months after Nixon had been elected with an overwhelming Electoral College majority, his attorney, John Dean, fearing a prison sentence for himself, began cooperating with the U.S. Attorney's office. He implicated several of Nixon's aides.**

In May of 1973, **the U.S. Senate formed a committee to investigate** the whole Watergate affair. The hearings were televised live, and the entire country watched with rapt attention as the story unfolded through the testimony of **John Dean** and other members of Nixon's inner circle.

One bit of tantalizing information Dean revealed to the committee was that Nixon secretly audio taped all of his meetings. **The committee asked Nixon to turn over the tapes, but he refused.** It took a series of court battles that eventually led to a decision by the U.S. Supreme Court that he had to comply with the request and turn over transcripts of the tapes. Although forensic analyses of the tapes showed that some conversations had been intentionally erased, they did reveal that Nixon was aware of hush payment to some of the Watergate defendants. The tapes also revealed that Nixon tried to get the CIA to claim that the Watergate break-in was part of a national security investigation.

In July, the House filed **articles of impeachment against Nixon, citing three articles: 1) obstruction of justice, 2) abuse of power, and 3) contempt of Congress.**

At first, **some Congressional Republicans stood firm in their support of Nixon**, but when more tapes came to light showing how actively Nixon was involved in the cover-up, they too said they would vote for impeachment.

When Nixon heard that even the Republicans in Congress were abandoning him, he went on TV to announce he was resigning the presidency. He left the White House the next day. He was **the first, and only, U.S. President ever to resign**.

Vice President Gerald Ford succeeded him and soon **granted Nixon a full pardon for any crimes he might have committed while president.**

A total of 25 officials from the Nixon administration, including four cabinet members, were eventually convicted and imprisoned.

The Presidential Election of 1976

After Nixon resigned, **Gerald Ford** served out the remainder of the presidential term and ran for reelection in **1976**. Ford was handicapped both by Nixon's Watergate scandal and by the fact that he had never been elected to any national office

In 1976, more and more people were aspiring to be president. Fifteen candidates competed in the Democratic primaries, including governors, senators, U.S. representatives, an ambassador, and a housewife.

As the Democratic primaries went on, it became clear that **Jimmy Carter**, the former governor of Georgia was going to prevail. He was nominated at the Democratic nominating convention, and he went on to mount an effective campaign as an outsider who would go to Washington to change the kind of dirty politics Nixon had been engaged in.

STORY

Although televised debates had played a significant role in the Kennedy-Nixon election of 1960, no televised debates occurred after that until the election of 1976.

In 1964, President Johnson was so far ahead of the Republican candidate, Senator Barry Goldwater, he saw no need to risk that lead by debating.

And then, in 1968, Johnson decided not to run for reelection. His vice-president, Hubert Humphrey, wanted to debate candidate Nixon, but Nixon was not about the revisit his 1960 problems with television. And then, once Nixon had managed to win the White House, he was not about the risk losing it again by participating in any of those dreaded televised debates.

In 1976, after President Ford feel behind in the polls, he felt he had no choice but to debate Carter.

Unlike the previous televised debates, the debates of 1976 were held before a live audience.

The first debate began after a long delay due to technical problems with the television feed. Although both candidates had chairs available to them, neither of them sat down while they waited for fear that they would look weak.

When the debate finally got going, Carter launched the expected attack on President Ford regarding the weak economy the country was going through. Carter said the country was in an inflationary spiral, and there was no chance of balancing the budget until we found a way to get people back to work. He suggested tax cuts and some incentive programs. He said the present tax structure was a disgrace to the country, a welfare program for the rich.

Ford said he also favored tax cuts and incentive programs. In fact, he said he had already made some of those kinds of suggestions to the Congress, but they had not gone along with his ideas. Ford was also challenged about how to deal with the many draft-dodgers who had refused induction because of the Vietnam War. Carter asked Ford why, if he had pardoned Nixon, he would refuse to pardon the draft-dodgers.

The consensus was that although Carter had made some good points, Ford had adequately held his own.

Unfortunately for Ford, he did not do as well in the second debate when he made a blunder about foreign affairs. He said, "There is no Soviet domination of Eastern Europe and there never will be under a Ford administration." He went on to say

that he did not believe the people of Eastern Europe considered themselves to be "dominated by the Soviet Union."

After the second debate, Carter surged ahead in the polls
and President Ford was never able to recover.

Carter and his running mate, **Walter Mondale from Minnesota**, won all the Southern states except Virginia (which they lost
by only 22,658 votes).

Ford won most of the Midwestern and Western states, but **his
controversial full pardon of Nixon hurt him the East**.

The popular vote was fairly close with 40,831,881 votes going
to Carter and 39,148,634 votes to Ford. **The Electoral College
vote was 297 for Carter and 240 for Ford.** Carter thus became
the first president from the deep South since Zachary Taylor in
1848.

Eugene McCarthy, a former Democratic senator from Minnesota. was known for his anti-Vietnam position. He ran as an independent and got 756,631 popular votes, but he didn't win any
electoral votes.

The Presidential Election of 1980

As the 1980 presidential election season began, the American
people were dismayed about the continuing poor economy, and
they were upset about the taking of American hostages in Iran, an
incident that became known as the **Iran Hostage Crisis**.

Many were also upset with Carter's decision not to allow U.S.
athletes to compete in the 1980 Olympics in Moscow. It was his
way of protesting the Soviet invasion of Afghanistan, but many
felt the international Olympic movement was a venue to honor the
world's best athletes and not a place for political statements. They
felt if President Carter's Olympic boycott was allowed to stand,
other countries would retaliate and every Olympics from then on
would be marred by political posturing.

President **Jimmy Carter** led in most of the Democratic primaries, but **Senator Edward M. (Ted) Kennedy** of Massachusetts was making a strong showing.

By the time the Democratic national presidential nominating convention came around, Carter had enough votes to win, but a strong anti-Carter mood on the convention floor resulted in a last minute **"draft Muskie"** movement to replace Carter with Secretary of State **Edmund Muskie** from Maine. It failed and Carter was nominated.

STORY

The **Iranian Hostage Crisis** took place in 1979 when a group of Islamist students and militant revolutionaries took over the American embassy in Tehran.

The revolutionaries were involved in a power struggle with Mohammad Rezā Shāh Pahlavī, **the Shah of Iran,** who was supported by the United States. With the support of Revolutionary leader Ayatollah Ruhollah Khomeini, the militants captured American citizens who had been in the embassy and held them as hostages.

As the months went by, President Carter came under increasing criticism for not doing something about it. Finally, Carter approved a rescue mission code named **Operation Eagle**. The plan was to use helicopters and U.S. Army Delta Force troops to fly into and rescue the hostages, but some of the helicopters suffered mechanical problems and the mission was called off. Unfortunately, as one of the helicopters was being refueled, it collided with the refueling tanker aircraft. The helicopter crashed and soldiers were killed.

The new government of Iran under the control of Ayatollah Ruhollah Khomeini, agreed to release the hostages if the U.S. would agree to release several billion dollars of Iranian assets that had been frozen in American banks when the hostages were first taken. President Carter was secretly working with various international banks to make the deal come about, but it took so long to finalize the details that **by the time the hostages were flown out of Iran, Carter had already been defeated by Ronald Reagan. It was the new president that welcomed the hostages home.**

The early 1980 Republican primaries indicated that their nominee would likely be former **California Governor Ronald Reagan**. Reagan was fairly well known outside of California because before being elected governor, he had been a movie actor, and he had also appeared in many TV commercials. Baring any unexpected developments, Reagan was sure to win the Republican nomination at the Republican national nominating convention.

Reagan won the nomination and selected one of his opponents, **George H. W. Bush** of Texas as his running mate.

In the general election, Reagan based his campaign on what he called "**conservative values**," giving Carter ammunition for his accusations that Reagan was a dangerous right wing radical who would take the country down the wrong path.

STORY

Although Ronald Reagan had previously been a registered Democrat who supported Roosevelt's very liberal "**New Deal**" policies, his two terms in office as California's Republican governor established his credentials as a **conservative**. His tenure as California's governor took place during a time of **great dissonance in the state over the Vietnam War**. California was a fairly liberal state, but Reagan soon showed that he was going to support the conservative side on most issues. He had plenty of liberal opposition in the state due to his defense of the Vietnam War and his frequent **sarcastic attacks on student antiwar protesters** (he called them "welfare bums").

There was a recall effort against him, but when it failed Reagan took that as a sign that his policies had the support of the people.

When the anti-Vietnam protests began to grow at California state universities, **Reagan began to crack down on the protesters, calling them "communist-inspired."** Reagan frequently used the California state police against the student protesters, and when a large "**people's protest**" was staged at the University of California campus in Berkeley, he called in state National Guard troops. They occupied the area of the city around the campus for two weeks. **When one student, James Rector, was killed by police gunfire, Reagan's response was, "If it takes a bloodbath, let's get it over with. No more appeasement."** His strong actions against the student protesters **had the approval and support of J. Edgar Hoover, the director of the FBI. It was later learned that Reagan had secretly been working for Hoover when he was in the Hollywood actor's union** in order to root out "communists" in the movie industry. From then on, Hoover and the FBI were reported to have done everything they could to help Reagan's political career.

Another hotly debated national issue that arose during Reagan's term as governor was debate about the legalization of abortion. The liberal State Legislature passed a bill legalizing abortion in California and sent it to Reagan for his signature. After many days of indecision, he signed it. However, during his run for the presidency, he would say he regretted signing it.

The election of 1980 was not even close. **Although Carter was a Southerner, the South was now firmly in the Republican camp.** Carter won his home state of Georgia and a handful of Northern states, but Reagan won all the other Southern states and all of the Midwest and West.

Reagan's Electoral College win of 489-49 was the largest in U.S. history for a candidate running against an incumbent.

Republican Congressman John B. Anderson of Illinois also managed to get himself on the ballot in many states, running as an independent. Carter refused to debate Anderson, but Reagan agreed, and most observers felt Anderson had done very well against Reagan.

In the general election, **Anderson got 5,719,850 votes, but he won no electoral votes.**

The Presidential Election of 1984

In the presidential election of 1984, Reagan ran for reelection, but being **the oldest president in U.S. history**, there were questions about whether he should be elected for another term. Nevertheless, he dominated the primaries and easily won the nomination at the Republican presidential nominating convention.

After Senator Ted Kennedy again declined to run for president, the Democratic primaries indicated the nomination would come down to three candidates, former vice president, **Walter Mondale** of Minnesota, Senator **Gary Hart** of Colorado, and civil rights leader **Jesse Jackson** of Illinois.

At the Democratic nominating convention, Mondale won, and he chose **New York Congresswoman Geraldine Ferraro** as his running mate. **It was the first time a woman had been on the ticket of any major political party**. The Democrats hoped she would attract at least some of the women's vote.

Mondale and Ferraro immediately began an attack on Reagan's so-called conservative values, saying he was using the threat of communism to scare Americans into going along with his extreme right-wing policies. They also said **his so-called anti-socialist**

economic policies were being used to turn average Americans against the poor and minorities.

The Reagan campaign focused mostly on his "cold war" foreign policy and on his approach to American economics that had became known as "**Reaganomics**." Reaganomics was the idea that if you get rid of business regulations and cut taxes on the rich, the resulting benefits to the most wealthy would "**trickle down**" to the middle class.

During the primaries, Reagan had little opposition, although another Republican candidate, George H. W. Bush, derided Reaganomics as "**voodoo economics**."

After the nominations, the nation tuned in to the **televised debates**. After the first debate, which was limited to domestic policy, most observers felt Reagan had done poorly against Mondale. **Reagan seemed hesitant and at times confused**. But in the second debate, which was about international policy and national defense, Reagan seemed much more confident.

Even as the debates were going on, the Reagan campaign was producing **slick television ads that emphasized the threat from Russia** and fostered a "peace through strength" approach to foreign policy. The ads said it was the only way to **stop the spread of worldwide communism**. These ads drew attention to how much Reagan had strengthened the U.S military.

COMMENT

Reagan's cold war foreign policy of fighting communism on all fronts was quite vividly demonstrated in 1983 when a military coup in Granada, a small island off the coast of Venezuela, replaced the government with one that was sympathetic to communist ideals. Reagan immediately sent in 7,000 troops, consisting of ranger battalions and airborne paratroopers to depose the new Granada government.

Although most Americans supported the invasion as a necessary part of the fight against communism, it was criticized by the United Kingdom, Canada and the United Nations General Assembly as "**a flagrant violation of international law.**"

Reagan's campaign approach, plus his personal appeal, worked. **He won easily.** He even won 55 percent of the women's vote **despite the presence of a woman on the opposing Democratic ticket. The Mondale-Ferraro ticket won only Mondale's home state of Minnesota and the District of Columbia.**

Reagan was a popular president, but information began to leak out that he had created a special task force not unlike the one that had resulted in Nixon's resignation. Further investigation led to what is now known as the **Iran-Contra scandal** (sometimes referred to as **"Irangate"**).

STORY

The **Iran-Contra scandal** began when **President Reagan created a secret organization known as "the Enterprise."** It was originally created as a way to deal with Iran in order to gain the release of hostages being held by terrorists in Lebanon. **The Enterprise group** worked out a deal with the Iranian Army wherein the U.S. would sell weapons to Iran to help with their ongoing war with Iraq, and in return, they would try to secure the release of the hostages.

National Security Adviser Robert McFarlane told President Reagan about the potential deal, but **they were stymied because there was an embargo against selling arms to Iran. Reagan wanted to go ahead with the deal anyhow.** Secretary **of Defense Caspar Weinberger** and **Secretary of State George Shultz** opposed the deal, but McFarlane and **CIA director**

William Casey supported it. With the backing of President Reagan, the plan was put into action. The result was that **arms, including thousands of missiles, were sent to Iran**, and in exchange, a few hostages were released. Unfortunately, they were soon replaced with new hostages. It appeared that Iran had discovered a way to get military arms from the U.S.—just take hostages and then trade them for weapons.

When the Lebanese newspaper, **Al-Shiraa**, printed an exposé of the deal in November of 1986, **President Reagan went on TV to vehemently deny any such deal had been made**. A week later, he admitted some kind of operation *had* occurred, but said it was definitely not an arms-for-hostages deal. Insiders in the Reagan administration continued to support him and defend him. Later, some said the president was having memory problems at the time and may have simply forgotten the details of the operation.

Polls indicated most Americans **believed President Reagan was not telling the truth,** and his popularity declined. But he still had plenty of support among Republicans. They felt that **although what he had done might have been illegal, it had been done with good intentions**.

That might have been the end of the affair, but it was soon discovered that **eighteen million dollars out of the thirty million dollars the Iranians had paid for the American weapons had disappeared**. A member of the National Security Council, **Lieutenant Colonel Oliver North**, admitted he had been diverting funds from the arms sales to **the Contras**, a group that was fighting against the communist government in Nicaragua. Although **direct support of the Contras was against U.S. law**, Reagan was well known as a supporter of the Contras, calling them **"the moral equivalent of our Founding Fathers."** It was also revealed that **North had been working with drug smug-**

glers and with Panamanian dictator Manuel Noriega to assist the Contras. North said everything he did had been done **with the full knowledge of National Security Adviser Admiral John Poindexter and, he assumed, with the full knowledge of President Reagan**.

Poindexter resigned and North was fired, but Reagan continued to claim he didn't know anything about it.

To many members of the national media, the connection between the arms sale and the diversion of the money to the Reagan-supported Contra seemed like the same kind of secret operation run out of the White House that had driven Nixon out of office. They hounded the president about it at every press conference, but Reagan continued to deny any knowledge of what his closest advisors were up to.

Some of Reagan's aides were tried and convicted, but when Reagan's vice president George Bush was elected in 1988, **he pardoned most of them**, including a **pardon of Secretary of Defense Caspar W. Weinberger just days before he was to go to trial**.

Oliver North was indicted on sixteen felony counts, but they were all later overturned.

Using the publicity he got during the Iran-Contra hearings, North ran for the U.S. senate in 1994 as a Republican against **Democrat Charles Robb**, son-in-law of President Lyndon B. Johnson. North was able to raise over twenty million dollars to fund his campaign, but the Iran-Contra affair continued to haunt him, and he was defeated.

Since then, North has been a regular commentator on cable news programs and has written several best-selling books.

Chapter Thirteen
Foreign Wars and Presidential Scandal

The Presidential Election of 1988

The presidential election of 1988 saw Vice President **George H. W. Bush** winning **the Republican nomination** by promising to continue the policies of outgoing president Ronald Reagan. He chose Senator **Dan Quayle** from Indiana as his running mate.

With the Iran Contra scandal continuing to dominate the news, Democrats were optimistic that they could take back the presidency. **Due to the Iran-Contra scandal, they had regained control of the senate** after six years of Republican domination.

In 1988, a large number of candidates fought for the Democratic nomination. At first, Gary Hart seemed to be the most likely nominee, but questions were raised about his extramarital affairs.

Senator Edward M. Kennedy of Massachusetts again decided against running in 1988, and Arkansas Governor Bill Clinton also declined to run.

Eventually, the convention nominated **Michael Dukakis**, the governor of Massachusetts. He chose U.S. Senator **Lloyd Bentsen** as his running mate.

The 1988 campaign was one of finger pointing. Bush said Dukakis was too liberal, and Dukakis said Bush was too conservative and too militaristic.

Dukakis tried to tie Bush to the Iran-Contra scandal, saying Bush's involvement in the sale of arms to Iran showed Bush had "failed the test of leadership."

In the general election, Bush won the popular vote by about seven million votes (out of ninety million votes cast). **In the Electoral College vote, the margin was larger, 426 to 111.**

The Republican candidate, Bush, won the South, as was becoming the trend, but he also won California and most of the Midwestern and Northern states.

It turned out to be the last election in which a Republican presidential candidate would win California.

Libertarian Ron Paul from Texas and his running mate, **Andre V. Marrou** from Alaska were also on the ballot in many states. They gathered 431,750 votes nationwide, but no electoral votes.

At first, Bush was a popular president. But a 1990 jump in the price of oil was tied to a brief war in **the Middle East** (now known as the **first Gulf War**). In addition, a weak economy and **huge government budget deficits** hurt his popularity.

As the 1992 presidential elections approached, his chances of being reelected seemed in doubt.

STORY

The **first Gulf War** was a military action waged by a UN-authorized coalition of forces against Iraq in response to Iraq's invasion of Kuwait.

In August of 1990, **Iraqi troops invaded Kuwait with the intention of annexing the country**. The invasion was met by widespread condemnation and immediate economic sanctions against Iraq by some UN member nations.

President Bush sent American ships to the area and **deployed forces in Saudi Arabia** to gather near the Kuwait border. Military forces from Saudi Arabia, Britain, and Egypt also sent troops and promised financial support.

Starting **in January of 1991, the U.S. began an aerial bombardment** on Iraqi positions. **Much of the aerial attack was shown on American television, and for some time, it dominated the news.**

Ground troops were sent in after the aerial attack, and within a few days, the **Iraqi forces had been pushed back into their own country**. At that point, President Bush ordered a cease fire. The war had lasted only a few days, and some in the U.S. criticized the president for not continuing the war. It was seen as a chance to oust the presiding regime in Iraq. However, both Bush and his Secretary of Defense, Dick Cheney, pointed out that **the UN mandate** was only to push the Iraqis out of Kuwait. They felt **further action would have made the United States, with its overwhelmingly powerful military machine, seem like an invading bully, and that might create new enemies in the Middle East.**

By the end of the hostilities, it is estimated there were between 20,000 and 35,000 Iraq military fatalities plus many thousands of civilian deaths (one estimate put the number of civilian deaths as high as 100,000).

According to the U.S. Department of Defense, **U.S. forces suffered 148 battle-related deaths, 35 of them from so-called "friendly fire"** (killed by their own troops). Another 145 deaths occurred in non-combat accidents. The United Kingdom reported 47 deaths, 9 to friendly fire. Other countries that were involved reported 37 deaths.

The Presidential Election of 1992

In 1992, **President George H. W. Bush ran for reelection** and was again nominated by the Republicans. Although there was some discussion about replacing Dan Quayle as the vice presidential candidate, Bush again chose **Quayle.**

After a long and contentions primary season, with many well-known candidates, the **Democrats** finally nominated the popular **Arkansas Governor, Bill Clinton.**

Clinton chose **Tennessee Senator Al Gore** as his running mate.

The Bush campaign chose a personal attack strategy. They accused Clinton of marital infidelity and draft dodging.

The **Clinton campaign focused almost entirely on the economy,** pointing out that the Republicans had a long history of increasing the size of government and thereby increasing the national debt.

Political polling was getting ever more sophisticated, and the polls were indicating that **Bush's personal attack strategy wasn't working.** People were more concerned with their own pocketbooks.

Another problem for the Republicans was that the cold war was finally cooling down. After a political moderate, **Mikhail Gorbachev,** was named the General Secretary of the Communist Party of the Soviet Union in 1985, **much of the Republican rhetoric about the worldwide communist threat fell on deaf ears.** By 1989, the Berlin Wall had come down and the phrase "Iron Curtain" was relegated to history. With no looming enemy abroad, all Bush had left to campaign on was his record, and many observers felt Bush's famous 1988 campaign promise of **"Read my lips: no new taxes"** hurt him in the 1992 election because he had in fact been forced to raise taxes as part of a compromise with Congress.

STORY

The surprise of the presidential election of 1992 was the candidacy of **Texas billionaire Ross Perot.** At one point during the campaign, **he was leading both Bush and Clinton in the national polls.** It seemed as if the public was ready to consider an outsider for president.

Midway through the 1992 race, Clinton was still leading in the polls, but when the presidential debates began, Ross Perot made some gains by attacking *both* Bush and Clinton.

Some felt Perot would pull votes away from Clinton, improving Bush's chances for reelection, but Perot was also talking about the poor economy and pointing out how much the Republicans were running up the national debt.

Perot managed to get 19,743,821 votes, but he wasn't able to win a single state and therefore didn't get any Electoral College votes. **It seems Perot pulled votes away from** *both* **Clinton and Bush.**

In the end, Clinton's message about the Republican's handling of the economy won out. **Clinton won the popular election by 5,805,256 votes (out of 104,423,923 votes cast), and he won the Electoral College vote even more convincingly, 370 to 168.**

The Presidential Election of 1996

By the time the election of 1996 rolled around, **Clinton was being credited with improving the economy**, and he was reducing the national debt. **He was also successful at keeping the U.S. out of any foreign wars**. The absence of a Russian threat, meant he was able to cut some military expenditures which helped reduce the national debt even more.

As soon as President **Clinton announced that he would seek reelection in 1992**, the Republican began to criticize his "liberalism" even before they had selected a candidate.

Ten serious candidates **fought for the Republican presidential nomination** during the Republican primaries.

Pat Buchanan, a well-known conservative, won some of the early Republican primaries, but eventually **Bob Dole** pulled ahead and was nominated as the Republican's 1992 presidential candidate. He chose **Jack Kemp**, a former congressman (and former professional football player) as his running mate.

As the campaign began, Ross Perot once again jumped into the race.

With no serious competition for the Democratic nomination, Clinton was able to get his campaign started early. **He raised**

huge amounts of money and used it to mount a intensive TV campaign.

In order to secure the Republican nomination, Dole had to appeal to the more conservative elements of the Republican party, especially in the South. **That gave Clinton the ammunition he needed to paint Dole as a right-winger** who would cut popular social programs like Medicare and Social Security.

The relatively young and talkative Clinton came off well in the election debates. In contrast, Dole seemed much older and more hesitant.

Ross Perot's chances of winning any Electoral College votes were dashed when he was left out of the televised presidential debates. (He later sued, claiming an unfair lack of coverage by the TV networks, but his lawsuit was thrown out of court.)

In the 1996 general election, **Clinton lost most of the South and the Midwest, but he was able to regain Democratic dominance in California and in the East.** He won the popular vote by 8,201,370 votes and **won the Electoral College vote 379 to 159.**

In his second term, Clinton continued his policy of budget reductions and reduced military expenditures, but in 1998, **there was talk on the internet that he was involved in a sexual relationship with a 22-year-old White House intern named Monica Lewinsky.** At first Clinton denied the affair, but eventually admitted he had engaged in some sexual "fooling around" with Lewinsky.

The Republicans, who were in control of the House of Representatives at that time, impeached him for trying to cover up the affair.

Although a few past presidents have been threatened with impeachment, President Clinton was only the second president in the history of the United States to **actually be impeached** by the House of Representatives.

STORY

The **Lewinsky scandal,** sometimes referred to as "**Monica-gate,**" came to light in the fall of 1997 when White House intern, **Monica Lewinsky,** confided to a coworker named **Linda Tripp** that she had been having a sexual affair with President Clinton.

Tripp reported it to **literary agent, Lucianne Goldberg,** who advised Tripp to engage Lewinsky in more conversations about it and secretly record whatever Lewinsky said.

When Tripp did that, Goldberg urged Tripp to take the tapes to **Kenneth Starr.** Starr had been appointed by President Reagan to a federal judgeship, but was at that time a private practice lawyer acting as an independent counsel to investigate some of President Clinton's past real estate investments.

Goldberg began speaking to reporters about the existence of the tapes, and in January of 1998, the Washington Post reported the accusations.

Clinton immediately **denied having "sexual relations" with Miss Lewinsky.**

His wife, Hillary Clinton, stood by her husband throughout the scandal, describing it as "a vast right-wing conspiracy that has been conspiring against my husband."

By the summer of that year, Lewinsky had been called before a grand jury and had received transactional immunity in exchange for her testimony. **She told the grand jury about the affair, and later turned over a semen-stained dress to Starr as DNA evidence proving she was telling the truth.**

When Clinton was called before the grand jury, he admitted he had had an "improper physical relationship" with Lewinsky that was "not appropriate." But he defended himself against the charge that he had lied about the affair when he said he had not had sexual relations with her by saying he had not understood that letting her perform oral sex on him could be included in the strict definition of "sexual relations." He said he had never been "the actor," in the affair and had never made physical contact with Lewinsky's "genitalia, anus, groin, breast, inner thigh, or buttocks."

That argument didn't carry much weight with the Republicans in the House of Representatives. They were in the majority and they initiated impeachment proceedings against him. **Almost all of the Republicans in the House voted for the majority of the articles of impeachment, and four Democratic representatives from the South voted with them,** as did Representative Paul McHale of Pennsylvania.

If a president is impeached by the House of Representatives it is sort of like being on trial. and it was shown on live TV throughout. The hearings take place in the senate, and upon their conclusion, it requires a two-thirds majority of the senators to remove the president from office.

After the senate hearings, 45 Republican senators voted guilty on the charge of perjury, and 55 senators (all of the Democrats and 10 of the Republicans) voted not guilty.

On the charge of obstruction of justice, 50 Republicans voted guilty; 45 Democrats and five Republicans voted not guilty. The vote did not meet the two-thirds majority requirement, so President Clinton was acquitted of all charges and was able to serve out the remainder of his second term in office.

Chapter Fourteen
The Electoral College System Fails Again

The Presidential Election of 2000

Now we come to the significant presidential election of 2000. I hope in the preceding pages I have clarified the complex and often unwieldy way presidents are elected in the United States. With that understanding in mind, let's closely examine the 2000 presidential election to try to understand **how a candidate could win the popular vote by 543,895 votes and yet not get to be president.**

After the revelation of President Clinton's sexual exploits in the White House and his impeachment for trying to deny it, many wondered how much it would hurt the Democratic party in the next election. Everybody knew it would hurt, but no one knew if it would be enough to overcome the positive effect of the Democrats having been in power **during a time of peace with a good economy.**

Al Gore, Clinton's vice president, ran for president and took the position that the Clinton's affair had nothing to do with him. He won the nomination easily and selected **Joseph I. Lieberman,** a senator from Connecticut, as his running mate. Lieberman was the first observant Jew to be named on the ticket of any major party, and many wondered it that fact was to have important ramifications in the election.

The **Republican primaries** were wide open. There were no fewer than 13 candidates vying for the nomination.

In the **Republican presidential primaries, Arizona Senator John McCain** took the early lead by winning the New Hampshire primary, but from then on it was mostly wins for George W. Bush, son of former president George H.W. Bush.

At the Republican presidential nominating convention, Bush won easily. He named **Texan Dick Cheney, the CEO of**

military contractor Halliburton Company as his running mate. Cheney had been Secretary of Defense under Bush's father, George H. W. Bush.

When somebody remembered that the Electoral College section of the U.S. Constitution states that the president and vice president cannot come from the same state, Cheney quickly got a driver's license from Wyoming and put his Texas home up for sale.

A third-party candidate, **Ralph Nader**, nominee of the **Green Party**, was on the ballot in many states, and as it turned out, **his presence on the ballot in Florida undoubtedly cost Gore the presidency.**

The 2000 presidential campaign was mainly **a battle of television ads**, many of them negative (meaning they attacked the opponent rather than extolling the virtues of the candidate who placed the ad).

The three October debates were also important. In the first televised debate, those present in the auditorium felt Bush had performed very badly. In fact, right after the debate ended, Bush's handlers went on TV to attribute his poor showing to rthe fact that he had been ill. They also said he had not had adequate time to prepare for the debate.

But when the polls came out the next day, a majority of the television viewing audience said they liked what they saw in George Bush. Many of those polled said he seemed like **"a regular guy."**

Gore accused Bush and the Republicans of being too "right wing" and too militaristic. There was also a lot of talk about where Bush's campaign funds were coming from.

Gore talked about the tax breaks **the wealthiest one percent** were getting, pointing out that it was **the other 99 percent** that were responsible for the country's current prosperity and the budget surplus, so why should the 99 percent have to pay more in taxes and the rich less.

The Bush campaign focused on the "Clinton-Gore" years in an attempt to tie Gore closely to the now-unpopular Bill Clinton.

Gore tried to distance himself from Clinton personally, but did often make reference to how Clinton had turned the budget deficits of the Republican years into a budget surplus.

Bush responded by saying Gore was using "fuzzy math."

In the end, Gore won the entire West Coast accounting for 7,829,197 of his popular vote total. Gore also won **the East**, except for New Hampshire which he lost by only 7,211 votes.

In just three of the eastern states he won -- New Jersey, New York, and Pennsylvania -- he got 7,878,047 popular votes. As you can see, Gore racked up large pluralities in the states with the largest populations.

In **the Midwest**, Bush won the all-important state of Ohio with it's 21 Electoral College votes. However, Bush only won the Ohio popular vote by 165,019 out of almost five million votes cast. In other words, in Ohio, Gore got **almost as many** votes as Bush in Ohio, but got **zero Electoral College votes there**.

In the **central Midwest, Gore won** Illinois, Iowa, Michigan, Minnesota, and Wisconsin, which gave him 7,809,214 more popular votes.

It is important to note that in the states Gore won, **Nader was also strong**. Some say Gore would have won as many as a million more votes **if Nader had not been on the ballot** in those states, but that wouldn't have resulted in Gore wining **any more** electoral votes. Without Nader in the race in those states, **it is likely Gore would have won the popular vote by more than a million votes, but he still would not have been elected president in the Electoral College.**

Bush won Western states with small populations, including Colorado, Idaho, Kansas, Montana, Nebraska, Nevada, North Dakota, Oklahoma, South Dakota, Utah, and Wyoming to accumulate **60 Electoral College votes**. The total number of voters in those states in 2000 was 9,394,171. In comparison, California had 10,965,856 voters, more than a million and a half more voters than all of the small Western states, and yet **California only gave Gore 54 Electoral College votes**. It clearly illustrated the advantage the smaller-population states have in the Electoral College.

Of course the Republican Bush won every Southern state, but in some of those states **the vote was close**. The only Southern states Bush won convincingly were Texas, his home state, and Alabama. In the other Southern states, the vote was surprisingly close. In Tennessee, Bush won the popular vote by only 80,229 (out of more than two million votes cast). In Arkansas, he won by only 50,172 votes (out of almost a million votes cast). That meant Bush was picking up **all** the Electoral College votes in the South, but he wasn't gaining much advantage in the popular vote count.

In Florida, the outcome was extremely close, with Bush pulling out a very narrow win of 1,784 votes (out of 6 million votes cast).

However, the state-mandated recount found many irregularities. Somehow, a lot of votes for Gore had been missed. After the recount was finished, Bush's lead had been cut to only 537 votes. A second, more careful recount was ordered, and **the more votes that were recounted, the more Bush's lead dwindled**. When Bush's lead was down to only 154, Republicans went to court to put a stop to the recount. The Florida state Supreme Court said the recount was legal and should go on, but **in an extremely controversial decision, the U.S. Supreme Court, in a 5 to 4 vote, ordered the recount stopped.** The votes of the court's five conservative members was quite surprising because they generally were not willing to overturn decisions of a state's supreme court; they were bitterly denounced by the four dissenting members of the court for doing that kind of blatant turnaround in policy.

Although **Gore won the nationwide popular vote by 543,895 votes**, with the addition of Florida's 25 electoral votes, **Bush had 271 Electoral College votes, just one more than the required 270 needed to win the election**. Gore ended up with 266 electoral votes (one Gore elector from the District of Columbia left her ballot blank to protest their lack of representation in Congress). **In the end, it meant that even though Al Gore had won the general election by more than half a million votes, he would not get to be president**.

It is interesting to note here that the framers of the Constitution intentionally left the members of the Electoral College free to vote for anyone they wanted to, possibly for just such a situation. A few Republican electors could have realized it was unfair that the candidate who won the national vote was losing in the Electoral College and **they could have legally switched their votes to the winner of the popular vote**, Al Gore.

COMMENT

The **Florida voting outcome in the 2000 presidential election** was very controversial, to say the least. With Bush's conservative Republican brother serving as the governor in Florida, most observers thought Bush would win the state's presidential election easily.

But Clinton had been a popular president, and the state also had **a large Hispanic and African-American population that traditionally voted Democratic**. Although the fact that Gore's running mate, Joe Lieberman, was Jewish might have hurt the Democrats in the rest of the South, the large Jewish population in Florida voted mostly for the Gore-Lieberman ticket.

The early pre-election polls showed the race was going to be closer in the state than people thought. Based on exit polling (the pollsters questioned voters as they left the polling places), **the national TV networks declared Gore the projected winner in Florida**. That meant Gore would win the Electoral College vote and would become the nation's forty-third president.

A significant moment in the election came after the TV networks had officially declared Gore their projected winner. Reporters asked if Bush was ready to concede Florida based on the exit poll results. **Bush reminded them that his brother was the governor of Florida and went on to say we haven't given up yet, we are "working the phones."** When the reporters asked what good "working the phones" would do now that the polls were already closed, there was no answer from either George Bush or his brother. Later that night, more and more last-minute results began to come in favoring Bush. That kind of thing, along with the many voting irregularities that were being reported in Florida, made the Democrats suspicious. When the final voting results came in, they showed Bush had somehow overcome Gore's lead and had won Florida by 1,784 votes (out of 5,963,110 votes cast), they got even more suspicious.

Under Florida law, an election that close requires an an automatic recount. The closely scrutinized recount found Bush to have won **by only 537 votes. Somehow, the recount had taken 1,247 votes away from Bush.**

The Democrats starting looking for voting irregularities. They found out that **in traditionally Democratic districts**, large numbers of votes had been thrown out for unexplained reasons. They pointed out that **in Escambia County, a predominately African-American district, 16% of the ballots were thrown out without explanation. In Columbia County, another predominately African-American district, 17% of the ballots had been rejected.**

Next, the Democrats began to analyze the 54,000 Florida citizens that had not been allowed to vote for one reason or another. **Again, they found that the majority of citizens that had not been allowed to vote were African-Americans.** Further analysis discovered that many African-American voters had been turned away because **their names had mistakenly been listed as felons.**

One thing that drew special attention from the Democrats was a confusing type of paper ballot used in Palm Beach that became known as the "**butterfly ballot.**" They said the Palm Beach voters were mostly Democrats who had been confused by the ballots which had **made them mistakenly vote for Pat Buchanan of the Reform Party** when they thought they were voting for Al Gore. Buchanan received 3,407 votes on the so-called butterfly ballots, and later, the chairman of the Palm Beach County's Reform Party said he believed there were only 400 to 500 Buchanan supporters in that Democratic stronghold. An analysis of the ballots showed **most of those who had voted for Buchanan had otherwise voted Democratic, and** exit polls indicated that most of the voters in that district said they had voted straight Democratic. Later, **Buchanan himself said, after looking at one of the so-called butterfly ballots, he could see how voters might have mistakenly voted for him when they thought they were voting for Al Gore.**

For all these reasons, the Gore campaign requested that **disputed ballots in four counties be counted by hand,** Under Florida law, such a recount was allowable.

Although thousands of spoiled Bush-favoring absentee ballots from overseas soldiers **had been** recounted by hand to determine "the **voter's intent," the Bush campaign fought hard against a manual recount of the rest of the votes.**

As things started to look bad for Bush, Katherine Harris, the Republican Secretary of State in Florida suddenly stopped the recount. That prompted the Democrats to go to court to say that under Florida law, a manual recount was required. **Harris argued against the recount** in courts until it was finally brought before **the Florida Supreme Court. They ordered the recount to be completed, and it was resumed.**

The problem for Bush was that the more the ballots were recounted, the more votes Bush lost. After careful scrutiny of the ballots, Bush's 1,784 vote lead soon shrank to only 154. **It was clear that if the recount continued to find more votes for Gore, Bush would lose.**

In desperation, the Republicans **asked the U.S. Supreme Court for an emergency meeting in hopes they would stop the recount. They said Bush would suffer "irreparable harm" if the recount was allowed to continue.**

The court's decision came quickly: **the Supreme Court voted five to four to stop the recount.**

To this day, that decision is still one of the most controversial in the Supreme Court's history. The decision, and more importantly, the close 5-4 vote, is often used as an example when people talk about the president's power to "stack" the Supreme Court. Cynics would say you could have told in advance which of the judges were going to vote to stop the recount by simply noting which president appointed them.

The five judges who voted to stop the recount were **Anthony Kennedy**, appointed by Republican President Ronald Reagan. **Antonin Scalia**, appointed by Republican President Ronald Reagan. **Sandra Day O'Connor**, appointed by Republican President Ronald Reagan. **William Rehnquist**, appointed by Republican President Richard Nixon. **Clarence Thomas**, appointed by Republican President George H. W. Bush.

The four judges who voted against stopping the recount, Ruth Bader Ginsburg, Stephen Breyer, David Souter, and John Paul Stevens were quite vocal about their **opposition to the decision.** They denounced the decision as **a violation of both constitutional procedures and democratic principles.** They said **the Florida Supreme Court had clearly made the right legal decision when they ordered the recount to continue.** They said it was not appropriate for the U.S. Supreme Court to step in and override the highest court in the state of Florida. **Justice Stevens pointed to historical legal precedent, saying, "On questions of state law, we have consistently respected the opinions of the highest courts of the states."** The four dissenting judges said **the Republicans had failed to provide a legal basis** for stopping of the recount. They said there was no evidence that Bush would suffer irreparable harm if the recount went on, other than he might lose the election. **They asked how, in a democracy, carefully counting every vote could be a bad thing. They said the only danger of "irreparable harm" was to the public and to the democracy, and that going against Florida law to stop a recount would "cast a cloud on the legitimacy of the election."**

Four of the five judges that had voted in favor of Bush's request to stop the Florida recount had nothing to say about why they had made that decision. Only Antonin Scalia commented, saying only that the decision had been made because there was no way to know if the ballots that were being counted were "legally cast."

The dissenters pointed out that **there was nothing in the Bush request to stop the recount that said anything about "legally cast ballots."** On the contrary, they said, that was exactly the reason for continuing the recount, to make sure every ballot counted had been legally cast.

Nevertheless, even though the Supreme Court had voted along party lines, it is the final law of the land. The recount was stopped. Katherine **Harris certified the election in favor of Bush and there was nothing Gore or the Democrats could do abut it. Bush would become the next president.**

Perhaps the most surprising outcome of the 2000 presidential election was the **lack of outrage by the public over the fact that the winner of the popular votes did not get to be president.**

Remember the 1824 election when Andrew Jackson won the nation's popular vote, but didn't get to be president? Back then, the nation erupted in outrage. They said the people's wishes had been trampled. Many demanded that the election be overturned and that Jackson be put into his rightful place as president.

When that didn't happen, Jackson demanded an end to the Electoral College system of electing the president. He said it was ridiculous that the people didn't get to vote for the most important office in the country. Nearly everyone agreed with him, but of course, the states with smaller populations were not about to give up their voting advantage in the Electoral College, so nothing was done.

So what was different in 2000? Why did Gore, unlike Andrew Jackson, give up so easily?

In 1824, Jackson immediately said he would run again for president in the 1828 election, and he used the unfairness of the 1824 election as his main reason why he should be president. As a result, he won the 1828 election in a landslide.

So why didn't Gore do the same thing that Jackson had done in 1824? **Many think that if he had run again and kept on reminding people of the fact that he had actually won the 2000 election by 543,895 votes, he would have won the 2004 presidential election easily**. But Gore didn't speak out about it, so that didn't happen.

Chapter Fifteen
Presidential Politics and the War on Terrorism

By the time **the 2004 presidential election** rolled around, Al Gore and the Electoral College debacle of 2000 was long forgotten because the nation was in an uproar over the events that had been put into motion on **September, 11, 2001**. On that date, young men from Egypt, the United Arab Emirates, Lebanon, and Saudi Arabia commandeered four airliners in order to crash them into important American buildings.

STORY

The events of September 11, 2001 were put into play many months before when a groupof young Arab-looking men entered the U.S. on tourist, business, or student visas. They spoke little English, but they asked about pilot training in San Diego and in Florida. **Through a translator, they said they wanted to learn to fly big Boeing passenger jets**, but they were told they would have to learn to fly small airplanes first. They said **they were only interested in learning how to fly big passenger airliners**. The flying instructors testified later that they thought the young men had big unrealistic dreams.

After the flying instruction began, the instructors said the students focused only on in-flight maneuvering and **had little interest in learning about takeoffs and landings**. They never actually got the chance to fly any large planes, but in the spring of 2011, they were able to get training on a Boeing 737 simulator in Arizona. That triggered an alert and somebody notified the Arizona FBI. **The Arizona branch of the FBI immediately alerted the Washington D.C. FBI headquarters that several Middle Easterners were training to fly large passenger jets**. They recommended that other aviation schools nationwide be contacted to find out if other Arabs might be trying to learn how to fly large airplanes. It is not known if anybody in the FBI, or in any other antiterrorist agency, took note of the warning. However, the FBI and other agencies must have been aware that airliner hijackings had long been a favorite way for militant groups to bring their causes to the public's attention. **Over the previous forty years, there had been several instances where airliner hijackers reported that they were planning to crash hijacked airliners into important buildings.** It is not known how far up the line the Arizona FBI report went, but it is now known that at least two of the hijackers were already on an FBI watch list. Nevertheless, nothing was done.

On September 11the, the hijackers bought tickets on four flights leaving from Eastern cities with **destinations in California to make sure they would have heavy loads of fuel.**

Using box cutters as weapons and with the threat that they had bombs, one group took control of American Airlines Flight 11 from Boston and **flew it into the North Tower of the World Trade Center.** A second group took control of American Airlines Flight 175 from Boston and **flew it into the WTC South Tower.** Another group took control of American Airlines Flight 77 from Washington D.C and **flew it into the Pentagon Building.** A fourth group took over United Airlines Flight 93 from Newark, but **reportedly, several of the passengers tried to overcome the hijackers** and the plane crashed into the ground near Shanksville, Pennsylvania.

Video of the two World Trade Center towers burning was soon being broadcast live on every TV news network, and the nation watched in horror.

Unexpectedly, the south tower, the second tower to be hit, collapsed after burning for 56 minutes. Twenty one minutes later, the north tower also collapsed.

Later analysis determined that the collapse of both buildings was caused by the fire, not by the impact. The heat of burning jet fuel had melted important steel structural elements of the buildings. **According to the 9/11 commission report, the buildings would not have collapsed if more fireproofing had been installed.**

By the end of that day, **2,606 people had died in the two towers and 125 had died at the Pentagon.** On the airliners, **246 passengers and crew had died,** along with the hijackers.

The attacks on 9/11 brought about many changes in the United States. **In less than a month, U.S. military forces launched attacks in Afghanistan.** It was the first stage of President **Bush's new "war on terror."** He said from now on, it would be U.S. policy to go after terrorists anywhere in the world. He said the U.S. would not distinguish between terrorist organizations and governments that harbored them.

Bush focused on one particular group of terrorists known as **al-Qaeda,** a group of Islamic militants led by a Saudi citizen named **Osama bin Laden** who was believed to be in Afghanistan. Many thought **al-Qaeda** was in league with the Taliban, an Islamist group that controlled Afghanistan at that time.

As U.S. forces, with support from Britain and Australia, approached Kabul, the capital city of Afghanistan, the Taliban retreated. By the middle of November, the allied forces were in control of the country. As of this writing, all these years later, the war in Afghanistan is still going on. Although it has now become America's longest war, but there is little public interest in it.

In the spring of 2003, President Bush's war on terror had expanded to Iraq. Alleging that **Iraq was harboring al-Qaeda** and that **Iraqi President Saddam Hussein** was in the process of developing **weapons of mass destruction,** President Bush sought approval from Congress to invade Iraq. Although Congress did not approve a formal declaration of war against Iraq, they did pass a joint resolution **authorizing military action** against Iraq. It was not an uncontested vote. In the House, the Republicans were nearly unanimously in favor of it, 215 to 6, but the Democrats voted against it, 126 to 82. The dissenters pointed out that United Nations inspectors had done a complete search of Iraq and had found **no evidence of any weapons of mass destruction** development and **no evidence of an al-Qaeda presence.** In fact, the United Nations experts said the brutal government of Iraq had been making sure there was **no support for al-Qaeda in Iraq.**

In the Senate, the Republicans, of course, supported their Republican president and voted in favor of military action, 48 to1. But what was surprising was that the majority of the Democratic senators also voted for it (29 to 21). Essentially all of the senators from the conservative Southern and middle Western states voted in favor of military action in Iraq, but it was a surprise to many that some senators from the more liberal Northern states also voted in favor of it. Senators like Kerry from Massachusetts, Clinton and Schumer from New York, Biden and Torricelli from New Jersey, Carper from Delaware, Feinstein from California, and Cantwell from Washington voted in favor of taking military action in Iraq. (However, most of the Democrats in Congress later said they would have voted against the measure if they would have known the truth about what was going on there, which meant it would have failed in the senate, and Bush would not have had the authority to send U.S. troops to Iraq.)

With congressional approval in hand, President Bush soon ordered air attacks on Iraq, and on March 20, 2003, the ground invasion of Iraq began. With the support of extensive air power, the U.S. forces moved quickly, and within a few weeks, they took the capital city of Baghdad.

A month later, speaking from the deck of a U.S. aircraft carrier, USS Abraham Lincoln, President **Bush said the war in Iraq was over** and a new era in Iraq could begin. In reality, it took many more years and a new president before most of the U.S. troops were withdrawn from Iraq.

All told, **well over a million members of the U.S. military** served in Iraq, and despite the best medical care in any U.S. war, **4,484 American soldiers died** in Iraq, many of them from insurgent ambushes and from so-called "**improvised explosive devices**" (IEDs). **317 coalition forces** from countries other than the U.S. also died in combat. Estimates of the numbers of wounded American soldiers **vary widely from 100,000 to more than half a million**, depending on what type of injuries are counted.

The number of deaths and injuries to Iraqi civilians is unknown. **Civilian death estimates vary widely, from 151,000 to over a million.** The number of injuries and deaths of Iraqi civilians **will probably never be known.**

The Presidential Election of 2004

In 2004, with two wars still going on, the Democrats thought they had a good chance of regaining the White House. The Democratic primaries saw 10 candidates come forward.

Howard Dean was the early favorite, but **John Kerry** pulled out a win in **New Hampshire**.

Then, in the **South Carolina** primary, **John Edwards** won.

In **Oklahoma**, **Wesley Clark** won, but Edwards was a close second.

But then, **Kerry started to win some primaries. He won Hawaii, Idaho, Maine, Michigan, Nevada, Tennessee, Washington, and Washington, D.C. He went on to win at the Democratic national nominating convention.** He selected North Carolina Senator **John Edwards** as his running mate

---

STORY

From the beginning, it was clear that the presidential election of 2004 was going to be **a referendum on the war in Iraq.** Despite a flawed homeland security program that had allowed the 9/11 attacks to happen, **most people had not blamed the Bush administration.** After the 9/11 attacks, **Bush had quickly gotten the nation involved in two foreign wars, and presidents almost always gain popularity in a time of war.** When, in March of 2003, Bush proclaimed that the war in Iraq was all but over, he attained some of the highest presidential popularity ratings in history. However, it soon became clear that **no weapons of mass destruction had been found** in Iraq, and as time dragged on, it became clear that **the war *was not* over, and American soldiers were still dying there.** There was also widespread criticism of Bush's conduct of the war, especially after **evidence of torture of military prisoners came out.** Of special concern was the **Abu Ghraib prison in Iraq and the Guantanamo Bay detention camp in Cuba**, both of which were managed by the U.S. military.

Nevertheless, despite Bush's steadily declining popularity ratings, no serious challengers appeared during the Republican primaries, and as a result, **Bush was nominated by the Republican party to run for reelection.** There were calls for him

---

to dump his vice president, Dick Cheney, because he was such a strong advocate of torturing prisoners of war (he referred to it as **"enhanced interrogation"**). But Bush refused, and the Bush-Cheney ticket went forward.

The 2004 presidential campaign was, as predicted, mostly about Iraq and U.S. foreign policy. **Kerry attacked Bush's handling of the war in Iraq**, and he especially criticized **the treatment of prisoners in Guantanamo Bay** which he said were in violation of the Geneva Convention (a set of international laws that regulate the treatment of prisoners of war). Kerry said Bush had repeatedly acted without the support of the United Nations, and that his actions were hurting America's reputation abroad, even among America's allies.

Bush's campaign focused on the **worldwide terrorist threat**, and it seemed eerily similar to earlier Republican presidential campaigns during the Cold War that had focused on the **worldwide communist threat**.

During the campaign, Bush defended his approach to fighting terrorism. His ads suggested Kerry would be weak on fighting terrorism, and in a crisis, he would be slow to act.

STORY

During the presidential campaign of 2004, the Kerry campaign often compared Kerry's record of service in Vietnam to Bush's lack of service. They pointing out that Kerry had voluntarily served in Vietnam and had won service metals while Bush was "hiding out" in the Texas National Guard." They said **Bush had used his father's political connections in Texas to get into easy (and safe) Texas National Guard assignments**, and even then, Bush had rarely even bothered to perform his National Guard duties. A news investigation found evidence that showed Bush was actually out of the state when National Guard records showed he was in attendance at Texas National Guard meetings.

The Republicans **found some Vietnam veterans willing to say that Kerry's "dangerous" service in Vietnam was exaggerated, and that he didn't deserve the medals he had won**. They pointed out that upon his return to the United States, Kerry had joined the **veterans against the war in Vietnam** movement, and they felt that was a betrayal of his former comrades.

Meanwhile, Bush was defending his conduct of the **"war on terror,"** and his ads often focused on an Arab threat.

The implication was clear, if the voters liked his "preemptive" approach to fighting Arab terrorism in Afghanistan and Iraq, they should vote for him. He defended the harsh treatment of Arabic prisoners, implying that it was a fitting response to the Americans who had died on 9/11. His campaign staff also defended the reported torture of captives as a way to get information that might help the U.S. military.

Bush and Cheney won every Southern state, of course, and many of the Midwestern and Western states. Kerry won the West Coast, the upper Midwest, and the East.

While **the popular vote was relatively close**, 50.73 percent to 48.27 percent in favor of Bush, **the Electoral College vote was not as close—286 for Bush and 251 for Kerry**.

The Presidential Election of 2008

In 2008, President Bush's approval rating was very low, The American public was tired of hearing about continuing deaths of American servicemen in Iraq and Afghanistan. As a result, the

Democrats were confident that they could take back the White House in 2008. Ten candidates came forward to compete in the Democratic primaries.

STORY

Many were surprised that Al Gore, the winner of the popular vote in 2000, wasn't among the candidates. At first he expressed interest, but eventually he decided against running again. The speculation was that he felt he was doing more good as an ambassador in **the fight against global warming.**

In the Iowa caucuses, the relatively unknown, but very eloquent, **first-term Senator Barack Obama** won. **John Edwards** coming in second, and **Hillary Clinton, the senator from New York and the wife of former president Bill Clinton,** came in third. **Clinton then won in New Hampshire, Michigan and Florida,** but the Democratic National Committee disallowed those votes because they were held too early in the primary season. (Eventually, the Michigan and Florida votes were divided between Clinton and Obama.)

At the end of January, **Obama won Nevada and South Carolina**, and from that point on, Obama and Clinton alternated wins in the rest of the primaries. As the Democratic national presidential nominating convention approached, many expected a contentious floor fight between Obama and Clinton. However, midway through the voting, **when it became clear that Obama was pulling into the lead, Clinton asked for Democratic unity and told her delegates to vote for Obama. Barack Obama** was nominated by unanimous acclamation. He was the first person of African-American heritage to be nominated by a major party (his mother was white, but she had married a Kenyan, Barack Hussein Obama Sr., while he was in the U.S going to college). Obama chose **Delaware Senator Joe Biden** as his running mate.

The Republicans, on the other hand, knew they were going to have an uphill battle because of President Bush's very low approval ratings. Eleven candidates came forward to compete in the Republican primaries.

The **Republican primaries** began, as usual, with the Iowa caucuses. **Mike Huckabee** won, but then he faded badly in New Hampshire. **McCain** won New Hampshire, with **Rudy Giuliani** and **Mitt Romney** having disappointing finishes.

After a third-place finish in Florida, Giuliani withdrew from the race and endorsed John McCain. **From then on, McCain won most of the primaries**, and he was nominated at the Republican national nominating convention in Minnesota. He surprised everyone by picking the outspoken conservative governor of Alaska, **Sarah Palin**, as his running mate.

STORY

While the 2004 presidential election had been about the wisdom of invading Iraq, the **Presidential Election of 2008** was clearly going to be a referendum on how well Bush had been handling the so-called war on terror. By the time the 2008 presidential election season began, national polls were indicating Bush would leave office as **one of the most unpopular presidents in U.S. history**. Some polls showed he was even **more unpopular than Richard Nixon**, even though President Nixon had been forced to resign in the Watergate scandal. It was quite **a contrast to Bush's 90 percent approval rating** when he stood on the deck of the aircraft carrier USS Abraham Lincoln and declared "mission accomplished" in Iraq. Paradoxically, when asked in 2008 why they disliked Bush's performance in office so much, most people mentioned the same thing that had formerly made him popular, the war in Iraq.

Vice President Dick Cheney's ratings were even lower than Bush's, with only thirteen percent of Americans saying they approved of his performance in office.

As expected, **the 2008 election campaigns focused on the two ongoing wars in Afghanistan and Iraq.** Obama came out strongly against the Iraq war in particular, and **McCain, who had supported the two wars all along, was forced to defend them**.

Focusing on Bush's unpopularity, Obama reminded the voters that McCain had voted to support Bush 90 percent of the time.

McCain, as a long-time member of the U.S. Senate, focused on Obama's inexperience. He pointed out the fact that Obama was **a first-term senator**.

Obama countered that charge by saying it was **time for a change**. He pointed out how the Republicans had turned Clinton's healthy economy and budget surplus into an unhealthy economy and a rapidly-growing budget deficit. He said he would enact universal health care, make America "green," and bring back respect for America abroad.

COMMENT

By the time voters went to the polls in 2008, the country was in the midst of a financial crisis. Only a few weeks before the general election, Lehman Brothers, one of the world's largest financial institutions was **forced to file for bankruptcy** because of its exposure to newly-created risky and speculative financial instruments that were based on shaky subprime mortgages. Many other financial institutions around the world were also highly exposed to the new and very complicated financial instruments. As a result, the situation was **threatening to bring down America's entire financial system, along with**

serious economic problems quickly spreading to the rest of the world. Bush's Secretary of the Treasury, Henry Paulson, the former head of the Goldman Sachs investment banking company, had gone before Congress to ask for hundreds of billions of dollars to bail out financial institutions. After much controversy, Congress finally authorized the money, and the crisis was averted for the time being. Nevertheless, investors in the stock market lost billions and the so-called "housing bubble" collapsed and many Americans found they owed much more on their homes than they were worth. With unemployment rising, many faced foreclosure.

As election day neared in 2008, the polls were showing it was the economic crisis that was the most important issue, more important even than the ongoing foreign wars. Although Americans were aware of Obama's inexperience, that seemed to be less important than the fact that people were hurting economically. They were ready for a change in Washington.

The election took place in an environment of financial anxiety and uncertainty. Although the Republicans again held most of the South, this time they lost Florida in a very close vote (McCain lost Florida by 236,148 votes out of eight million votes cast). McCain also lost Virginia in another close vote, and he lost North Carolina, but by only 14,177 votes (out of more than four million votes cast).

Obama won the East, some of the Midwest, and the West Coast. But McCain won 28 states, more than Obama's 22. However, McCain's wins were all in states with smaller populations and fewer Electoral College votes. Obama won all the larger population states *and* enough of the South and Midwest to secure the Electoral College vote, 365 to 173.

The Presidential Election of 2012

The presidential election of 2012 **turned out to be closer than most would have predicted**. Although the war in Afghanistan was still going on, most assumed it would play only a minor role in the campaign because nobody expected the Republicans to be against it, even if it was now "President Obama's war."

It was said that if the states that had been voting Republican in the past went back to voting that way in 2012, Obama would have a hard time getting elected. It was even possible that the election would be a replay of 2000 when the Democratic candidate won the general election but lost in the Electoral College.

With President Obama assured of the Democratic nomination, all attention was on who the Republicans would nominate. The Republican primaries began, as usual, with the caucuses in Iowa and primary balloting in New Hampshire. And as usual, a great deal of attention was paid to these first two primaries; however, in 2012, they did little to predict which candidate would win the Republican nomination. The outcome of the primary in Iowa was essentially a three-way tie between former **Pennsylvania Senator Rick Santorum, former Massachusetts governor Mitt Romney**, and **Texas Representative Ron Paul**.

The New Hampshire primaries were held a week later. As an indication of how wide open the Republican race was, **33 candidates filed to appear on the ballot**.

Mitt Romney won in New Hampshire, and Ron Paul came in a distant second. The next primary, in South Carolina, was expected to clarify the situation, but it did the opposite. Newt Gingrich won, and Romney came in a distant second. If Romney couldn't find a way to win the South, it would be unlikely that he would win the nomination. Romney managed to win Florida, and then he also won the most states on "Super Tuesday," the day ten states were to hold their primaries. Romney carried six states, and Santorum carried three. Gingrich won his home state of Georgia. It meant Romney was again in the lead, but it was not a decisive lead.

COMMENT

The primary elections of 2012 were the first presidential primary elections to be held after **a landmark Supreme Court five-to-four decision that had lifted the restrictions on corporate contributions to political campaigns.** As expected, the amounts spent on the candidates' campaigns broke all prior spending records.

Over the next few weeks, twelve more primaries were held, with Romney winning most of them. Baring any unforeseen surprises, **it was beginning to look like Romney would be the nominee.**

While the Republican primaries were going on, President Obama's approval rating was gradually going down. The early polls about a Romney-Obama presidential race indicated Romney might do surprisingly well, given that he was up against a sitting president who had been elected by a large margin.

At the Republican National Convention, Romney was nominated.

Early on, the polls consistently showed President Obama in the lead, but **the margin was never all that great.**

At the time, it seemed likely that **the two biggest campaign issues would be foreign policy and the domestic economy**. President Obama had withdrawn most of the U.S. troops from Iraq after the long war there, but the situation was still unstable. **What would happen to Iraq without a U.S. military presence was an open question.** And then there was the issue of the ongoing war in **Afghanistan, the longest war in U.S. history**. The Republicans revealed statistics that indicated Obama's war policies in Afghanistan were failing. They said **Afghanistan was a more dangerous place now than it was when he took office.**

During the 2008 campaign, Obama had been critical of President Bush's handling of the war in Afghanistan, but after taking office, he had **retained President Bush's Secretary of Defense, Robert Gates, and had approved the same "surge" approach** (increasing the number of troops and fighting resources) Bush had used in Iraq and Nixon had used in Vietnam.

No one really knew what Romney's position would be in Afghanistan. He would need to appear to be tough on terrorism, but was the country ready for another escalation of the conflict in Afghanistan? President Obama had promised to get U.S. troops out "soon" and turn the defense of the country over to the Afghans. That was the approach he had used in Iraq, but it was still an open question as to whether it was going to work either there or in Afghanistan. There had been a sustained increase in violence in Iraq after the U.S. troops were pulled out. **Some people worried that Iraq would go the way of Vietnam, with anti-American militants taking over the government.**

In the past, Republican presidential candidates had tried to paint the Democrats as weak on defense. Republican candidates generally supported a strong military and showed more of a willingness to get involved in foreign civil wars than the Democratic candidates.

After the 9/11 attacks on the twin towers in New York City, President Bush had not only approved the military invasions of Iraq and Afghanistan but had also created **a huge new division of government, the Department of Homeland Security**. Those moves had the approval of most Americans, but his administration had also instituted new policies that many said were an attack on privacy and freedom.

However, Obama had kept all of those policies in place, and he had stepped up the "assassination by drone" program that Bush had initiated. That meant Obama had taken away one of the strongest Republican talking points.

> **STORY**
>
> Another fact turned out to play an important role in the presidential election of 2013: Obama had ordered a successful CIA and Navy SEALs operation that went into Pakistan and **killed Osama bin Laden**, the supposed leader of the al-Qaeda terrorist organization. During the election campaigning, Obama brought that fact up as often as possible.

The issue of **the country's ongoing economic problems was also a major campaign issue**. A sitting president must always run on his record, and from the outset, it was clear Mitt Romney would campaign against President Obama's handling of the economy. Although the financial crisis of the Bush administration had passed, **the unemployment rate had stayed stubbornly high throughout Obama's four-year term**. Obama had constantly pointed out that it was the previous Republican administration that had handed him an economy that was near collapse, and he had done his best to stabilize the situation through bailouts and government economic stimulus programs. **He said the economy was recovering as well as could be expected**, given how bad it had been.

Romney told the voters that he, as an experienced businessman, could do a better job of getting the U.S. economy back on its feet. That raised questions as to where he stood with regard to those in the financial industries who were widely seen as *causing* the country's severe economic downturn. President Obama tried to portray Romney as a member of that group.

Even the people who supported President Obama were not sure he had done enough to rein in the perpetrators of the near economic collapse. Many of the leaders of the nation's largest financial institutions were still in power, and no one had been sent to jail.

Romney said the bailouts and the economic stimulus packages

were the wrong approach. He laid out a five-point plan that had the blessing of many top economists. But more importantly, he asked the voters to look at their own lives and ask themselves if they were better off after four years of an Obama presidency. Many believed the outcome of the 2012 election would be determined by how people answered that question.

One thing was clear: in the spring of 2012, **the polls were already indicating that the race would be very close**; Obama would not coast to the kind of easy victory he had enjoyed in 2008.

When the pollsters asked the public which candidate would better solve the nation's economic problems, Romney consistently came out ahead. But only if the respondents were male. When the same question was asked of female voters, Obama always came out ahead.

There were also **differences in the polling data depending on which demographic group was polled**. Among polled voters who identified themselves as Hispanic, Obama consistently lead by a margin of nearly two to one. Among polled voters who identified themselves as African-American, only three percent said they would even consider voting for Romney.

In every speech, Romney talked about the stubbornly high unemployment rate, pointing out that far from delivering an improved economy, as President Obama had promised in 2008, the unemployment figures had grown worse since he had taken office four years before. In response, Obama pointed out the fact that it had been Republican policies under George Bush that had put the economy into such bad shape in the first place. Obama said the economic situation would have been much worse without the policies he had put in place.

Romney laid out a five point economic plan which he said had been endorsed by five Nobel laureates. In response, Obama said the numbers in Romney's plan just didn't add up.

Neither candidate's argument seemed to sway many voters. **The polls continued to show a near dead heat**, and there were always enough undecided voters to change the outcome.

STORY

A turning point in the 2012 presidential election came when a video turned up of Romney's meeting with supporters at a dinner at the Boca Raton, Florida, home of Marc Leder, a financier. Unbeknownst to him, one of the catering staff was secretly making a video of Romney's comments at that dinner. The video was kept secret for some time, but on September 17th, Mother Jones magazine published an article titled "SECRET VIDEO: Romney Tells Millionaire Donors What He REALLY Thinks of Obama Voters: When he doesn't know a camera's rolling, the GOP candidate shows his disdain for half of America."

The article included a clip from the video in which Romney is heard to say " . . . **there are 47 percent who are with him [Obama], who are dependent on government, who believe they are victims, who believe the government has a responsibility to care for them . . . .**"

The national news media picked up the story and for several weeks it was mentioned and the video was re-shown nearly every time Romney's name came up.

At first, Romney said his comments at that dinner were speculative and that they hadn't come out exactly the way he wanted them too. But later, he completely disavowed what he had said at the dinner, saying in no way did it reflect his true feelings. That did little to stop members of the media from using the video against him, and the Obama campaign also used it frequently.

Soon after the secret video came out, the polls began to show voters turning against Romney. Commentators on TV began to talk about an inevitable Obama victory.

As the election neared, someone in the U.S. put together a short, very **amateurish video that poked fun at the founders of the Muslim religion** and posted it on the YouTube internet site. Although few people had actually seen the short video clip, it set off a series of **anti-American demonstrations** in the Muslim world. From Egypt to Australia and in some European countries, there were protests and burnings of the U.S. flag. In countries like Yemen and Tunesia, the protests turned violent.

After several U.S. embassies were attacked on September 11th, the anniversary of the 9/11 attacks in New York in 2001, government officials in Washington, and elsewhere, were closely watching the situation. However, **when reports starting coming in that the U.S. diplomatic mission in Benghazi, Libya was under attack, there was apparent confusion about what was going on there**. **The attack ended with four Americans dead, including U.S. Ambassador J. Christopher Stevens.**

Although al-Qaeda claimed responsibility for the attack, in the weeks that followed, representatives of the Obama administration were saying it was just another protest against the anti-Muslim video that had gotten out of control. In the middle of a closely contested presidential election, such an event was bound to come under close scrutiny, which **brought Obama's foreign policy (and the policies of his Secretary of State, Hillary Clinton) into question.**

When the video was released, showing that there were no demonstrations in that area of Benghazi and that the men who attacked the embassy were heavily armed, some people began to suspect that the Obama administration was trying play down the attack. They suggested the attack showed that anti-American extremists were well entrenched in Libya, despite the administration's support of the uprising there that had removed Libya's leader. President Obama strongly denied that accusation, but the attacks from Republicans continued. They included accusations that Ambassador Stevens and others had been worried about just such an attack, and that they had asked for more security, but his requests had been denied. In fact, instead of providing more security to the embassy, some of the existing security forces had been pulled out, apparently to show trust in the new Libyan government.

Eventually, the facts came out: **the attack was a well-coordinated mission, pre-planned to take place on the anniversary of the 9/11 attacks**. Reports surfaced that the attackers were militants related to al-Qaeda, and that the group included seasoned al-Qaeda fighters that had been brought in from Tunisia and Iraq.

President Obama announced that they were trying to track down the killers, and he said he was beefing up security at all U.S. facilities in the region.

But that didn't end the controversy. Critics said the Obama administration had tried to cover up the true nature of the Benghazi attack because it might reflect badly on U.S. foreign policy in the region. Republican lawmakers started hearings on the matter.

President Obama, and other members of his administration, denied that there had been any sort of cover-up. They said they had not been given correct information about the true nature of the Benghazi attack from intelligence sources.

Nevertheless, the Benghazi attack and the aftermath continued to be a topic of dispute throughout the rest of the campaign.

In the three presidential debates, Romney was eager to talk about the economy. He mentioned the rapid rise in the deficit, and he described people who had come up to him with stories of lost jobs and difficult times.

But Obama said he had created five million jobs in the private sector, that the automobile industry had come roaring back, and housing sales had begun to rise. He attacked Romney for his unwillingness to raise taxes on the wealthy. He pointed out that it was the previous Republican administration that had created the economic problems and that Romney wanted to take the country back there by reducing taxes on the rich and by taking away regulation of Wall Street.

Romney again talked about his five point plan to bring back the economy and said his goal was both to lower taxes on the middle class and to create new jobs. He said he would close tax loopholes and work toward energy independence through the use of clean coal and by increasing offshore and Alaskan oil drilling. He said Obama was going to take huge amounts of money out of Medicare to pay for his new "**Obamacare**" program. (He apologized for using the term "Obamacare," but the president said he had come to actually like the term.)

After the first debate, **Romney closed on Obama in the polls nationwide *and* in the crucial "swing states,"** the states that historically do not consistently vote either Republican or Democrat (also known as "battleground states"). Some polls indicated Romney had pulled ahead in Colorado, Florida, New Hampshire, and Virginia, but not by very much. A few polls suggested Romney had even pulled ahead in Ohio, but most polls showed Obama holding onto a narrow lead there.

In the two debates that followed, Obama was more aggressive, hitting Romney on his comments that had been captured in the secret 47% video.

Romney again referred to the 23 million people who were still struggling to find a job, and he again brought up the high unemployment rate in the country.

Obama disputed Romney's plan, saying Romney's five-point plan was actually only a one-point plan that was designed to make sure that folks at the top got to play by a different set of rules.

Romney also said he would put in place an employment verification system to make sure employers didn't hire people who had come into the U.S. illegally.

Obama responded by saying "**We are a nation of immigrants.**" He said he had streamlined the legal immigration system to make it easier for people to come into the country legally. On the other hand, he said his administration had put a lot of focus on securing the border, and the flow of undocumented workers across the border was less than anytime in the last 40 years

Romney pressed Obama about the Benghazi attacks and about turmoil in the Middle East. He said there was a rising tide of chaos, with al-Qaeda and other jihadist groups gaining strength.

Obama responded by saying his first job as commander-in-chief was to keep the American people safe. He said he had ended the war in Iraq and refocused attention on "those who actually killed us on 9/11." He said **al-Qaeda's core leadership had been decimated**, and that the war on terror would continue.

After the debates were over, **the polls indicated the race was still very close**, but there were some indications that Obama's aggressive tactics in the last two debates had at least slowed Romney's momentum.

Back on the campaign trail, President Obama kept up his relentless attacks on Governor Romney, **trying to portray him as out-of-touch rich man who wanted to take the country back to the Republican policies that had caused the recent economic problems**. He said Romney was only interested in helping the rich, and that he would destroy Social Security and Medicare.

Romney tried to keep the focus on the president's record. He said Obama's 2008 campaign slogan had been "change," but now he wanted to "go forward" with no change. Over and over again, he recited statistics that he said showed the country had gone backward economically under Obama.

COMMENT

Some of the very conservative Republican senatorial candidates were not helping Romney's attempts to sound more moderate. Republican **tea party favorites were taking a hard line on abortion and illegal immigration,** and the Democrats were using Romney's endorsement of those candidates against him.

Surprisingly, with the country's longest war still going on, there was little campaigning that had anything to do with foreign policy issues (except for talk about the recent attacks on the U.S. consulate in Benghazi).

The Green Party presidential candidate, Jill Stein, was getting some national attention by talking about U.S. wars and military adventures. She pointed out that President Obama had dramatically increased the frequency of deadly "**assassination by drone**" attacks by U.S. unmanned drones and that he had also started to use drone attacks in Yemen and Somalia. She said the drone attacks resulted in 75 percent of Pakistani civilians believing the U.S was their chief enemy, not the Taliban or al-Qaeda.

COMMENT

The changing demographics of the United States was to play an important role in the 2012 presidential election. In the last two U.S. censuses, the number of people that identified themselves as of Hispanic origin had increased dramatically. In fact, Hispanics accounted for more than half of the nation's growth in the last decade. That hurt Romney's chances because only 20 percent of Hispanics polled said they were planning to vote for him.

The 2010 census also showed that the segment of the population that identified themselves as black or African-American **had increased from twelve percent of the population in 2000 to over sixteen percent** in 2012, and nearly all of the polled African-American voters said they were planning to vote for President Obama.

Because of the design of the Electoral College, even non-voters were to play a role in the 2012 presidential election. Since 1964, the number of electors has been fixed at 538. **States are assigned electors based on their total population, not the number of eligible voters.** Based on the most recent census, the number of electors assigned to a state are recalculated before every presidential election. States gain electors if their populations increase, which means electors have to be taken away from states whose populations have not increased. In 2012, it is notable that states like Arizona and Texas gained electors. **Since the presidential election of 2000, Arizona has gained three electors, and Texas has gained six electors.** Those nine electors were taken away from other states that did not have such large increases in their populations. It is known that much of the increase in population in Arizona and Texas is due to the influx of undocumented people from south of the border. Therefore, in 2012, we had the unusual situation that some states gained electors even though they did not gain voters.

As the election campaign entered its last few weeks, the polls were showing that **the race couldn't be closer in the all important "swing states."** In **Nevada**, all of the polls had Obama in the lead, but by only a few percentage points. In **Colorado**, Romney had a slight lead in some of the polls, and Obama had a slight lead in other polls. In Iowa, the polls were showing Obama with a lead, but it was very narrow. In the crucial swing state of **Ohio**, Obama had been holding a small lead in the polls throughout the campaign, but some polls indicated a tie there. In **New Hampshire**, some polls indicated Romney would win that state, but other polls indicated Obama had a slight lead there. In normally-Republican **Virginia**, the polls were mixed, with some showing Romney with a slight lead, while others showed Obama with a slight lead. In **Florida**, most of the polls were showing Romney with a very slight lead.

The media was full of Electoral College analysis. It looked like **Romney would have to win Florida, Virginia, and Ohio, plus at least two of the other swing states to become president.**

Nevertheless, Romney was sure he would win. He said **the polls were wrong** because they were overestimating the number of minorities that would turn out to vote for Obama.

After both campaigns were suspended for several days due to the huge hurricane that hit the upper East Coast, the candidates engaged in nearly non-stop campaigning in the swing states.

STORY

In some past presidential elections, there have been last minute events that may have changed the outcome. Known as an "**October surprise**," events such as Henry Kissinger's statement just days before the 1972 election that "**peace is at hand**" in Vietnam helped assure Nixon's reelection despite the news that was starting to come out about the Watergate break-ins. Another example came about in 2000. Just days before the election, it was reported that Republican presidential candidate **George W. Bush had once been arrested for drunk driving** (Gore won the popular vote, but Bush became president anyhow by winning the Electoral College vote).   An October **non-surprise** took place in the presidential election of 1980. The Iran hostage crisis had dragged on for years and was hurting incumbent Jimmy Carter's chances of being reelected. Carter thought he had a last minute deal to free the hostages before the election, but the deal fell through. Later, the president of Iran said Reagan's campaign aides had **struck a deal with Iran to delay the release of the hostages until after the election. Reagan denied it, but the later arms-for-hostages scheme in Iran carried out by members of Reagan's executive branch gave credence to the idea.**

As the 2012 presidential campaign neared its end, there was widespread discussion as to **the likelihood of an October surprise** in such a close and hard-fought election.

As it turned out, the only October surprise in 2012 was the weather. An unusual fall hurricane hit the upper East Coast the week before the election. President Obama canceled his scheduled appearances in hard-hit Virginia, and his campaign aides said it would only be fair for Romney to also cancel his scheduled appearances. Romney announced that out of respect for those who were suffering from the hurricane's impact, he would cancel all of his campaign appearances until the crisis was over. He went to Ohio to organize a relief effort to send food and clothes to the hardest hit areas. As a result, the president got to be constantly in the news by holding many official press conferences about the government's ongoing disaster relief effort; Meanwhile, the news media was hardly covering Romney. It gave the president a slight boost in many of the polls, but whether it had any affect on the outcome of the election is still an open question.

When all the votes were counted, Obama **squeaked out wins in the key swing states** of Colorado, Iowa, Virginia, Florida, and Ohio. **He lost two of the states he had won in 2008 (Indiana and North Carolina), but he held onto all the other swing states, even though** his margins of victory in those states was much lower than in 2008: in most of the swing states, Obama won by less than two percentage points. As in the 2000 presidential election, Florida was a near tie, with Obama winning by only 74,309 votes out of 8,401,203 votes cast.

In the end, **Obama won the popular vote by about two million** votes, meaning the election was not as close as the polls had been indicating. **He won in the Electoral College, 332 to 206**.

Chapter Sixteen
Hillary Wins, but Trump Becomes President

The Presidential Election of 2016

Right from the start, it was clear that the presidential election of 2016 was not going to be "normal." With no incumbent president running for reelection, the field of potential candidates was wide open. In fact, according to the Federal Election Commission, 1,817 candidates filed a Statement of Candidacy. Of course, only a handful of them would ever be known to more than a few friends and relatives.

The way the voting public gets to know the candidates is through televised pre-primary debates.

The Democratic Debates

The Nine Democratic debates gave the lesser-known candidates a chance to present their views to the public on national television. Based on the early poll results, **five candidates were invited to participate in the initial Democratic debate: Lincoln Chafee**, former governor of Rhode Island, **Hillary Clinton,** former U.S. Senator from New York and U.S. Secretary of State, **Martin O'Malley**, former governor of Maryland, **Bernie Sanders**, U.S. Senator from Vermont, and **Jim Webb**, former U.S. Senator from Virginia. In addition, Vice President **Joe Biden** was invited to debate, but he declined.

They were all well prepared, but the news media mostly focused on Clinton and Sanders.

By the time the second Democratic debate came around, the field had been narrowed down to Clinton, Sanders, and O'Malley. With a terrorist attack in Paris having just occurred, the focus was on terrorism and foreign policy. Each of the candidates **defined terrorism as a great threat to the world**, and each of them promised to find a way to defeat the Islamic terrorist group known as ISIS. **Hillary Clinton reminded the audience of the depth of her experience** in foreign affairs.

Sanders focused more on domestic affairs. He hammered on one main theme, that **the country was being run (and ruined) by Wall Street and the big banks**. He said, "I'm running for president because our economy is rigged because working people are working longer hours for lower wages and almost all of new wealth and income being created is going to the top one percent,"

O'Malley tried a two-pronged approach, saying we had economic problems here at home and the threat of terrorists attacks from abroad.

In the debates that followed, **Clinton showed her experience** at debating, parrying any and all attack while still managing to get her main points across. **She focused more on the Republicans** than on her Democratic debate opponents.

The early polls indicated Hillary Clinton was in the lead, but **the message of inequality that Bernie Sanders was focusing on was also getting quite a bit of support**.

In the early polls, O'Malley hardly registered, so it was looking like a two-horse race between "Hillary" and "Bernie" (as the news media had begun to refer to them).

As a result, only Hillary and Bernie participated in the final few debates.

Hillary continued to talk about her experience in foreign affairs, but being aware that Bernie's progressive message was getting through to a lot of voters, **she also began describing herself as "a progressive."**

Bernie insisted college should be free for all, and Hillary agreed that it should be "affordable" for all, but not free because the country had no way to pay for that.

They both agreed that the minimum wage should be raised and that health care should be affordable for all. However, **their approaches to the health care issue differed**. Hillary supported the existing Affordable Care Act, but wanted to strengthen it and make it more affordable. Bernie was floating a "Medicare for all" plan, essentially saying we should take advantage of the existing infrastructure of the popular Medicare program.

The two candidates did agree that there needed to be more control over who could buy a gun, especially assault rifles.

The last few Democratic debates took place after the primary elections had begun, and the rhetoric of the debates sharpened, especially from Bernie who criticized Hillary for making too much money speaking to the wealthy and for accepting campaign money from financial institutions. He also tried to tie her past tenure as the U.S. Secretary of State to current terrorist problems in Egypt, Libya, and Syria.

Hillary, in turn, criticized Bernie for some of his past votes in the Senate, suggesting that they differed from his current stands on some of the important issues.

Both candidates also talked about the problems of racial discrimination in the country and agreed that "something" needed to be done about it, especially in policing.

They also talked about immigration because it was sure to be a leading topic from the Republican side. They both agreed there should be a path to citizenship for those who had entered the country illegally but who had been good citizens since.

Both of the Democratic candidates were aware of **how much attention Donald Trump was getting** in his bid for the presidency on the Republican side. Hillary criticized "Trump" (as the news media was calling him) for his hate rhetoric, his demagoguery, and his trafficking in prejudice and paranoia. **She said such talk had no place in our political system**.

Bernie agreed and said the American people would never elect a president who insults Mexicans and Muslims and African-Americans. He also reminded the audience that **Trump was a supporter of the so-called birther movement** that was championed by bigots who were trying to keep an African-American from becoming president by suggesting he hadn't been born in the U.S.

By the time the Democratic debates were over, Bernie was seen as having done a good job of using the debates to make himself and his progressive message better known to the public.

The Republican Debates

The Republican debates brought together a lot of candidates. **Based on the early polls, ten candidates were invited to the initial televised debate**. Five other candidates who had not scored as high in the polls debated in a "second-level" debate.

Several of the Republican candidates were well known. **Jeb Bush** was the former governor of Florida, the son of President George H. W. Bush, and the brother of President George W. Bush. Others had held high political offices: **Chris Christie,** Governor of New Jersey, **Ted Cruz,** U.S. Senator from Texas, **Mike Huckabee**, former Governor of Arkansas, **John Kasich**, Governor of Ohio, **Rand Paul**, U.S. Senator from Kentucky, **Marco Rubio**, U.S. Senator from Florida, and **Scott Walker**, Governor of Wisconsin

There were also two "outsiders" who had never held public office. **Ben Carson** was a retired neurosurgeon who had written several books and was well known in the African-American community. **Donald Trump** was a well-known businessman and TV entertainer. He said he was one of America's wealthiest men, so he knew how to get things done. However, **Trump had filed for bankruptcy several times in the past, so his actual worth was not known**. He said he was going to fund his own campaign and would not take donations from anybody.

The Republican debates were often decidedly uncivil. It started in the very first Republican debate when the moderator asked if all the candidates would pledge to support to the eventual nominee of the Republican party and pledge to not run an independent campaign. Only **Trump refused**, and that encouraged the other candidates to immediately begin to attack him. Despite getting booed by the audience, Trump wouldn't back down. Instead, he just said if he did win the Republican nomination, he would promise not to run as an independent.

After that odd beginning, attention turned to Jeb Bush who, although not leading in the early polls, was **still considered to be the favorite** because of name recognition and the amount of money he was getting through campaign donations. When asked why the county needed another Bush in the Oval Office, he said that as governor of Florida, he had cut taxes and saved the state money by vetoing unneeded budget line items.

When the moderator asked Trump why he had **referred to women as "fat pigs, dogs, slobs, and disgusting animals,"** he said he just liked to kid around. But when she pressed the issue with more examples, he said, "I think the big problem this country has is being **politically correct.**"

Huckabee and Walker said abortion should be illegal, even if it would cost the life of the mother.

Paul said Christians should not be forced to conduct business that conflicts with their religious beliefs.

Trump found a variety of ways to insult President Obama, saying **"We have a president who doesn't have a clue.** I would say he's incompetent, but **I don't want to do that because that's not nice."**

Cruz said he believed Russia and China had committed cyber war against the U.S. and added that as a result of the Obama-Clinton foreign policy, Iran was on the verge of acquiring a nuclear weapon.

Carson talked about value of personal responsibility, hard work, creativity, and innovation.

Walker said he had defunded the Planned Parenthood organization before any of the other governors.

The moment that refocused the debate was when **Trump turned to his signature issue, illegal immigration from Mexico.** He said he alone had brought the immigration issue to the public's attention. He said he would send the estimated eleven million illegal immigrants back home, and **he would build a wall to keep them out.** Furthermore, he said **he would make Mexico pay for that wall.** He said the immigration problem existed "because our leaders are stupid." He said, "The Mexican government is much smarter, much sharper, much more cunning. And they send the bad ones over because they don't want to pay for them. They don't want to take care of them. **Why should they when the**

stupid leaders of the United States will do it for them?"

When questioned about his business practices and his bankruptcies, Trump said, on four occasions he had **"used the laws of this country** just like the greatest people that you read about every day." He added, "I'm very proud of the job I did."

Regarding the deal President Obama and Secretary of State Kerry had made with Iran, **they all agreed that it had been a mistake.** Huckabee said Obama "trusts our enemies and vilifies everyone who disagrees with him."

The moderator asked the candidates how they felt about God.

Cruz said he was "blessed to receive a word from God every day in receiving the scriptures and reading the scriptures." He said his father was an alcoholic and not a Christian, but then he gave his heart to Jesus and became a pastor.

Kasich said he believed in miracles.

Walker said, "I'm certainly an imperfect man. And it's only by the blood of Jesus Christ that I've been redeemed from my sins." **He said God calls us to follow his will** and that is what he was going to try to do.

Rubio said, "God has blessed the Republican Party with some very good candidates. The Democrats can't even find one."

Carson did not answer the question directly, but instead said, "The bully pulpit is a wonderful place to start healing."

In the second Republican debate, **former Hewlett Packard CEO Carly Fiorina** was added to the list.

When Paul said there was **a sophomoric quality about Mr. Trump,** Trump said **I never attacked him on his look, and believe me, there's plenty of subject matter right there**." He also attacked Governor **George Pataki**, saying he was "a failed governor" in New York. He said **he wouldn't be elected dog catcher right now.**" When Trump attacked Governor Walker on how he handled the Wisconsin budget, Walker fired back, saying, "You took four major projects into bankruptcy over and over and over again. **You can't take America into bankruptcy**."

As it turned out, that second debate was to set the tone for the rest of the Republican debates. There were **numerous attacks on**

Trump, and he aggressively responded to every one with counterattacks. Trump was apparently feeling more confident because he was leading in the polls, and he often interrupted the other candidates. On the topic of foreign policy, **Trump said he thought he would "get along" with world leaders like Putin that Obama couldn't get along with.** He also continued to press his main agenda, **deporting all the illegal immigrants.** He was even against birthright citizenship. He said, immigrant women were walking across the border to have babies, and then "we take care of the baby for 85 years." He said the U.S. was the only country dumb enough to do that.

During the Republican debates, there were quite a few ugly exchanges between the candidates. One of the first was between Trump and Bush over some things Trump had said about Bush's Mexican-American wife. He demanded that Trump apologize, but Trump refused. **Trump also criticized Bush for speaking Spanish on the campaign trail.** He said, "We have a country, where, to assimilate, you have to speak English."

There were also plenty of other personal attacks. After **Trump dismissively called Rubio "little Marco,"** Rubio responded by calling him "big Donald, which eventually **let to an innuendo battle between Rubio and Trump about the size of Trump's hands (and other body parts).**

Trump also attacked Jeb Bush by questioning the record of his brother, former President George W. Bush, reminding the viewers about Bush's invasion of Iraq and saying **Bush hadn't kept the country safe from terrorism on 9/11.**

Bush said Trump was "not a real Republican." He pointed out that **Trump had been a registered Democrat** and reportedly had donated money to the Planned Parenthood organization.

As the campaign went on, the polls were showing that some of the Republican candidates had little chance to win, so they dropped out of the debates.

Trump refused to participate in the Iowa debate, and some speculated that he was done with debating. But he was back for the next one, and the rancorous debating continued.

Trump was turning attacks on his fellow Republicans into something of an art form, constantly coming up with new and ever more degrading insults offhandedly tossed at every one of his challengers. He even continued the attacks outside of the debates by sending out "tweets" on his online Twitter account. He went after Bush, tweeting, "Low energy Jeb Bush **just endorsed a man he truly hates, Lyin'** Ted Cruz. Honestly, I can't blame Jeb in that I drove him into oblivion!"

After twelve debates, only Cruz, Rubio, and Trump remained. There was supposed to be one more debate in Salt Lake City, but Trump said he wasn't going to attend. He said he'd done enough debating (the fact that he was by then leading in the polls probably influenced his decision). That led the other candidates to also back out, and that signaled the end of the Republican debates.

The Democratic Primaries

The first test of the Democratic candidates was in the **Iowa** "caucuses." The result was close between Hillary and Bernie.

In the **New Hampshire primary**, 28 Democratic candidates got votes (including perennial candidate, Vermin Supreme, whose promise to give every American a free pony garnered him 260 votes, placing him ahead of 24 other candidates).

Of the "serious" candidates, only **Bernie Sanders** and **Hillary Clinton** got a significant number of votes.

O'Malley got only a few votes and soon thereafter announced his withdrawal from the race.

From that point on, most of the primaries were close contests between Hillary and Bernie. Hillary won 34 of the state primaries and Bernie won 23. The clincher turned out to be the largest state, California. Hillary won that state convincingly and was thereby assured the nomination at the Democratic National Convention.

Nevertheless, **the passionate Sanders supporters were not happy about it. Many of them refused to accept the results**. Some of them went so far as to call the whole primary election system a conspiracy to get Hillary nominated. They especially didn't like the Democratic Party's system of including "superdelegates," elected officials and party activists who would be unpledged delegates at the Democratic National Convention. Most of them were known to support Hillary. Sanders supporters vowed to battle "the process" at the convention.

The Republican Primaries

The Republican primaries were wide open. **In Iowa, twelve candidates got votes,** led by Ted Cruz and Trump.

Most of the candidates got less than 2% of the votes, even though some of them should have been well known to the voters **(four current and former governors, four current and former senators).** Of special note was the fact that **Jeb Bush got less than three percent of the vote.** That first primary narrowed the field somewhat as **Huckabee, Paul and Santorum withdrew.**

The next primary, New Hampshire, was the first win for Trump who got 35% of the vote. It was not a good primary for Ted Cruz: he only got 12% of the vote. The rest trailed far behind.

Trump also won the next significant primary, South Carolina, with 32.5% of the vote. This time, Rubio came in second with 22.5% of the vote, and Cruz was close behind with 22.3% of the vote. **Jeb Bush only got 7.8% of the vote in South Carolina, and for him, that meant it was time to check out of the race.** His announcement was simple: "Tonight I am suspending my campaign. "He made no reference to Trump, but he did say, "In this campaign, I have stood my ground, refusing to bend to the political winds."

After "super" Tuesday, the day 10 states held primaries, it was clear Trump was pulling into the lead.

After Rubio lost his home state of Florida to Trump, he too decided it was time to give up. Some speculated that both he and Jeb Bush had decided that Trump would fail to win the general election, so it was better for them to drop out quickly and **wait for a better opportunity** to run for president in the future.

The 2016 Republican National Convention

The 2016 Republican National Convention was held first, and **Trump had easily won enough votes in the primaries to secure the nomination.** He chose Governor **Mike Pence** of Indiana as his vice presidential running mate.

However, the "Dump Trump" and the "Never Trump" movements were still notably present at the convention. They worked both overtly by planning to disrupt the convention, and covertly, with innuendo and rumors about Trump's business dealings.

Part of the problem was that although Trump's main rival in the primaries, Senator **Ted Cruz** of Texas, *was* invited to speak at the convention, he still pointedly refused to endorse Trump. In response, **Trump heaped insults on his one-time rival,** saying he didn't even want Cruz's endorsement. It was clear that even after his resounding victory, **Trump was not willing to try to mend fences** with the other Republicans that had opposed him. In fact, he said he might try to raise money to orchestrate Cruz's defeat in his bid to be reelected to his Texas Senate seat.

Trump tried to link Cruz's father to the Kennedy assassination, referring to **a conspiracy theory fed by an old news photo that seemed to show Ted Cruz's father, Rafael Cruz, a one-time supporter of Fidel Castro, joining Lee Harvey Oswald** on a street corner to pass out flyers that supported Castro.

Trump even attacked Ohio Governor John Kasich, despite the fact that he would need the governor's support to help him win the crucial swing state of Ohio.

A problem for Trump was that **he had had alienated many Republicans** with his seemingly racist attacks on illegal immigrants and Muslims. During the run-up to the convention, he had proposed **a "temporary" ban on allowing Muslims into the country**, and he continued to proclaim that **he would send all the (estimated) eleven million illegal immigrants back** to their home countries.

The convention got off to a rocky start with the delegates that were opposed to Trump's nomination demanding a roll-call vote to change the convention rules. When that motion was denied, there were accusations of secret manipulation of the process, and **the entire Colorado delegation got up and walked out in protest**.

Nevertheless, Trump's supporters were still solidly behind him. His slogan of "**Make America Great Again**" appealed to those Republicans who were dissatisfied with the direction the country was going in.

After the nominating process was over, Trump himself took the stage and gave **a long speech that was described by most observers as "dark."** He said there was a dramatically increasing level of crime in the country and great danger of terrorist attacks by what he called "**Radical Islamic Terrorism**." Much of his speech was an attack on President Obama who he blamed for all kinds of trouble, both here and abroad. He said Hillary Clinton, as Secretary of State was also to blame, and he said that **if he was elected president, "the violence that today afflicts our nation will soon come to an end."** He again **blamed many crimes on illegal immigrants**. He said **America was far less safe and the world was far less stable** than when Obama made the decision to put Hillary Clinton in charge of America's foreign policy.

At that point, for some reason, the crowd began to chant, "Lock her up. Lock her up."

STORY

It was hard to tell who or what prompted the often heard chant of "Lock her up" at the Republican National Convention, but it was **probably a throwback to the Republican hope that the justice department or the FBI would find Hillary Clinton guilty of some kind of criminal wrongdoing** in how she handled her e-mail. What was clear was that Trump liked that kind of chanting and encouraged it.

Although there was nothing wrong with government employees having private e-mail accounts in addition to their office government e-mail accounts (most did), a private e-mail account wasn't supposed to be used to send or receive confidential information. **Secretary Clinton said she was following the same e-mailing methods that had been established by all prior Secretaries of State** and by other government officials. This was true, but by the time she became Secretary of State, **the rules regarding private mail servers had been changed** for security reasons. Private mail servers could still be used, but not for classified information. Therefore, **the main issue was not over her use of the private server for personal e-mailing, but whether she had sent or received correspondence marked as secret or classified.** Secretary Clinton had repeatedly stated that she hadn't used her personal e-mail account for anything so designated.

Under pressure from Congressional Republicans, **the FBI investigated her e-mail in great detail** and found that text in few e-mails, out of the many thousands they examined, *had* **been marked as classified, although they lacked classified headers and were only marked with a small "c" in parentheses somewhere within the body of the text.** The director of the FBI stated that Hillary, and the Secretary of State office in general, had been **"extremely careless in the handling of very sensitive, highly classified information,"** but that it was possible **Ms. Clinton was not "technically sophisticated"** enough to understand what that small "c" symbol, in the middle of text meant. His recommendation to the Justice Department was that "no charges are appropriate in this case."

Trump, in his convention speech and afterwards, accused the government of "covering up her crimes." He said the FBI and the U.S. Justice Department were **complicit in "saving her from facing justice for her terrible, terrible crimes."**

Some were shocked that a presidential nominee from a major party would suggest out loud that the FBI and the U.S. Justice Department were involved in a cover-up in order to influence a presidential election, but many of Trump's supporters said they believed it.

Later, **Trump tried to cast suspicion on Hillary by saying she had deleted 30,000 e-mails "to hide something."** Her staff, who had done the erasing, said those e-mails were personal, mostly about family matters, like anybody else's normal day-today e-mails. Nevertheless, as the campaign went on, Trump at first implied, and then later flat-out said, she had deleted all those e-mails because they would have incriminated her. He offered no proof of that accusation. However, the charge was repeated so often during the campaign that **the press began referring to it as the e-mail "scandal."**

Many people said they didn't understand what all the hoopla about: **were they really expected to vote for or against a candidate based on how they handled their e-mail?**

In the end, the e-mail issue probably didn't change how many people voted. However, some polls indicated that **the constant Republican attacks on her related to the e-mail "scandal"** *did* **have the desired effect of creating a feeling of mistrust about Hillary.**

A good part of Trump's convention speech was dedicated to attacking Hillary. **For some unexplained reason, he had begun calling her "crooked Hillary."** He often said she was a liar, and made other vague statements about her trustworthiness. Although **he never said what she had done that was "crooked,"** the nickname and the vague statements about trustworthiness had some effect: the polls indicated that despite her many years of government service, many began to say there was something untrustworthy about her.

If nothing else, **it shows the remarkable effectiveness of a relentless propaganda campaign that repeats the same accusation over and over again.** In concert with Trump's attacks on Hillary, his supporters began to bring professionally-printed signs onto the convention floor saying things like, "Lock her up" and "Hillary for Prison in 2016."

Trump portrayed Hillary as the ultimate "insider." He went so far as to **blame Hillary for the rise of ISIS** and for all the other unrest in the Middle East. He said "The problems we face now – poverty and violence at home, war and destruction abroad – will last only as long as we continue relying on the same politicians who created them in the first place." He said, "**Americanism, not globalism**, will be our credo." He said he would create "reforms to add millions of new jobs and trillions in new wealth."

After his long acceptance speech, most in the news media said he was trying to paint **a dramatically dark picture of America** in order to appeal to those who were dissatisfied. It was true that the polls were indicating that a lot of people felt the United States was "going in the wrong direction."

After the conclusion of the Republican National Convention, many were eagerly awaiting the next round of poll results. **Presidential candidates always get something of a "bounce" in the polls after all the TV exposure** their conventions give them, and Trump did move up a bit in the polls. However, a Gallup poll soon came out that had asked people if they were more or less likely to vote for Trump based on what they saw at the Republican convention.

The data, which went all the way back to 1984, showed that **every single candidate had gotten a two to forty-five percent increase in voters approval** after their national convention.

But this time, after the Republican convention, the results indicated **voters were now *less* likely to vote for the Republican candidate.**

It was a historical divergence and it turned out to be **the first sign that Trump's poll numbers were about to start dropping**.

STORY

After Trump was chosen to be the Republican nominee for president, a lot more information came out about him. The people soon learned Donald Trump's story was not your usual American politician's story. He was the first nominee of a major party in U.S. history to have **never played in role in elected politics**. Since he had no experience in government, he talked about his experience in business. He said that his skills in becoming rich would be applied to making the United States a better country. Right from the start, he made it clear he was running as an outsider, and that **only an outsider could "fix" the nation's many problems**.

Trump's father was a well-known real estate developer in New York. Donald was sent to a prestigious college-prep school, but he soon left that school (reportedly because of behavior problems) and was enrolled in the New York Military Academy where he later said **he "got more training militarily than a lot of the guys that go into the military."**

After military school, he went to college at the Wharton School of Finance and Commerce which is part of the University of Pennsylvania. He majored in real estate studies.

After college, he was in danger of getting drafted and sent to Vietnam, but he got a medical deferment for what he described as "heel spurs."

Back in New York, **he joined his father's construction firm** that had expanded from building single-family homes in Queens, New York to building apartment buildings. The senior Trump had received some unwanted publicity when **Woody Guthrie**, the famous folksinger, became a tenant in one of his apartment buildings and **accused him of being a racist slum landlord**.

In 1973, **the U.S. Justice Department filed a suit against the Trumps**, charging that they had systematically refused to rent to African-Americans. The Trumps hired a top lawyer, and after a lengthy court battle, the suit was settled in 1975 with a consent decree.

With a large amount of seed money from his father, Donald Trump began to make real estate deals and soon got a reputation as a rough and tough, self-promoting deal maker who had mastered the art of "creative" financing.

However, after making a number of high-profile real estate investments in Manhattan, **he decided to go into the casino business in Atlantic City**.

He formed a partnership with Harrah's and opened his first casino. It didn't do well, but that didn't slow him down; he bought a partially completed building that wasn't on the famous Atlantic City Boardwalk like all the other casinos, but instead, was in the nearby Marina District. He named it Trump Castle. He followed that up by buying another casino on the Atlantic City boardwalk. He named this new one the Taj Mahal.

Unfortunately, developing all those casinos put Trump heavily in debt, and as it turned out, the casinos could not earn enough money to service his many loans. One by one, **the casinos all filed for Chapter 11 bankruptcy**.

But **Trump himself never went personally bankrupt because his creditors gave him time to sell off the casino properties before paying them back**. (He was later to say, "**I do play with the bankruptcy laws** – they're very good for me.")

After the Atlantic City casino fiascoes, Trump went back to making real estate deal and starting other enterprises. He began developing hotels and golf courses, and **he got involved in developing beauty pageants**. He created **Trump University**, a for-profit education company that offered expensive courses in real estate management.

Beginning in the 1980s, Trump **began to publish books** about how to get rich in the real estate business. His first, *Art of the Deal* with co-writer Tony Schwartz, reached number one on the New York Times Best Seller list. He published several more, including *The Art of the Comeback* and *Never Give Up: How I Turned My Biggest Challenges into Success*.

In 2003, **Trump was featured on an NBC reality show called "The Apprentice."** He hosted the show in which competitors battled for management jobs. In order to get the job, contestants were required to "apply" for the job by answering questions. One by one, the contestants are successively "fired" and eliminated (Trump has filed a trademark application for the phrase "You're fired"). For a while, the show was popular, and it helped Trump market his name as a "brand." Some real estate developers paid Trump a fee to let them name their buildings after him. **He allowed merchandisers to put the Trump name on many other thing**s, including a board game, bottled water, clothing (made in Bangladesh), cologne, a luxury airline, steaks, vodka, a watch, a magazine, restaurants, and wine, not to mention all the campaign paraphernalia.

Trump also got involved in a large number of partnerships and foundations that took on his name, including the Donald J. Trump Foundation, Trump Follies, Trump Equitable Fifth Avenue, Trump Books Manager, Trump Brazil, Trump Caribbean, Trump Canadian Services, Trump Classic Cars, Trump Carousel, Trump Drinks Israel, Trump Endeavor, Trump Ice, Trump Golf Swing, Trump Korean Projects, Trump Ferry Point, Trump Productions, Trump Restaurants, Trump Payroll, Trump Ruffin, Trump RHF, Trump Ocean, Trump Project Management, Trump Vineyard Estates, plus other Trump holding corporations registered in nearly every country on earth, 271 in all. Obviously, the Trump name and the Trump empire is unbelievably complicated. Many wondered how he was going to be able to continue to manage all this while running for president. And then there was the issue of **what would happen to all these business relationships, especially the foreign relationships, if he was elected president**.

Although Trump had no experience in politics or government service, he often said he was thinking about running for president of the United States. In 1999, despite having been a Reagan supporter and a member of the Republican Party, **he joined the Reform Party, and for three years, he ran a presidential exploratory committee** within that party. After that, **he joined the Democratic Party**. However, in 2008, **he switched back to the Republican Party** and endorsed John McCain for President. In 2011, **he switched to the Independent Party** and **became a voice in the "birther" movement**, questioning Barack Obama's citizenship. But he was soon **back to the Republican Party** where he stayed until, in 2013, he began to again plan a run for the presidency.

The 2016 Democratic National Convention

At the 2016 Democratic National Convention, **Hillary had already locked up the nomination**. She chose Virginia Senator, **Tim Kaine**, a political moderate and a Catholic, to be her running mate.

But the convention did have its **moments of dissent**. When the supporters of Bernie Sanders found out about some leaked e-mails from the Democratic National Committee, they started to protest on the convention floor. The **leaked e-mails indicated that the**

Democratic National Committee didn't want Sanders, a registered Independent, to be the Democratic Party's presidential candidate. The Sanders supporters made such a fuss about that kind of bias within the party, the chairperson of the Democratic National Committee was forced to resign. From that point on, **most of the speakers (including Hillary) were sure to show their approval of Sanders,** and many of his main talking points were included in the party's official platform.

By bringing on numerous African-American speakers, gospel singers, and even rap artists, **the Democrats made it clear they were the multicultural party.** And they also made it clear that they strongly disagreed with the "make American great again" theme of the Republican convention by repeating over and over again that **America *already was* the greatest country on Earth.** Several of the convention speakers criticized what they saw as Trump's decidedly negative view of America.

All three of the living Democratic presidents addressed the convention in support of Hillary. That was in marked contrast with the Republican convention where **the two living Republican presidents were noticeably absent**, and were not willing to endorse the Republican nominee.

Senator Kaine quickly demonstrated that he was willing to attack the Republican nominee, making fun of Trump's vague promises to fix everything that was wrong with America. As a clear message to Hispanic voters, he also showed off his fluency in Spanish.

STORY

A highlight of the Democratic convention was the appearance of **the father of a U.S. soldier, Humayun Khan**, an American Muslim who had been a captain in the U.S. Army. He had been killed in Iraq while protecting his men. Appearing on the stage along with his wife, Mr. Khan spoke directly to Donald Trump, saying, "If it was up to Donald Trump, my son never would have been in America. Donald Trump consistently smears the character of Muslims. He disrespects other minorities, women, judges, even his own party leadership. He vows to build walls and ban us from this country. Donald Trump. You are asking Americans to trust you with our future. Let me ask you: Have you even read the U.S. Constitution?" Then, **Mr. Khan pulled out a pocket-sized version of the U.S. Constitution and waved it in the air.** "I will gladly lend you my copy. In this document, look for the words 'liberty' and 'equal protection of law.'" Mr. Khan went on to say that **people of many different religions and backgrounds had made sacrifices for America,** and then he **questioned what Trump had sacrificed**.

Trump's reaction was quick, and as was typical of him, he responded with a counterattack. He questioned Mr. Khan's honesty, saying, "Who wrote that? **Did Hillary's script writers write it?**" He also questioned why the man's wife didn't speak. "Wasn't she allowed to speak?" (Mrs. Khan later said that the large picture of her dead son on the stage had left her too overcome to speak.) Trump went on to say, "**I think I've made a lot of sacrifices. I work very, very hard. I've created thousands and thousands of jobs, tens of thousands of jobs, built great structures. I've had tremendous success.** I think I've done a lot."

There was nearly universal condemnation of Trump's attack on the Khan family, and it put Trump in a bad position. He had based a lot of his bid for the presidency on painting Muslims as dangerous people who should not even be allowed into this country. Many felt it had contributed greatly to his resounding primary wins in the South and Midwest. But now he was being presented with a Muslim hero in the U.S. military who had died for his country. It undercut his whole message, and the incident would continue to plague him throughout the rest of the campaign.

Hillary's acceptance speech started out by calling attention to the fact that this moment was a historic milestone, **the first time in our nation's history that a woman would be a major party's nominee** for president of the United States.

She then said she wanted to congratulate Senator Sanders for the extraordinary campaign he had run, and she made reference to his long career in public service fighting for progressive causes and principles. **She said she and Sanders were in complete agreement** that they both wanted to create a society that was tolerant, inclusive, and fair.

She then immediately launched an attack on Donald Trump, saying he was "**temperamentally unfit**" to be president and commander-in-chief." It was the first mention of the word "temperament" with reference to Trump, and it was a word that would be heard from many different sources throughout the campaign.

She said Trump was not just trying to build a wall between America and Mexico, he was **trying to wall off Americans from each other.** She said his "Make America great again" slogan was code for talking **America backwards**, back to a time when opportunity and dignity were reserved for the few.

She pointed out that **Trump had said a distinguished judge born in Indiana couldn't do his job because of his Mexican heritage**, and that he had mocked a reporter with disabilities and called women "pigs."

COMMENT

Hillary didn't need to clarify her reference to Trump's attack on a judge's Mexican heritage. The news media had made much of **Trump's attack on U.S. District Judge Gonzalo Curiel, the judge overseeing the fraud case against Trump University.** Trump said the judge had "an absolute conflict" in presiding over the litigation because he was of Mexican heritage" and a member of a Latino lawyers' association. Despite the fact that Judge Curiel was born in Indiana, Trump took the position that the judge was **biased against him because of his campaign stance against illegal immigration** and his pledge to "build a wall." He said it was "an inherent conflict of interest."

Even when **some prominent Republicans called Trump's attack on the judge racist**, he refused to back down, saying there would be no apologies to Judge Curiel, who he accused of "judicial activism."

As a direct reference to Trump's saying he was going to build a wall between the U.S. and Mexico, Hillary said, **"Bridges are better than walls."** She said she believed "we are stronger together." That concept, **"Stronger Together,"** was to become her main slogan, and those two words were soon to be found printed on most of her campaign materials.

After her relatively short speech at the convention, many in the news media commented on **how upbeat her speech was as compared to that of Donald Trump**. And of course, everybody was waiting for the next round of poll results to see if her speech had made Americans more or less willing to vote for her.

STORY

After Hillary was chosen to be the Democrat's nominee for president, a lot more information came out about her. The people soon learned Hillary Rodham Clinton's story was not your usual American politician's story.

Growing up in a conservative family in a conservative suburb of Chicago, she was a standout in high school where she was a National Merit finalist and voted "most likely to succeed." She went on to **major in political science at Wellesley College,** a private women's liberal-arts college in Massachusetts that was well-known as a breeding ground for women who were destined to go on to "big things." As a freshman, she already stood out and was soon to become **the president of the Wellesley Young Republicans**. But the Vietnam War and the Civil Rights Movement eventually convinced her to switch her allegiance to the Democratic Party, and **she became a supporter of Eugene McCarthy**, an anti-war Democratic candidate for president.

In 1968, **she was elected president of the Wellesley College Government Association, and was described as not only a leader of her group, but as the de facto leader of the entire student body**. Despite the school's tradition of not allowing students to speak at commencement, the other students forced the school's administration to let her speak. She gave an inspirational, and political, speech, and it fired up all the students. **Some of them began to suggest that she might someday be the nation's first female president**.

Hillary went on to attend **Yale Law School** where she served on the editorial board of the Yale Review of Law and Social Action and **volunteered at New Haven Legal Services** to provide free legal advice for the poor.

At Yale, **she met fellow student, Bill Clinton, who soon asked her to marry him**. She said no, but they did move in together, and in 1972, they campaigned together for Democratic presidential candidate George McGovern.

She did **postgraduate work as a staff attorney for the Children's Defense Fund** in Cambridge, Massachusetts, and she then **became a member of the House of Representative's Watergate inquiry staff, researching procedures of impeachment**. That job ended when Nixon resigned before he could be impeached.

People saw a bright future for Hillary in politics, but she decided to "follow her heart." She went with Bill Clinton back to his home state of Arkansas. There, she became only the second **female faculty member at the University of Arkansas School of Law**, and she became the first director of the school's new legal aid clinic.

In 1975, she finally **agreed to marry Bill, but chose to keep her own last name, Rodham**. That didn't go over well in conservative Arkansas, especially after Bill decided to enter Arkansas politics.

In 1976, he was elected Arkansas Attorney General, but Hillary continued her own career, joining a prestigious law firm. She also **continued to provide free legal aid to the poor**.

In 1978, **Bill was elected Governor of Arkansas, and Hillary soon became known as a most unusual first-lady** of Arkansas by maintaining her own law career.

In 1980, Bill was defeated in his bid for reelection, and some said it was because of his "uppity" wife.

That same year, their daughter Chelsea was born.

In 1982, Bill again ran for governor, and this time he was successful. Back in her position as Arkansas's First Lady, she changed her name to **Hillary Rodham Clinton**, but she continued to practice law.

In 1992, Bill ran for president. In the middle of the election campaign, **a potential scandal arose when a woman came forward to say she had been having an affair with Bill. But Hillary stood by him** and nothing was ever proved.

Bill was elected president, and as the nation's first-lady, Hillary was not content to merely host diplomatic dinners. **She had her own office in the West Wing near the president's office and took an active role in presidential affairs.** Most notably, she **chaired a task force designed to reform health care** in the United States. However, the Republicans in Congress called it "**Hillarycare**" and were able to stop any type of new health program from being put in place. She was able to help create the **Office on Violence Against Women** at the Department of Justice, and she **initiated the Adoption and Safe Families Act**.

When the House impeached her husband for the Monica Lewinsky affair, she again stood by him.

After leaving the White House, in 2000, **Hillary ran for the open Senate seat in New York.** She won easily, thereby becoming the first former first-lady to hold a major elective office.

In 2008, Hillary decided to run for president, and in the early polls, she was in the lead over challengers Senator **Barack Obama** of Illinois and former Senator **John Edwards** of North Carolina. However, they both came in ahead of her in the Iowa caucuses. It was a blow to her campaign, but she rebounded with a win in the next primary in New Hampshire. Edwards dropped out of the race for personal reasons, and as primary after primary was held, Hillary and Obama continued to be neck and neck. But then, in the later primaries, with very strong support from African-Americans, **Obama began to pull ahead.** By mid-summer, Obama had gained enough delegates to become the presumptive nominee. **Hillary had garnered over 17 million votes, almost the same number as Obama, but she immediately suspended her campaign and threw her support behind Obama.**

Obama was elected president, and he appointed Hillary as his Secretary of State.

Her tenure in that position was not without controversy. **She supported an increase in the number of troops sent to Afghanistan, and she was involved in a controversial agreement with Iran** that lessened some of the sanctions against that country in exchange for them stopping their nuclear development program.

She was one of the cabinet members **in favor of a raid into Pakistan to kill Osama bin Laden.** The raid was successful, but other terrorists soon filled the void left by the death of bin Laden, and with more and more terrorist attacks taking place in the Arab world and elsewhere, she had to deal with heightened public concern about the possibility of terrorist attacks in the United States.

When Arab Spring protests spread throughout the Middle East, it was a challenge for her and Obama to find the appropriate response.

In 2012, on the anniversary of the 9/11 attacks, **terrorists launched an attack on a U.S. diplomatic mission in Benghazi,** Libya. The U.S. Ambassador there and three other Americans were killed. There was some controversy about possible security lapses, for which Hillary took personal responsibility.

Three months later, Hillary ended her tenure as Secretary of State and **launched her second bid for the presidency.**

"Third-Party" Candidates

As I pointed out earlier, if someone wants to be president of the United States, all they have to do is file a Statement of Candidacy with the Federal Election Commission. In 2016, thousands did so. The next step is to **get enough signatures to appear on a state ballot**, and several also did that.

However, few of those candidates had the money or the connections to publicize their candidacy much beyond their own circle of friends and supporters.

Nevertheless, as we have seen, a few "third-party" candidates were able to use heated issues (for example, slavery and civil rights) to garner some attention, and therefore, some votes.

However, in 2016, a new phenomenon arose to bring two third-party candidates into the limelight: an **"anti" vote**.

As the nation's attention was focused on the extensive TV coverage of the Republican and Democratic national conventions, **other political parties were also holding national conventions**. Although they didn't get the extensive media coverage that the Republicans and Democrats were getting, there was more interest than usual in these "secondary" conventions.

In 2016, voter polling showed that some people who traditionally voted Democratic or Republican were expressing interest in the **Libertarian Party** and the **Green Party**.

COMMENT

In addition to the **Libertarian Party** presidential candidates (on the ballot in all 50 states) and the **Green Party** presidential candidates (on the ballot in 40 states), **more than thirty "third-party" candidates for president were "ballot qualified" in at least one state**.

The **Constitution Party, a conservative party with the goal of restoring American jurisprudence to its Christian Biblical** foundations and limiting the federal government was ballot qualified in at least 15 states.

Various parties referring to themselves as either "Independent" or "Independence" were ballot qualified in at least 14 states. Some of the most prominent Independent parties had goals that were similar to those of the Constitution Party; that is, making the United States a Christian nation with states' rights being predominant over control by a federal government.

The Socialist Party, opposed to oppression including capitalism and authoritarian forms of communism, was a successor to several older Socialist parties. It was ballot qualified in only a few states.

The **Peace and Freedom Party, which had been around since the sixties,** promoted socialism, democracy, ecology, feminism and racial equality. It had seen its popularity fade in the twenty-first century, but it was ballot qualified in several states.

In 2016, none of the so-called "third parties" was able to get any electoral votes, but in a few states they may have taken enough votes away from Hillary to cost her the election.

At the **Libertarian National Convention, two former governors were nominated, Gary Johnson** from New Mexico and **William Weld** from Massachusetts. The Libertarian Party said they stood for individual freedom and rights and limited government. They said they were against foreign military involvement and that the U.S. should maintain a military devoted only to national defense. They wanted to shut down both foreign military aid and economic aid.

The two former governors nominated by the Libertarian Party were relatively strong candidates, and early polls that included them as candidates indicated they might pull votes away from traditionally conservative Republicans that objected to Trump's decidedly "different" campaigning style. However, later in the campaign, voter polls indicated that they were actually pulling a lot of votes away from Hillary, essentially "protest votes" by voters who normally voted for Democrats.

At the **Green Party's National Convention**, they once again chose **Dr. Jill Stein** from Massachusetts as their presidential candidate, and they nominated **William Kreml** from South Carolina as their vice-presidential nominee.

Traditionally one of the more liberal third parties, **the Green Party had long been anti-war, and Stein had been a vocal voice against the U.S. "assassination by drone" program**. Their party platform took a stand against inequality, the death penalty, and the "war on drugs." A lot of environmentalists favored the Green Party.

The Presidential Campaigns

After national conventions had determined who the candidates would be, the "real" campaign began. Hillary started touring the swing states, at first by bus, but then later in her own campaign jet. She avoided the so-called "red" (Republican) states where the polls were indicating Trump had an insurmountable lead.

COMMENT

Ever wonder where the terms "**red state**" and "**blue state**" came from? Most believe those terms originated from the large map NBC News displayed on TV during the very close 2000 presidential election. To clarify which way states were leaning, they showed the Republican-leaning states in Red and the Democratic-leaning states in blue. That kind of visual representation of where the states stood became the standard way to represent them, and the two terms "red state" and "blue state" eventually also caught on.

Trump was also hitting many different states in his campaign jet, which he said was bigger than the president's Air Force One jet (it wasn't). His campaign slogan continued to be "make America great again," and **his campaign speeches were mostly about what bad shape the country was in**. He emphasized how bad the economy was, insisting that **Obama and Hillary had hurt the livelihoods of working-class people by making trade deals** with other countries that sent American jobs out of the country.

He also focused on **law and order**, saying that Obama and Hillary had made America a dangerous place to live. He said police needed to have more power to enforce the laws, and that good policies like "**stop and frisk**" had been taken away from the police, (The stop-and-frisk policy had been declared unconstitutional because it had been found to unfairly target people of color.)

On the campaign trail, Hillary was also talking about the economy. **She said President Bush had handed Obama a very challenging economic situation after the worst recession since the great depression** and President Obama had been successful in bringing it back.

She said Trump was creating a divisive climate with his negativity about America and his never-ending claim that he was going to "build a great wall" and deport all illegal aliens. Her slogan of "stronger together" was designed to point out Trump's saying he would ban Muslim from coming into the country and deport Mexican "rapists and killers."

COMMENT

When the polls showed Trump was losing badly among African-Americans and Hispanics, **Trump began to talk about how terrible conditions were in "the African-American community."** He said things were so bad, few African-Americans had jobs, their schools were a disaster, and **they were afraid to go out in the street lest they get shot.** He said **things had never been worse in the African-American community, and it was Hillary's fault.** He began saying, "What do you have to lose?"

Even after Hillary supporters disputed his grim statistics and pointed out that schools in America were no longer separated by race, he kept on saying, "What do you have to lose?"

When polling among African-Americans indicated that his "What do you have to lose" strategy was not working, he abandoned it and went back to focusing on what the polls were showing was his base, non-college education white men and Evangelicals.

To deal with his lack of support among Hispanics, his campaign staff announced that **he was going to "moderate" his harsh plan** to immediately deport all illegal immigrants. **He made a trip to Mexico to meet with the Mexican president**, followed by a nationally televised speech in Arizona in which he tried to walk a fine line between insisting he was going to "build a wall and Mexico was going to pay for it" and a supposedly more moderate policy of first deporting illegal immigrants that had been convicted of crimes. **He said he would "deal with"** all the other illegal immigrants later, but he still emphasized that **"we are a country of laws,"** and that meant illegal immigrants had to be deported.

He then **brought up onto the stage with him a series of people who claimed that their loved ones had been killed by**

illegal immigrants. The message was clear: **illegal immigrants were killers** and had to be gotten rid of.

From that point on, there was no more talk from the Trump campaign about moderating his hard stance on immigration policy. In fact, **he began to constantly suggest that Hillary wanted an "open border" policy**. He said that would mean "we no longer had a country."

As the campaign went on, **Trump and his supporters kept up their attacks on Hillary with regard to how she had handled her e-mail**. At the same time, Republicans in Congress continued to press the FBI for more information about their investigation of the matter. **The Democrats in Congress said the Republican efforts were "purely political."**

Out on the campaign trail, Trump was insisting that Hillary had "lied" to the FBI, even though the FBI never said that.

In the middle of the campaign, Congressional Republicans began to insist that the Justice Department should undertake a whole new investigation; this time they wanted to go after Hillary on perjury grounds, **suggesting that she had lied to Congress about how she handled her e-mail**. The FBI continued to say they had found nothing criminal in her actions or in what she had said to the FBI.

Trump also began to talk about **the relationship between the State Department and the Clinton Foundation** during Hillary's tenure, suggesting that the Clinton's had somehow personally profited from the non-profit foundation and that donors to the foundation might have been given special access to the State Department. However, Hillary denied it and Trump never produced any evidence.

Trump's campaign staff wanted him to stick to issues like that, but **Trump preferred to talk off-the-cuff**, sometimes saying things he would later have to take back.

During the campaign, **Trump fired some of the leading members of his campaign staff and replaced them with more aggressive anti-establishment muckrakers** who were more in tune with his desired image of being an "outsider" (he even wanted to be seen as outside of the Republican mainstream). He said, "I am who I am," and promised his followers he wasn't going to change.

In addition to attacking Hillary, Trump talked about the atrocities that had been perpetrated in the name of "radical Islam. In typical Trumpian style, he blamed President Obama and Hillary not only for the rise of ISIS, but also for other trouble in the Middle East. **He said the violence of "radical Islamic" terrorism all over the world only started after the election of President Obama** (he never mentioned the role President Bush's invasion of Iraq had played). After Hillary said the fight was not against Islam but again terrorism, Trump said Hillary was unwilling to use the phrase, "radical Islamic terrorism." **He asked how she would be able to fight Islamic terrorism if she couldn't even use the words. He said if he was elected president he would stop ISIS, even if it took "vicious" methods.** He said we "have to play the game at **a much tougher level.**" He suggested that tougher approach should include **killing the families of the terrorists.** When it was pointed out to him that killing the families of suspects was against international law, he backed off a bit, saying he had only said he would "go after" them." He repeated that "We're "not fighting it strongly enough." **He said he would keep open the prison at Guantanamo Bay and that he was in total support of waterboarding.** He said we should do "whatever it takes." **He also said he would cut off the terrorists' access to the internet all over the world.** His main message was that if he was elected president, he would "quickly" stamp out ISIS.

Throughout the campaign, Trump often made reference to "**political correctness,**" and said it was keeping the U.S. from effectively fighting illegal immigration and terrorism. He said if he was elected president, he would give the immigration authorities permission to engage in "**extreme vetting**" to make sure no bad actors got into our country.

In the midst of the campaign, Trump started talking about **teaming up with Russia to fight ISIS**. However, when it was revealed that his campaign chief had a business relationship with some Russians, that campaign manager was quickly replaced.

STORY

At one point in the campaign, **Trump called Hillary "a bigot."** Hillary immediately responded in a speech that **suggested the real bigots, white supremacists and KKK-related figures, were strongly supporting Trump.** Later, in another speech, she said, "**To just be grossly generalistic, you can put half of Trump supporters into what I call the basket of deplorables. Right? Racist, sexist, homophobic, xenophobic, Islamaphobic, you name it. The other basket of people are people who feel that government has let them down, the economy has let them down, nobody cares about them, nobody worries about what happens to their lives and their futures. They are just desperate for change. Those are people who we have to understand and empathize with as well.**"

It seemed to be a well-thought out statement designed to attract some of Trump's less radical supporters, the ones who felt the government and the economy had "let them down," and the ones who just wanted things to change.

But she failed to think through how the Trump campaign and the news media would pick and chose which of her words to report on. **They grabbed onto the words "deplorables, racist, sexist, homophobic, xenophobic, and Islamaphobic, and ignored the rest of her statement.** She quickly came out with an apology, saying she shouldn't have used the word "half." She said only meant that "some" of Trump's supporters were like that. Nevertheless, Trump continued to attack her on it, **saying what she really meant was that "all" of his sup-**

porters were "deplorable." His forces quickly created an anti-Hillary TV commercial that suggested she thought anyone who might think about voting for Trump was "deplorable." It didn't seem to hurt Hillary much in the polls, but it was a hard lesson for her about how words can be taken out of context and used against you.

Hillary's campaign mostly consisted of speaking engagements in the swing states and meetings with the group of reporters who had been attached to her campaign.

While Hillary frequently pointed out her extensive knowledge of foreign affairs, Trump's ventures into that subject sometimes got him into trouble. In interviews, he often praised Russian President Vladimir Putin, describing him as a leader who had high favorability numbers in Russia. Previously, Putin had praised Trump, describing him as "bright and talented" and the "absolute leader of the presidential race" in the U.S.

When asked about Putin's alleged killing of journalists and political opponents, Trump dismissed it, saying we have a lot of killing in this country too. **Of Putin, Trump said, "At least he's a leader, unlike what we have in this country."**

Earlier, in the GOP debates, **Trump had bragged that he knew Putin personally. He said, "I got to know him very well because we were both on 60 Minutes. We were stablemates, and we did very well that night."** (Actually, they couldn't have met because Trump was interviewed for the program in the United States and Putin was interviewed in Russia.)

Trump had also stated that he and Putin had spoken directly at a National Press Club luncheon in Moscow, and he said, President Putin "could not have been nicer."

Trump began saying Russia and the U.S. ought to be on better terms, and that **maybe the U.S. ought to back out of its commitments to NATO** if they wouldn't pay their fair share.

Trump's comments sounded like he was approving Putin's methods and policies, and that brought him a lot of criticism, even from members of his own party. **Trump quickly backed off, saying in actuality he had never met Putin.**

Many expected Trump to bring up Benghazi often—just as Romney had done in the presidential election of 2012—and at first he did. During the primary season, **he said Hillary's decisions as Secretary of State "spread death, destruction and terrorism everywhere she touched."** He said that Benghazi and the death of Ambassador Chris Stevens was one of her biggest failures, and he accused her of **"sleeping through"** the Benghazi attack. He said, "I mean what she did with him was absolutely horrible. **He was left helpless to die as Hillary Clinton soundly slept in her bed.** That's right. When the phone rang at three in the morning, **Hillary Clinton was sleeping.**" Actually, the Benghazi attack took place at about 3:30 in the afternoon, Washington D.C. time, and Hillary was in her State Department office monitoring the situation in Benghazi. Nevertheless, it wouldn't be the last time Trump would imply that Hillary just wasn't up to the task of being president.

COMMENT

In the 57 prior U.S. presidential elections, there had never been a female candidate nominated by either the Republicans or the Democrats. When Hillary was nominated by the Democrats in 2016, many said she would have an uphill battle. That turned out to be true. Despite the fact that she had twice been elected a U.S. Senator and had served as the U.S. Secretary of State, many voters said they didn't trust her. Few ever said why that was, but some came right out and said it was because she was a woman. They said they didn't think a woman would have "the strength" to be a president. Others said they "wanted a man in charge."

In the 2016, campaign, **Trump was quick to jump on that idea, but he couched it in vague terms.** He said Hillary didn't have "the presidential look," and **he often referred to her as weak and lacking stamina.** Sometimes, on stage at his rallies, he would parody her by pretending to walk in a very feeble way. He said she was so weak, she was often "barely able to make it back to her car." In fact, late in the campaign, he said "she should be drug tested," **implying that she was so weak she must be using performance-enhancing drugs to be able to keep going.**

And then, in the middle of the campaign, **Hillary was videotaped looking tired and weak on her way to her car** after she had attended a public event on a hot day. It was then discovered that **she was suffering from pneumonia,** and on doctor's orders she had to take a few days off of campaigning. Trump made fun of her need to "rest" all the time.

However, **a few days later, despite the pneumonia, Hillary was back on the campaign trail,** and when Trump mentioned her "stamina" in one of the debates, she replied, **"As soon as he travels to 112 countries and negotiates a peace deal, a cease fire, a release of dissidents, an opening of new opportunities in nations around the world, or even spends 11 hours testifying in front of a congressional committee he can talk to me about stamina."**

Nevertheless, during the campaign, even though **Hillary held a huge polling advantage over Trump with women,** many men and some women still didn't feel comfortable about electing a woman as president. There was **a religious divide among voters,** with some quoting **passages from the Bible that suggested a woman should not try to lead men.** Previously, a staff member of Rick Santorum's presidential campaign had sent an e-mail that said, "Is it God's highest desire, that is, his Biblically expressed will, ... to have a woman rule the institutions of the family, the church, and the state?"

Others pointed out that the Bible says **Eve's origin was subordinate to Adam**, and to an Old Testament passage that seemed to say it was **"shameful" when a woman has to step up and lead when male leaders falter**. Others mentioned a New Testament verse that says, "The husband is the head of the wife as Christ is the head of the church."

A number of Republican-led congressional investigations into Benghazi were launched, but **despite bringing Hillary before Republican-led Congressional committees with many very long sessions that featured seemingly endless attacks on her, they were unable to shake Hillary or prove that she was in any way responsible for what happened**. The Democrat's claim that the "investigations" were "purely political" was soon given credence when it was revealed that some Republicans were **congratulating themselves for how their congressional investigations had managed to drive down Hillary's poll numbers**.

When Trump heard that the Russian intelligence agencies had apparently hacked computers belonging to the Democratic National Committee, and had released damaging DNC e-mails through the Wikileaks organization in order to try to influence the U.S. elections in Trump's favor, **Trump suggested that they should also try to hack into U.S. computers to find Hillary's missing e-mails**. He said, "Russia, if you're listening, I hope you're able to find the 30,000 e-mails that are missing . . . I think you will probably be rewarded mightily by our press."

That statement, which seemed to invite a foreign power to get involved in the U.S. presidential election by hacking U.S. computers, outraged a lot of people. Some went so far to describe it as treason. (Later in the campaign, there were hacks of Hillary's staff e-mails that the U.S. government said were being done by the

Russians. Hillary's campaign manager said it was Russian intelligence agencies attempting to influence Americans to vote for Trump.)

Years before, when Trump was a Democrat, he had been a supporter of the Planned Parenthood organization. But now that he was a candidate for president on the Republican ticket, he said he was against abortion. In an interview, he even said if he was successful in making abortion illegal in the United States, **he would punish a woman for having an abortion**. That unleashed a firestorm of criticism, and he backed off, saying he would only punish the doctor that had performed the abortion.

After a number of such controversial statements, even his supporters began to say they wished he would just stick to attacking Hillary. And for a short time, he did that, but soon he was back to making his usual outrageous statements. Trump said that's just the way he was, and he wasn't about to change.

STORY

As has become common in modern presidential elections, the candidates try to keep themselves in the media spotlight as much as possible. Buying TV time in placed ads is very expensive, so the **candidates try to get free "air time"** by making news.

It didn't take long for the experienced entertainer Trump to show that he was a master at that. **His outlandish statements (and frequent retractions) were sure to grab the news headlines the next day**, or in the case of the TV cable news networks, within minutes. **Trump seemed to be going for the "any publicity is good publicity" approach.**

However, he soon began banning certain news reporters from his press conferences.

The TV cable news networks took varying approaches to reporting on the presidential campaign. Some news outlets obviously favored one or the other of the candidates, but one cable TV network was so blatantly in favor of Trump, it became well known, in essence, as an anti-Hillary, pro-Trump propaganda network. Trump routinely appeared on that TV network and none of the others.

If Trump wanted something to get out into the news, that TV network always obliged by immediately putting him on. They avoided asking him any tough questions. Obviously, Hillary stayed well away from that particular cable TV network.

Some of the other cable TV news networks sometimes sounded anti-Trump, mostly because **they liked to rebroadcast Trump's most outlandish statements** (many viewers were tuning in just to find out what Trump had done or said lately). Nevertheless, those news outlets usually presented the views of both candidates by putting together "panels" that included both pro-Hillary and pro-Trump people. Nevertheless, **Trump often said all those other networks were biased against him.** He called them "the mainstream media."

Meanwhile, there were few stories about Hillary in the news. **She just didn't have Trump's news-grabbing ability.** The only time she got any free air time was when she gave a major speech, and not all the networks were willing to cover them. If she was upset that Trump was being constantly covered by every TV network and every print news outlet, she didn't let on. **As long as she maintained her lead in the polls, she seemed willing to let Trump grab all the headlines.**

Throughout the 2016 presidential campaign, Trump got into the habit of making what became known as Trump's "outrageous statement of the day."

Here is a partial list of what might be called "outrageous Trumpisms":

- "I will be the greatest jobs president God ever created."
- "When Mexico sends its people, they're not sending their best. They're sending people that have lots of problems. They're bringing drugs. They're bringing crime. They're rapists."
- "I will build a great wall – and nobody builds walls better than me, believe me – and I'll build them very inexpensively. I will build a great, great wall on our southern border, and I will make Mexico pay for that wall. Mark my words."
- "Hey, I watched when the World Trade Center came tumbling down. And I watched in Jersey City, New Jersey, where thousands and thousands of people were cheering as that building was coming down. Thousands of people were cheering." (Trump made it clear he was describing Arab-looking people cheering the fall of the Trade Tower buildings, but no television network reported broadcasting such a thing. If it would have happened, they said, it would have been a major news event.)
- "The concept of global warming was created by and for the Chinese in order to make U.S. manufacturing non-competitive."
- "There is no drought in California. They're sending the water out to the ocean to protect a certain kind of three-inch fish." (At the time he made this statement, 80% of California was in the fifth year of devastating drought.)
- "John McCain is not a war hero. He's a war hero 'cause he was captured. I like people that weren't captured, OK?" (McCain was a Navy pilot that was shot down and captured and tortured during the Vietnam War. He spent more than five years as a prisoner of war in North Vietnam.)

- "Hillary wants to abolish, essentially abolish the Second Amendment. By the way, and if she gets to pick — if she gets to pick her judges, nothing you can do, folks. Although the Second Amendment people, maybe there is, I don't know." (This was widely seen as a suggestion that maybe the only way to stop Hillary from taking away everybody's guns was with a gun. After nearly universal outrage, Trump said he was only suggesting Second Amendment people should vote against her.)
- "I know more about ISIS than the generals."
- "Mr. Putin is very much of a leader . . . far more than our president." Many quickly pointed out that Trump's statement ignored the fact that Putin is a dictator who suppresses any and all dissent, has driven his country's economy into the ground and created a state-sponsored doping program that got many of Russia's greatest athletes banned from the Olympics.
- "Look, we're led by a man that either is not tough, not smart, or he's got something else in mind. And the something else in mind — you know, people can't believe it. People cannot, they cannot believe that President Obama is acting the way he acts and can't even mention the words 'radical Islamic terrorism.' There's something going on. It's inconceivable."

But perhaps the best example of Trump's strategy of getting media attention with outrageous statements was a claim he made after he started to fall behind in the polls: he said, "**Obama is the founder of ISIS.**" It is unknown whether or not Trump was aware of it, but it was a replication of the anti-American propaganda Russian state media had been pushing for some time.

He repeated it several times, in several different speeches and interviews. He repeated it over and over again, enough times to be sure everybody had it firmly planted in their consciousness. Trump's supporters quickly scrambled to try to say it was only a metaphor, but Trump wouldn't go along with them: he just kept repeating it. He said it was no metaphor. He said, "**Obama really is the founder of ISIS, and Hillary helped.**"

But then, the next day, he got himself a brand new set of headlines by saying it was "**only sarcasm.**" For a presidential candidate to employ that kind of say-it-and-then-retract-it approach to getting in the news might seem like a silly thing to do, but his supporters seemed to be going for it.

Although his radically new attack-oriented approach to campaigning seemed to be hurting him among moderates, his support in the solidly-Republican states never faltered.

When his handlers and other top Republicans tried to convince him to get back on track and quit making such outlandish statements, he said he was just going to keep on doing the same thing all the way to the end. "**It's either going to work or I'm going to have a very, very nice, long vacation.**"

That got people talking too, suggesting that maybe he was preparing for new enterprises after the election, and **there was a rumor that he was already preparing to launch his own post-election TV show, or maybe even an anti-establishment TV network.**

In the last few weeks of the campaign, Trump began making even more outrageous statements, such as "**The election of Hillary Clinton would lead to the destruction of our country**" and "**Hillary Clinton is the most corrupt politician ever to seek the office of the presidency,**" and "**Hillary Clinton's corruption is on a scale we have never seen before. We**

> **must not let her take her criminal scheme to the Oval Office.**" No prior presidential candidate had even made such unfounded outrageous accusations against an opponent, but by this time, the news media was so used to these kinds of outlandish statements from Trump that they were pretty much ignored.

As the two campaigns moved into the fall, the polls were making it clear to everybody (except for the die-hard Trump supporters) that **if Trump didn't change his approach to campaigning, he had little chance of being elected president.**

He did overhaul his campaign staff, but not to moderate his approach. In August, he got rid of some professional campaigners and hired people that were described as "ultra-conservative" or "Alt-Right," people that were known to favor aggressive attacks on anyone who didn't agree with them, even attacks against other Republicans that were seen as "**not conservative enough.**"

As fall approached, Trump **refocused his campaign to do even more attacks on Hillary and Obama. That strategy** *did* **strengthen his support in the "red" states**, but the polls continued to indicate that as long as nothing changed by election day, Hillary would easily get enough Electoral College votes to win the presidency.

Meanwhile, in speech after speech, Hillary's message was clear: she had the experience; her opponent did not. She mentioned how much she had learned by being a United States senator from New York, and **how much she knew about foreign affairs due to her service as the U.S. Secretary of State.** She laid out her economic plan, and she described what she saw as the best qualities of the United States: the best science, the best colleges, and the best clean-energy policies.

She said she had worked closely with the president and that Obama trusted her judgment. **She said she would be ready to as-**

sume the duties of president "on day one," and she was always ready and willing to discuss foreign policy on any front—region by region, country by country. She emphasized the strength of America's military, but said we need to work closely with other countries.

She also often suggested that **Trump didn't have the temperament to be president.** In her speeches and in her TV ads, **she used Trump's own words against him.**

STORY

In the heated 2016 presidential race, TV ads were even more significant than in prior elections. However, **unless you lived in one of the so-called "swing states," you probably didn't see any of them.** TV ads are very expensive, and the candidates were not about to waste money on the states they figured they were not going to win anyhow. **Many of the TV ads did not appear until mid-October,** the period when the candidates believed undecided voters where making up their minds.

The trend toward more negative ads continued in 2016, with **"attack ads" that often featured the candidate's own words.**

One of Hillary's ads that was aired on TV all over the nation showed young girls looking into a mirrors while Trump's words were spoken: "I'd look her right in that fat, ugly face of hers . . . She's a slob . . . A person who's flat-chested is very hard to be a ten" while the words, "Is this the president we want for our daughters?" was displayed on the screen.

Other Hillary ads used Trumps' words about how he treated women, including his words in the Hollywood Access audio tape about how he could get away with sexually molesting women because he was a star.

A Trump add, aired in New Hampshire, North Carolina, Ohio, and Pennsylvania, **used the "overkill" approach** to make reference to Hillary's words about "super predators" (while putting the words "African-American Youth" on the screen), "basement dwellers (while putting the words "Bernie Sanders Supporters" on the screen)," and "basket of deplorables" (while putting the words "Trump Supporters" on the screen).

Some of Trump's ads used fear and demagoguery to try to make people vote for him because they needed to be afraid of immigrants. One of them that aired in New Hampshire, North Carolina, Ohio, and Pennsylvania, featured a weeping mother describing how an illegal immigrant had murdered her child and set him on fire. The ad finished with her saying the words, "Hillary Clinton's border policy is going to allow people into the country just like the one that murdered my son."

Nevertheless, there were some "traditional" ads that promoted the candidate's vision for the country. Hillary's ads were often optimistic as she talked about education, jobs, and equal opportunity. She aired ads that talked about child care and quality education.

Some of her ads were "uplifting." In one, she said, "We are going to lift each other up. I want us to heal our country and bring it together . . . This is the America that I know and love. If we set those goals and we go together, there's nothing that America can't do." Those kinds of upbeat ads aired repeatedly in all the swing states.

Few of the ads were subtle. One ad that was reminiscent of the famous 1964 anti-Goldwater "daisy" as was put up by a pro-Hillary PAC (political action committee) that ran in Ohio. It showed Trump talking about nuclear weapons and then switched to **a video of an atomic bomb going off** behind a warning that one nuclear bomb could kill more people than live in Columbus, Ohio. The ad ended with the words, "Be careful who you vote for" displayed on the screen.

Another Hillary ad on the same subject featured a man who had spent many years as a nuclear missile launch officer saying, "The thought of Donald Trump with nuclear weapons scares me to death."

Hillary aired other ads that featured generals and former government security officials who said they were worried about Trump's ability to handle military situations.

In another Hillary ad, aired in all the swing states, Khizr Khan, father of the slain Muslim soldier, Captain **Humayun Khan,** is featured asking, "Mr. Trump, would my son have a place in your America?"

Hillary also aired a number of ads featuring Republican's saying they were going to vote for her, and ads that showed all the negative things elected Republican officials had said about Trump.

There were also "interview" ads that featured live interviews with supposedly average citizens. One Hillary ad, aired in Florida, Pennsylvania, Ohio, and North Carolina, was a live interview of people of color in a barbershop saying why they were voting for Hillary.

Some of Trump's ads tried to paint Hillary negatively as a Washington "insider." In one ad, he says, "Clinton won't change Washington. She's been there thirty years. Taxes went up. Terrorism spread. Jobs vanished."

The National Rifle Association paid $6.5 million to air an ad in Ohio, Nevada, North Carolina, Pennsylvania and Virginia that featured a woman who says a man with a knife tried to rob her, but he failed because "I carry a pistol." (She shot him twice.) She says, "Don't let politicians take away your right to own a gun."

In another of Trump's pure attack ad, aired only in Ohio, Pennsylvania, and Wisconsin, it says, "Jobs are gone. Factories closed. Because of bad trade deals pushed by the Clintons.

He also aired ads with innuendo and suspicion about Hillary and the Clinton charitable foundation. In one, he asked, "How did Hillary end up filthy rich?" He answered his own question with, "Pay to play politics. Staggering amounts of cash poured into the Clinton Foundation from criminals, dictators, countries that hate America. Hillary cut deals for donors, sold out American workers, exploited Haitians in need, She even handed over American uranium rights to the Russians. Hillary Clinton only cares about power, money, and herself."

Some ads made false statements. For example, at many of Trump's speeches and in some of his ads, he proclaimed that the FBI had said she lied to the FBI about her e-mails. The director of the FBI, James Comey contradicted that. In sworn testimony before Congress, when pressed by a Republican Congressman about whether Hillary had lied, he said, "We have no basis to conclude she lied to the FBI." Nevertheless, the ad continued to play on TV. Late in the campaign, some of Trump's ads claimed Hillary was "under investigation." That was not true. What *was* being investigated were some e-mails found on the laptop of her assistant.

Some of Trump's ads tried to play down Hillary's experience by tying her to "Chaos in Libya and Syria, the rise of ISIS, a failed reset with Russia, supporting the disastrous nuclear deal with Iran, and a terror attack in Benghazi. The ad stated, "Hillary has experience, but it's bad experience."

Some of Hillary's ads focused on Trump's business ties with Russia; others referred to the fact that many of his products were made in places like Bangladesh even though comparable products were available from American manufacturers. Other ads talked about Trump's refusal to release copies of his income tax statements, suggesting he had "something to hide."

Of course, some of Trump's ads talked about immigrants. One of them that aired in Florida, North Carolina, Ohio, and Pennsylvania said, "In Hillary Clinton's America . . . Syrian refugees flood in. Illegal immigrants convicted of committing crimes get to stay, collecting Social Security benefits . . . Donald Trump's America is secure. Terrorists and dangerous criminals kept out. The border secure. Our families safe."

In selected states, like Nevada, Hillary's forces aired some ads in Spanish using Trump's words about creating a "massive deportation force."

Hillary described herself as the daughter of a small business owner (silk screening fabrics) and the granddaughter of a factory worker. **It was a clear attempt to point out the contrast between her modest family history and the wealthy family of Donald Trump who had given him his start in business.** She said she couldn't imagine how average Americans would possibly support the self-proclaimed billionaire, Trump.

She released copies of her IRS tax filings and challenged Trump to do the same.

COMMENT

The issue of releasing copies of IRS tax filings was constantly in the news throughout the campaign. **Hillary released copies of her and husband Bill's tax filings,** which showed that they had made a lot of money from writing books and from giving speeches The tax forms showed that they had paid a very high tax rate in 2014 and 2015, despite giving almost 10% of their income to charity. (Some said the 35.7% rate they had paid was abnormally high and suggested that maybe they should get a better tax accountant.) Hillary then demanded to know what kind of tax rate Trump had paid on his supposedly very high income.

Early in his run for the presidency, **Trump promised to release copies of his tax returns, just as every presidential candidate had done for the past forty years**. But once the campaign had actually begun, when news reporters asked Trump about that, he said it was none of their business.

The Democratic vice-presidential nominee, **Tim Kaine, also released copies of his tax filing documents** and pointed out that every presidential candidate since Lyndon Johnson had released their tax statements to the public. **He said even Nixon had released his tax statements, so why couldn't Trump?**

Trump's only response was that he couldn't do it because he was undergoing "a routine audit" by the IRS.

Hillary's supporters said that he should at least release his earlier tax statements that were not under audit. Trump also refused to do that. Hillary asked him to at least state what tax rate he had paid, but **Trump again said it was nobody's business**.

After that, **Hillary started asking if the real reason Trump wouldn't release copies of this present or prior taxes was because he "had something to hide,"** something he didn't want the voters to know about. She also suggested that **maybe Trump, after claiming bankruptcy multiple times and "stiffing" his employees, wasn't as rich and successful as he claimed**. (She also said she would have read his books about how to get rich, but "they all seemed to stop at chapter eleven.")

In mid-campaign, even Trump's running mate, **Mike Pence released copies of his tax filing documents**. Many thought that would embarrass Trump into releasing his, but Trump stuck to his story about being under audit and refused to do it.

Late in the campaign, a story came out showing that in 1995, **Trump had declared a 916 million dollar loss on his income tax returns**. Tax experts said that meant **he might not have paid any personal income taxe**s for as many as 18 years after that. **Trump's response was that he had simply taken advantage of the tax laws.**

About that time, the IRS commissioner said that an audit didn't prevent anyone from releasing his or her taxes. Others pointed out that **Richard Nixon had released his returns while he was being audited.**

In many of her speeches, Hillary said she would work hard to raise the minimum wage and help college students from middle class families complete their educations debt free.

She said she realized the country was still recovering from the economic crash of 2007-2008, but **she disputed Trumps pessimistic views of the country's current economic state**. She said the economy was recovering well from the disastrous recession and that the stock market was at an all time high. (**Trump said the stock market was in "a bubble" and was about to collapse.**) Hillary pointed out that **the rich had been getting richer** while the middle class was stuck in low-paying jobs. She said **she would "make the rich pay their fair share"** by changing the structure of the tax code. She said jobs should not be allowed to be exported to other countries, and companies should not be allowed to move to other countries to avoid U.S. taxes.

She said, if elected, she would institute new, more effective regulations on big business and on the financial industry. She said that a big part of the problem was **gridlock in Congress**, created by **uncooperative Republicans who tried to suppress any regulations.**

Meanwhile, Trump was still saying the U.S. was in terrible shape. **He said we were becoming "a third-world country."**

Trump also promoted an economic and tax plan. In many ways, it was similar to what Hillary was proposing—more jobs and lower taxes—but he completely disagreed with her about how to do it. He said **the best approach would be fewer regulations on business**, not more. He also said he would dramatically slash corporate taxes and taxes on small businesses. When asked how he would deal with the loss in government income his plan would create, he said we could make it up by attracting more businesses to come to this country. He also said he would "get tough" on our trading partners (especially China). He said if they were "not playing by the rules," he would impose tariffs.

He also said he would repeal the Affordable Care Act (known as Obamacare).

COMMENT

After both Hillary and Trump had laid out their economic plans, economists began to analyze them. Moody's Analytics, a company that does economic research regarding risk, performance, and financial modeling analyzed Hillary's economic proposals and said, "Evident from her proposals is the belief that the country needs to invest more in education, infrastructure and workers, and that the well-to-do, and to a lesser degree financial institutions and businesses, should pay for it. **While her budget arithmetic does not completely add up, it is pretty close, and the nation's debt load under her plan is no different than under current law.**" Their analysis of Trump's plan **concluded that his policies would sharply re-**

duce economic output and reduce employment by 3.5 million jobs. They said it could produce a prolonged recession, and that heavy job losses would hit lower-income and middle-income workers very hard. Under almost any scenario, their report says, "the U.S. economy will be more isolated and diminished."

The Trump campaign said that the Moody analysis rested on flawed assumptions about policies that haven't been fully fleshed out by the campaign.

As Hillary was out on the campaign trail promoting her economic plan and emphasizing her experience in foreign affairs, Trump was busy tossing off one-liners that could only help make her point that he was inexperienced in world affairs. In an interview on ABC television, **he said the Putin was not going to make a military move into Ukraine**. He said, "He's not going into Ukraine, OK, just so you understand. He's not going to go into Ukraine, all right? You can mark it down. You can put it down. You can take it anywhere you want,"

When **the interviewer pointed out that the Russians had already moved into Ukraine**, seizing the country's Crimean Peninsula, Trump said, "OK - well, he's there in a certain way. But I'm not there. You have Obama there. And frankly, that whole part of the world is a mess under Obama with all the strength that you're talking about and all of the power of NATO and all of this. In the meantime, he's going away. He takes Crimea."

Trump's prepared speeches about foreign policy were very different from Hillary's. He was much less specific about how he would deal with foreign affairs, and **he focused mostly on the issue of terrorism**. He said he was sure he could take care of ISIS. In fact, **he said he knew more about ISIS than the top United States military generals. He said he was "the only one" who could deal with ISIS.**

In some speeches, he said the U.S. military was in terrible shape and needed to be dramatically rebuilt.

These kinds of statements did not endear him to military leaders and foreign policy experts. In fact, a number of them came forward to publicly denounce Trump's foreign policy ideas.

Something that got a lot of attention in the country was an open **letter against Trump from 50 foreign affairs and defense specialists. The most surprising thing about the 50 who had signed the letter was that they all had served in Republican administrations.**

The letter stated:

"From a foreign policy perspective, Donald Trump is not qualified to be President and Commander-in-Chief. Indeed, we are convinced that he would be a dangerous President and would put at risk our country's national security and well-being.

"Mr. Trump lacks the character, values, and experience to be President. He weakens U.S. moral authority as the leader of the free world. He appears to lack basic knowledge about and belief in the U.S. Constitution, U.S. laws, and U.S. institutions, including religious tolerance, freedom of the press, and an independent judiciary.

"In addition, Mr. Trump has demonstrated repeatedly that he has little understanding of America's vital national interests, its complex diplomatic challenges, its indispensable alliances, and the democratic values on which U.S. foreign policy must be based. At the same time, he persistently compliments our adversaries and threatens our allies and friends. Unlike previous Presidents who had limited experience in foreign affairs, Mr. Trump has shown no interest in educating himself. He continues to display an alarming ignorance of basic facts of contemporary international politics."

The letter signers included **Michael Chertoff** (Former Secretary of Homeland Security under Presidents Bush and Obama), **James Langdon** (Former Chairman of President Bush's Foreign Intelligence Advisory Board, **John Negroponte** (Former Director of National Intelligence under President George Bush), **Tom**

Ridge (Former Secretary of Homeland Security under President George Bush), and **Kori Schake** (Former Director for Defense Strategy under President George Bush).

Trump dismissed them all as "the dangerous Washington elite" who deserved the blame for making the world such a dangerous place.

Nevertheless, the fact that 50 such high ranking defense experts would make such inflammatory statements about the Republican nominee got everybody's attention, and it clearly hurt him in the polls that came out soon thereafter.

The 50 foreign affairs experts who had served in Republican administrations were not going to be the first or the last Republicans to turn against Trump. One after another, prominent Republicans were starting to come out against him. The New York Times reported that more than 160 Republican leaders were not supporting Trump. This degree of lack of support of the nominee of your own party was something unheard of in any modern presidential election.

Characteristically, Trump brushed them all off, saying he didn't want their support anyhow.

In fact, many other well-known Republicans had already come out against Trump, and he had previously either ignored them or verbally attacked them.

COMMENT

Below are only a few of the many well-known Republicans who came out publicly against Trump early in the 2016 presidential campaign.

Barbara Bush, wife of former President George H. W. Bush. (Her husband and two sons, Jeb and the former president, George, refused to support Trump but didn't say how they would vote; they all pointedly stayed away from the Republican National Convention).

Michael Bloomberg, former Republican Mayor of New York City. (He not only disavowed any support for Trump; he also spoke on behalf of Hillary Clinton at the Democratic National Convention).

Colin Powell, a retired U.S. general who had served as Secretary of State President George W. Bush, said he was going to vote for Hillary.

Susan Collins, U.S. Senator from Maine. (She said Trump would slash and burn and trample anything and anyone he perceived as being in his way or an easy scapegoat).

Bob Dole, Republican Congressman from Illinois. (He said, "Whether it be Mr. Trump's comments about women, his comments about Muslims, his comments about Latinos, for me it was very personal his comments about POWs." He said he might write in a name.)

Lindsey Graham, U.S. Senator from South Carolina. (After Trump's attacks on Judge Gonzalo Curiel, Graham said his fellow Republicans should all withdraw their endorsements, adding, "This is the most un-American thing from a politician since Joe McCarthy.")

Richard Hanna, Republican Congressman from New York. (He said he would vote for Hillary, adding, "For me, it is not enough to simply denounce Trump. . . He is unfit to serve our party and cannot lead this country.")

Gordon Humphrey, former Republican Senator from New Hampshire. (He called Trump "a sociopath without a conscience or feelings of guilt, shame or remorse.").

Larry Pressler, former three-term Republican senator from South Dakota. (He not only said he wouldn't vote for Trump; he endorsed Hillary Clinton).

Hank Paulson, former Secretary of the Treasury under George W. Bush. (He said he was going to vote for Hillary "with the hope that she can bring Americans together to do the things necessary to strengthen our economy, our environment and our place in the world.").

Sally Bradshaw, aid to Jeb Bush. (She said she "could not abide the hateful rhetoric of Donald Trump and his complete lack of principles).

Marc Racicot, chair of the Republican National Committee from 2001 to 2003. (He said, "Trump has demonstrated neither the aforementioned qualities of principled leadership, nor offered any substantive or serious conservative policy proposals consistent with historical Republican Party platform positions").

Vin Weber, former Minnesota Republican congressman. (He said he would not remain a Republican if Trump became president).

George Will, conservative columnist. (He said he had left the Republican Party because of Trump's nomination).

Mitt Romney, the 2012 Republican nominee. (He said, "I wanted my grand-kids to see that I simply couldn't ignore what Mr. Trump was saying and doing, which revealed a character and temperament unfit for the leader of the free world.")

In addition to the Republicans listed above, **seventy-five former ambassadors, including 57 that had been appointed by Republican presidents,** released a letter endorsing Hillary Clinton and criticizing Donald Trump as "entirely unqualified" for the office.

Although no prior candidate had ever failed to receive the support of so many well-known officials in his own party, Trump brushed it off, describing all of them as "just jealous," and described them as Washington establishment people and said, "Look at the terrible job they've done."

A number of terrorist events in the U.S. and around the world happened during the 2016 presidential campaign. They all became fodder for Trump's campaign. He bragged that he'd predicted that kind of thing would happen, and said it proved his plan to keep Muslims from entering the U.S. was right (the shooter was actually born in the United States). At his rallies, he said immigration "from areas of the world where there is a proven history of terrorism" should be prevented.

COMMENT

At one of his boisterous campaign rallies, Trump said that the "Second Amendment people" should do something to stop Hillary. It was part of a warning that if she wasn't stopped, she would get to pick the next Supreme Court justice. The assumption was that Hillary would pick a Supreme Court justice that Trump's followers wouldn't like. Trump said if he was elected, he would appoint a justice like Antonin Scalia (Justice Scalia had died in the early days of the campaign). Underlying Trump's words was a widespread belief that Supreme Court justices were not objective about the law. There was plenty of evidence to support that belief. Justice Scalia had consistently voted on cases in a way that most Republicans would approve of. You can often predict how Supreme Court justices will vote simply by knowing which president appointed them, Republican or Democratic.

But how can that be? Aren't judges who are at the very highest level of jurisprudence supposed to be making their decisions based on the law, not on personal preferences?

The problem turns out to be what psychologists call cognitive dissonance reduction. That is, once a person begins to look at something in a certain way, data that competes with that point of view tends to make that person psychologically un-comfortable. It will cause internal dissonance. Humans (even judges) will therefore strive to reduce that dissonance by inter-preting incoming data in a way that fits their established world view. As a result, if a president wants to "stack" the Supreme Court, all they have to do is analyze a judge's long history of decisions and find one that consistently votes in a certain way. Trump said he would do that if he was elected president, and he assumed Hillary would do the same thing.

After Justice Scalia died, President Obama did what the Constitution demanded and quickly named a replacement. As was typical of President Obama, to be accommodating with both sides, **he picked a moderate judge**, Merrick Garland, the chief judge for the U.S. Court of Appeals for the D.C. Circuit.

According to the Constitution, the judge chosen by the president then must go before the Senate Judiciary Committee to be questioned, and then the entire Senate is to vote on con-firmation.

But **the Republicans in the Senates did something un-precedented: they refused to even hold the required hear-ings**. They were so used to blocking any legislation President Obama sent to them, **they also refused to act on his Supreme Court nomination**, saying it would not be appropriate to do so in an election year (even though in the twentieth century, six Supreme court justices had been confirmed in a presidential election year). **A few Republican Senators did apparently ap-prove of the president's pick** and did want to hold hearings on Judge Garland, but they were overruled by the Republican leadership.

As the election season rolled on and it looked more and more like Hillary was going to be elected, one wonders if those

> same Republican Senators regretted not voting for a moderate Supreme Court Judge when they had the chance.

Meanwhile, **Hillary kept up her attacks on Trump's lack of experience**, making frequent comments about him not being "temperamentally fit to be president (the polls consistently showed her far ahead on the "temperament" issue).

She said it was not just that he is unprepared, he is temperamentally unfit to hold an office of such immense responsibility that requires knowledge *and* stability. She often suggested that Trump wouldn't know how to deal with crisis situations. She said we should not put the safety of our children and grandchildren in Donald Trump's hands: "This is not someone who should ever have the nuclear codes because **it's not hard to imagine Donald Trump leading us into a war just because somebody got under his very thin skin."**

Hillary often mentioned the fact that it is the president that makes the final decision about using nuclear weapons, suggesting that the experience of being a businessman does not prepare you for dealing with a global crisis. She said, "There's no risk of people losing their lives if you blow up a golf course deal. But it doesn't work like that in world affairs," and added, "The stakes in global statecraft are infinitely higher and more complex than in the world of luxury hotels."

Hillary even questioned Trump's supposed success as a businessman, suggesting that maybe the reason he wouldn't release his tax statements was because "he isn't a rich as he claims."

There were even suggestions that Trump was using his candidacy to enrich his businesses. Because Trump's various business interests included such things as airplanes and helicopters and hotels, several news organizations wondered out loud if the Trump campaign was paying money to any of those organizations.

COMMENT

The fact is, it can be quite a challenge to figure out the true worth of a man like Trump who is involved in so many different businesses. **There had never been a nominee with such complicated finances.** All that was known was that he bought and sold properties via an opaque maze of financial backers and hidden investment partnerships, both here and abroad. His businesses borrowed heavily, often from the same Wall Street financial organizations he was so fond of criticizing, and from foreign countries like China that he blamed for the loss of jobs in the U.S. What made his finances especially difficult to understand was that **the Trump organization is a closely held family-run business** that does not have the financial-reporting responsibilities of a publicly held company like IBM or General Electric. What that meant was that although much of his candidacy was based on his success as a businessman, little was actually known about his finances, either here or abroad.

Former presidents, upon being elected, placed their holdings in a blind trust so as not to have their businesses interests influence their presidential decisions. If Trump was elected president, that clearly would not be possible.

As the November election drew closer, Trump fell even farther behind in the polls. Hillary had always held a slight lead in most of the key swing states, but **the national polls and the swing-state polls began to steadily move in Hillary's favor**.

Nevertheless, members of Trump's staff continued to go on radio and TV to say the polls were wrong and the size crowds at Trump's rallies proved it. It was true that Trump was still drawing large crowds to his rallies, and the crowds were a boisterous as ever. When Hillary's name was mentioned, some yelled, "Hillary is a whore!" or "Kill the Bitch!" They often broke into a chant, "Lock her up! Lock her up!" Trump egged them on, and he never failed to call her "Crooked Hillary" and talk about how corrupt she was.

COMMENT

In presidential elections, there has always been propaganda. What varies is the amount and viciousness of it, and the 2016 presidential election set new levels in both.

Propaganda is defined as biased derogatory information used to promote a particular political point of view. In politics, in it's simplest form, propaganda is merely name-calling, but it can also be used to associate your opponent with something unsavory or illegal.

Early on in the 2016 presidential race, **Trump began calling Hillary Clinton, "crooked Hillary,"** an unsavory name that **implied that she had been convicted of something illegal**. When he failed to specify what made her "crooked," it showed he had decided to enter the world of political propaganda.

Soon thereafter, **he escalated the name-calling** by saying she was "a liar," often referring to her as "lying Hillary," adding that she was a **"dangerous liar."**

In a speech early in the summer, he called her "**a world-class liar,**" adding that she was the "most corrupt person to ever run for president." Again, he offered no proof of that, and in fact, didn't even say what he was referring to. Some speculated that he might be referring to how she handled her e-mail when she was the U.S. Secretary of State, but few could see how that made her "**the most corrupt person to ever run for president.**"

Next, he said her full name, Hillary Rodham Clinton, sounded a lot like "Hillary Rotten Clinton." **It was a sneaky, if childish, way to say she was "rotten,"** but if asked, he could say it was just how her name sounded to him.

A few weeks later, he said Bernie Sanders had "made a deal with the devil," adding, **"She's the devil."**

Later in the campaign, probably **in response to some psychologists getting themselves into the news by suggesting that *he* had mental problems**, Trump began saying *she* was "unhinged," and that she was an "unbalanced person."

For the next stage of the propaganda campaign, a group of people paid by the Trump organization, began hitting the TV and radio talk shows, all of them referring to Hillary as "a liar." Once the propaganda campaign was fully operational, they began to self-referentially remind people of that by saying she was **a "well-known liar."**

Members of Trump's staff also furthered Trump's unsubstantiated accusations of corruption by appearing on as many TV and radio shows as possible to call Hillary "corrupt." They eventually upped the level of their propaganda tactic by starting to call her *"totally* corrupt," and *"completely* untrustworthy." Instead of talking about policy and Trump's vision for the country, portraying Hillary as corrupt and as a liar eventually became the central tactic of his campaign.

But **does propaganda work?** It does, and many psychologists and social scientists have tried to figure out why. They say **the most effective propaganda works by associating a person or an idea with something unsavory or unpleasant, something people already have negative feelings about.**

But it only works if it gets repeated often enough, and the 24-hour availability of news radio, online news, and cable TV are the perfect venue for such repetitions.

But **did it work this time?** Was repeatedly associating Hillary's name with negative connotations like "crooked" or "corrupt," or "untrustworthy" able to change people's opinion about her even though she was so well known?

The polls provided the answer. Back **in 2013, only 26% of those questioned nationwide rated her unfavorably.** But by the fall of 2016, after a year of non-stop propaganda from Trump and his supporters about her honesty, **more than 50% of those polled rated her unfavorably.** Polls that focused specifically on a propaganda words Trump was using showed the trend even more clearly: **by the fall of 2016, polls were indicating that 67% were now rating her as "untrustworthy."**

Hillary mostly ignoring it. When asked about Trump's insults, she said she was not going to engage in "the kind of insult fest that he seems to thrive on." She added, "**It is beneath the character of the kind of dialogue we should have**, because we have serious problems to solve. Her running mate, Tim Kaine added, **"Most of us stopped the name-calling thing about fifth grade."**

However, Trump eventually pushed the propaganda too far: he said, "Hillary Clinton is a Bigot," and it was like a trial lawyer bringing a topic into a case that should have been kept out of the jury members' minds. **Hillary reacted.** She said, **"From the start, Donald Trump has built his campaign on prejudice and paranoia.** He's taking hate groups mainstream and helping a radical fringe take over one of America's two major political parties." **She pointed out that Trump had launched his campaign for president with racist lies about Mexican immigrants, portraying them as rapists and criminals.** In fact, she said, **his whole campaign was based on a steady stream of bigotry**, including banning people from entering the United States based on their religion. She reminded voters that Trump's campaign operation was headed by those that had been in charge of the right-wing web sites that appealed to the Alt-Right, a fringe group of ultra-conservative Republicans that opposed multiculturalism and had long been associated with white supremacist groups.

Hillary began to parody Trump's "Make America great again" slogan, saying his real was to **"Make America hate again."**

Hillary's strong response to Trump's "She's a bigot" accusation may not have undone the negative effect Trump's "she's a liar" and "crooked Hillary" propaganda campaign had done, but the polls showed **Trump's "likability" numbers stated to drop.** With the effect of the relentless propaganda campaign and Trumps attacking style, people began to talk about the 2016 presidential campaign being a race between two unlikable candidates.

As the first nationally televised debate approached, some were saying Trump had better get his act together or he was sure to lose the election. Most agreed that Hillary had far more experience at dealing with the debate format, but some said the debates would give entertainer Trump his chance to shine.

As Hillary retreated from the campaign trail to prepare for the debate, Trump continued to hold huge rallies so he would bask in the glory of his adoring fans. In fact, he made fun of Hillary's taking time out to prepare for the first debate, saying she wasn't actually preparing, but only resting. **He said he didn't need to prepare, and he guaranteed that he would easily win the debate.**

The First Debate

The first presidential debate of 2016 began with a straightforward question about how the candidates would create more jobs. Hillary responded as expected, by outlining her economic program, but Trump started talking trade deals. He said he would keep jobs from fleeing the country, and he would cut taxes on businesses.

Hillary responded by saying Trump's plan was a trickle-down economics plan to help the rich. She called it "trumped-up" trickle-down.

At that point, Trump accused Hillary of failing to solve the country's economic problems even though she'd had thirty years to do it.

The moderator kept on trying to interrupt, but Trump wouldn't stop talking about trade deals.

When Hillary finally got a chance to talk, she reminded the audience that eight years ago the country was in the middle of the worst financial crisis since the 1930s, due, in large part, to tax policies that slashed taxes on the wealthy. She said Trump had made money off of the collapse in the economy.

Trump interrupted to say, "That's called business, by the way."

Hillary went on to point out that nine million people had lost their jobs, and five million people had lost their homes. She added "Donald thinks that climate change is a hoax perpetrated by the Chinese."

Trump interrupted with, "I did not. I did not. I do not say that."

Hillary went on to say, "I think science is real."

Trump interrupted again to repeat, "I do not say that."

Hillary wanted to talk about investing in clean energy, but Trump kept on interrupting with comments about why she hadn't done anything in thirty years.

When Hillary responded that she thought her husband had done a good job of improving the economy when he was president, Trump interrupted with, "He approved NAFTA, which is the single worst trade deal ever approved in this country."

Hillary replied that if we actually look at the facts, incomes went up for everybody, and manufacturing jobs also went up. However, the more she tried to talk about facts and figures, the more Trump interrupted. He wanted to keep on talking about

NAFTA. Then, whenever Hillary tried to talk about her economic plan, Trump kept on interrupting with, "You have no plan."

Hillary reiterated that people have looked at both of their plans and concluded that hers would create 10 million jobs and his would lose 3.5 million jobs, and explode the debt which would cause a recession.

Trump replied by saying Hillary was going to drive businesses out of the country by increasing regulations "all over the place."

The moderator again tried to get the debate back on track to talk about taxes, but Trump interrupted him, saying, "She's going to raise taxes $1.3 trillion." He then went on to say, "She tells you how to fight ISIS on her website. I don't think General Douglas MacArthur would like that too much."

Hillary responded with, "Well, at least I have a plan to fight ISIS."

The moderator tried to intervene, but Trump said, "No, no, you're telling the enemy everything you want to do."

After more back and forth, Hillary just smiled and said she had a feeling that by the end of this evening she was going to be blamed for everything that's ever happened in the country.

Trump interjected, "Why not?"

She suggested he was saying crazy things and tried to go on, but Trump interrupted with, "There's nothing crazy about not letting our companies bring their money back into their country."

The moderator chided him, saying, "This is Secretary Clinton's two minutes, please."

Hillary went on, referring to his tax proposals as not providing a way to bring back money that's stranded overseas.

Trump interrupted with, "Then you didn't read it."

Hillary went on, referring to his tax plan and how it included a "Trump loophole" that would be an advantage for him.

Trump interrupted with, "Who gave it that name? The first I've — who gave it that name?"

The moderator again tried to get Trump to stop interrupting, saying, "Mr. Trump, this is Secretary Clinton's two minutes."

Hillary went on, saying it would create a four billion dollar tax benefit for Trump's family.

She tried to go on, but Trump again interrupted with, "How much? How much for my family?"

Hillary went on, saying "trumped-up trickle-down" doesn't work, and it is what "got us into the mess we were in, in 2008 and 2009."

Trump responded with, "Typical politician. All talk, no action. Sounds good, doesn't work."

The moderator then asked Trump why he hadn't released his tax returns like all previous candidates had.

Trump gave his usual response about being under audit, and added that he would release his taxes as soon as Hillary released her 33,000 e-mails.

Hillary responded by saying, "You've got to ask yourself, why won't he release his tax returns?" She suggested that either he's not as rich as he says he is, or that he's not as charitable as he claimed to be. She suggested he had something to hide, and that maybe he actually wasn't paying any federal taxes."

Trump interrupted with, "That makes me smart."

Hillary went on: "So if he's paid zero, that means zero for troops, zero for vets, zero for schools or health."

The moderator then asked Hillary about her e-mails.

She said, "I made a mistake using a private e-mail server."

Trump interrupted with, "That's for sure."

Hillary went on, saying, "And if I had to do it over again, I would, obviously, do it differently. But I'm not going to make any excuses. It was a mistake, and I take responsibility for that."

Trump said it was more than a mistake, that it was done purposely. He pointed out that some of her staff had taken the Fifth Amendment, and that he thought that was disgraceful. He went on to talk about what bad shape the country was in, suggesting that we were like "a third world country."

Hillary said "Maybe because you haven't paid any federal income tax for a lot of years."

Trump replied with, "It would be squandered, too, believe me."

Hillary said, "If your main claim to be president of the United

States is your business, then I think we should talk about that." She pointed out that his campaign manager had said he built a lot of businesses "on the backs of little guys."

Trump said, "It's all words. It's all sound bites."

After quite a bit of back and forth about topics such as race relations and law and order, they got into the topic of the controversial "stop and frisk" police policy. Hillary said the policy had been declared unconstitutional because it largely singled out black and Hispanic young men.

Trump defended the policy and talked about the terrible situation in the African-American communities. He said, "You walk down the street, you get shot." He added that in Chicago they'd had thousands of shootings, and he asked "Is this a war-torn country?"

Hillary replied that she thought it was unfortunate that Trump was painting such a dire picture of the black communities.

Trump interrupted with, "Ugh."

Hillary went on to describe the vibrancy of the black church and black businesses. She pointed out that violent crime is one-half of what it was in 1991, and that property crime is down 40 percent. She said, "We've got to address the systemic racism in our criminal justice system. We cannot just say law and order."

Then, the moderator asked if she believed that police are implicitly biased against black people?

Hillary answered that she thought implicit bias is a problem for everyone, not just police. She tried go on with some facts, but Trump interrupted with, "No, you're wrong." He said the African-American community had been let down by our politicians. "They talk good around election time, like right now, and after the election, they said, see ya later, I'll see you in four years . . . look at the inner cities . . . I've been all over the place while you decided to stay home."

Hillary said, "I think Donald just criticized me for preparing for this debate. And, yes, I did. And you know what else I prepared for? I prepared to be president. And I think that's a good thing."

The moderator then asked Trump about his false claim that the nation's first black president was not a natural-born citizen.

Trump said Hillary had started it. He then went on to talk about ISIS and having a strong border.

The moderator tried to press him on the "birther" story, but Trump brushed it aside saying nobody cared much about it.

Hillary said Trump was not going to be able to dismiss the whole racist birther lie that easily. She pointed out that Trump had started his political activity based on the "racist lie that our first black president was not an American citizen" when there was absolutely no evidence for it. She then mentioned the fact that Trump's businesses had been sued twice by the Justice Department for racial discrimination.

Trump said the lawsuit by the justice department happened when he was very young, and that they had settler the suit with no admission of guilt.

The moderator then asked about cyber crime,

Hillary mentioned the recent and troubling cyber attacks from Russia, and mentioned Trump's praise of Putin. She said she was shocked when Donald publicly invited Putin to hack into American systems, and she said it was one of the reasons why 50 national-al security officials who served in Republican administrations said Trump was unfit to be the commander-in-chief.

Trump said he had been endorsed by over 200 admirals and generals and by ICE, and he added that Hillary didn't know for sure it was the Russians. He said, "It could also be China. It could also be lots of other people. It also could be somebody sitting on their bed that weighs 400 pounds."

Hillary said she'd put forth a plan to defeat ISIS, and she reminded the audience that she had been involved in a number of efforts to take out Al Qaida leadership when she was Secretary of State, including taking out bin Laden.

The moderator then asked about acts of terror on American soil. Instead of answering that question, Trump said President Obama and Secretary Clinton created a vacuum for ISIS by the way they got out of Iraq. He said, "We should have taken the oil."

Hillary responded by pointing out that Trump had supported the invasion of Iraq."

Trump interrupted with, "Wrong."

Hillary said, "That is absolutely proved over and over again."

Trump said, "Wrong. Wrong."

Hillary said, "He actually advocated for the actions we took in Libya and urged that Gadhafi be taken out, after actually doing some business with him one time." She then went on to explain that it was President George W. Bush that made the agreement about when American troops would leave Iraq, not Barack Obama. She then moved back to the question that the moderator had asked about what we should do to protect out people here in the United States. She said we needed to have "an intelligence surge." She added that we should also work with NATO, the longest military alliance in history, and work with our friends in the Middle East, including the Muslim majority nations. She reminded the audience that Donald had consistently insulted Muslims.

Trump said, "We have the greatest mess anyone's ever seen. You look at the Middle East, it's a total mess under your direction. He then went on to talk about "the Iran deal, another beauty." He then went back to talking about how Obama and Hillary "had created a vacuum."

The moderator tried to say it was a topic already covered, but Trump went on to say, "You're talking about taking out ISIS. But you were there, and you were Secretary of State when it was a little infant. Now it's in over 30 countries. And you're going to stop them? I don't think so."

At that point, the moderator pointed out that "A lot of these are judgment questions. You had supported the war in Iraq before the invasion. What makes your—"

Trump interrupted him to say, I did not support the war in Iraq."

The moderator said, "In 2002—"

Trump again interrupted him to say, "That is a mainstream media nonsense put out by her, because she — frankly, I think the best person in her campaign is mainstream media."

The moderator tried to ask his question again, but again Trump interrupted him to say, "Wait a minute. I was against the war in Iraq."

The moderator said, "The record shows otherwise."

Trump said, "The record does not show that . . . the record shows that I'm right." He went on to say he had told Sean Hannity that he was against the war but nobody will call Hannity.

The moderator then tried to ask a follow up question, but Trump kept on interrupting him, saying, "I have much better judgment than she does. There's no question about that. I also have a much better temperament than she has, you know?"

That comment elicited quite a bit of laughter from the audience, but Trump went on: "I have a much better — she spent — let me tell you — she spent hundreds of millions of dollars on an advertising — you know, they get Madison Avenue into a room, they put names — oh, temperament, let's go after — I think my strongest asset, maybe by far, is my temperament. I have a winning temperament. I know how to win."

The moderator then asked Hillary to reply, but Trump went on: "Wait. The AFL-CIO the other day, behind the blue screen, I don't know who you were talking to, Secretary Clinton, but you were totally out of control. I said, there's a person with a temperament that's got a problem."

The moderator again asked Hillary to reply, and she said "Whew, OK."

That elicited even louder laughter from the audience.

She went on to talk about the importance of NATO and the negotiated nuclear disarmament deal with Iran. "That's diplomacy," she said. "That's coalition-building. That's working with other nations."

She went on to say that she had seen Trump saying that there were some Iranian sailors taunting American sailors, and he said if they taunted our sailors, he'd blow them out of the water and start another war. That's not good judgment."

Trump interrupted with, "That would not start a war."

Hillary said, "That is not the right temperament to be commander-in- chief, to be taunted. And the worst part . . . "

Trump again interrupted with, "No, they were taunting us."

Hillary went on to talk about what Trump had been heard to say about nuclear weapons. "He has said repeatedly that he didn't care if other nations got nuclear weapons."

Trump interrupted with, "Wrong."

Hillary tried to go on but Trump interrupted with, "It's lies."

She went on to say, "His cavalier attitude about nuclear weapons is so deeply troubling."

Trump replied with, "That line's getting a little bit old, I must say. I would like to—"

This time it was Hillary that interrupted with, "It's a good one, though. It well describes the problem."

Her comment again elicited laughter from the audience.

The moderator then asked about the use of nuclear weapons.

Trump said the U.S. was falling behind Russia. He said, "They have a much newer capability than we do." He then went on to talk about our aging military and about the 1.7 billion dollars in cash for the hostages deal with Iran. He said it was one of the worst deals ever made by any country in history.

The moderator said, Your two minutes is expired," but Trump went on: "And they're going to end up getting nuclear."

When Hillary was given her two minutes to answer the question, she started out by saying, "Words matter. Words matter when you run for president. And they really matter when you are president. And I want to reassure our allies in Japan and South Korea and elsewhere that we have mutual defense treaties and we will honor them." She said Trump claimed to have a secret plan to defeat ISIS, and added "The only secret is that he has no plan."

Trump said, "We cannot be the policemen of the world."

The moderator then tried to go on, but Trump continued with, "Where they're not paying us what we need."

The moderator was still trying to go on, but Trump wasn't finished: "And she doesn't say that, because she's got no business ability. We need heart. We need a lot of things. But you have to have some basic ability. And sadly, she doesn't have that."

The moderator then said, "Mr. Trump, this year Secretary Clinton became the first woman nominated for president by a major party. Earlier this month, you said she doesn't have, quote, "a presidential look." She's standing here right now. What did you mean by that?"

Trump replied, "She doesn't have the look. She doesn't have the stamina. I said she doesn't have the stamina. And I don't believe she does have the stamina. To be president of this country, you need tremendous stamina."

The moderator said, "The quote was, "I just don't think she has the presidential look.""

Trump replied, "You have — wait a minute. Wait a minute, Lester. You asked me a question. Did you ask me a question?" Then he went on to talk more about how countries ought to be paying us.

The moderator asked Hillary to respond, and she said, "Well, as soon as he travels to 112 countries and negotiates a peace deal, a cease-fire, a release of dissidents, an opening of new opportunities in nations around the world, or even spends 11 hours testifying in front of a congressional committee, he can talk to me about stamina."

That got loud applause from the audience.

Trump said, "The world — let me tell you. Let me tell you. Hillary has experience, but it's bad experience."

The audience also applauded that statement.

Hillary said, "You know, he tried to switch from looks to stamina. But this is a man who has called women pigs, slobs and dogs, and someone who has said pregnancy is an inconvenience to employers, who has said—"

Trump interrupted with, "I never said that."

Hillary went on: "Women don't deserve equal pay unless they do as good a job as men."

Trump interrupted with, "I never said that."

Hillary went on: "And one of the worst things he said was about a woman in a beauty contest. He loves beauty contests, supporting them and hanging around them. And he called this woman

"Miss Piggy." Then he called her "Miss Housekeeping," because she was Latina. Donald, she has a name."

Trump replied, "Where did you find this? Where did you find this?"

Hillary said, "Her name is Alicia Machado."

Trump replied, "Where did you find this?"

Hillary went on: "And she has become a U.S. citizen, and you can bet—"

Trump interrupted with, "Oh, really?"

Hillary said, "She's going to vote this November."

Trump said, "Hillary is hitting me with tremendous commercial . . . somebody who's been very vicious to me, Rosie O'Donnell, I said very tough things to her, and I think everybody would agree that she deserves it and nobody feels sorry for her. But you want to know the truth? I was going to say something . . . extremely rough to Hillary, to her family, and I said to myself, I can't do it. I just can't do it. It's inappropriate. It's not nice." But she spent hundreds of millions of dollars on negative ads on me, many of which are absolutely untrue. They're untrue. And they're misrepresentations. And I will tell you this, Lester: It's not nice. And I don't deserve that. But it's certainly not a nice thing that she's done. It's hundreds of millions of ads. And the only gratifying thing is, I saw the polls come in today, and with all of that money—"

The moderator said, "We have to move on to the final question."

Trump continued: "200 million is spent, and I'm either winning or tied, and I've spent practically nothing."

The comment elicited more applause from the audience.

The moderator said, "One of you will not win this election. So my final question to you tonight, are you willing to accept the outcome as the will of the voters? Secretary Clinton?

Hillary said, "Well, I support our democracy. And sometimes you win, sometimes you lose. But I certainly will support the outcome of this election.

The moderator then asked the same question of Trump.

Trump said, "I want to make America great again. We are a nation that is seriously troubled. We're losing our jobs. People are pouring into our country. The other day, we were deporting 800 people. And perhaps they passed the wrong button, they pressed the wrong button, or perhaps worse than that, it was corruption, but these people that we were going to deport for good reason ended up becoming citizens. Ended up becoming citizens. And it was 800. And now it turns out it might be 1,800, and they don't even know."

The moderator interrupted him to again ask the question: "Will you accept the outcome of the election?"

Trump replied, "Look, here's the story. I want to make America great again. I'm going to be able to do it. I don't believe Hillary will. The answer is, if she wins, I will absolutely support her.

The moderator then concluded the debate.

Discussion of the First Debate

Remember what I said earlier about the 16-year lapse in televised debates when both Lyndon Johnson and Richard Nixon refused to debate? After the first televised debate of 2016, Donald Trump might have wished he had follower their lead.

Immediately after the conclusion of the first presidential debate, **a national poll was conducted**. The results indicated that Hillary had won the debate convincingly. **62% of voters who watched the debate on TV said Clinton won, while only 27% said Trump did.** Most agreed that Trump seemed unprepared and was often on the defensive

Trump was quick to disagree. He said he won the debate, and **he criticized Hillary for being "over prepared."**

Many commented on the fact that Hillary had come well armed with facts and figures, to which Trump mostly responded "off-the-cuff" with vague assertions that he would "fix things."

Most of the commentators from the news media had predicted that Trump would come to the debate prepared to be calm and acting "presidential." He didn't. He was animated and aggressive throughout the debate, being what most observers described as very "Trump like."

Some thought Trump did fairly well when he was attacking Hillary's position on trade deals, but after the debate many **economists refuted his assertion that trade deals had hurt the U.S. economy**.

They also said **his assertion that trade deals had caused unemployment to spike in Michigan and Ohio was wrong**, and in fact, the rate of unemployment in those two states was less than the U.S. average. His attack on Hillary about NAFTA was also seen as off the mark. NAFTA was actually created during the administration of President George H.W. Bush, but Bill Clinton had been elected by the time it went into effect.

To many, **Trump seemed nervous and agitated**, maybe because he was doing a lot of "sniffing." His supporters were quick to say it was only seasonal allergies, but Trump denied that. He also denied having a cold, which got the internet going to try to guess what the sniffing was all about.

During most of the debate, Trump was in attack mode, but Hillary mostly refused to go on the defensive. She just disputed what he was saying and said the viewers should do fact checking.

One of the few truths in Trump's many attacks on Hillary during the debate was his assertion that the U.S. had paid Iran 1.7 billion dollars in cash as part of a deal to get American prisoners back. It was money that the U.S. owed Iran, and President Obama denied that it was payment for the release of the hostages. **Whatever it is called, it does seem unlikely that the U.S. would have paid the debt if the hostages had not been released.**

Part of the reason Trump was often defensive during the debate was because Hillary suggested he might not be as good at business as he claimed. After the debate, investigative reporters found evidence that his father had frequently bailed him out.

When Hillary accused him of bragging about making money off of the 2008 collapse in the economy, he replied, "**That's called business, by the way**." When questioned after the debate, many viewers thought that statement sounded so callous, **it seemed to support her allegation**.

During the debate, **Hillary had suggested that one of the reasons why Trump was refusing to release his taxes was because he wasn't paying any income taxes**.

After the debate, Hillary said his reply of "**That makes me smart**" meant he thought people who paid taxes were dumb.

After the debate, there was a renewed search for any evidence of Trump's assertion that Hillary had started the birther movement. None was found.

There was also a post-debate search for any evidence that Trump had been against the invasion of Iraq. There was some evidence found that he did support the war at first, and only later joined the many who were saying it had been a mistake.

One thing that Hillary brought up during the debate **seemed to catch Trump completely off guard was her assertion that Trump had degraded a former Miss Universe**.

Soon after the debate, **Trump sent out a tweet at 3:00 AM** pressing his attack on the Venezuelan woman. Hillary asked what kind off presidential candidate makes tweets at three o'clock in the morning in order to attack a woman.

After the debate, many disputed Trump's repeated assertion that Hillary and Obama fostered the rise of ISIS by setting a date for all U.S. troops to leave Iraq.

In fact, **it was President Bush who set the pullout date. President Obama tried to negotiate a deal to leave some troops in Iraq** after the pullout date, but the leaders of Iraq wouldn't agree to the terms.

All in all, the post-debate discussions were about Trump, but for the wrong reasons. The polls, especially in the all-important swing states, showed him losing support.

STORY

One of the most explosive events of the 2016 presidential campaign happened not long after the first presidential debate. It was **the release of an audio tape that had been made in preparation for a Trump appearance on the Access Hollywood TV show. The tape had been made when Trump was 59-years old**. In the tape, Trump can be heard using vulgar language to **brag about how he could get away with sexually accosting women. He said he could even get away with grabbing their gentiles because he was "a star."** Haring how Trump talked on that audio tape set off a media firestorm, and edited versions of the tape were heard on every radio and TV station and reproduced in every newspaper and news-oriented web site.

After the release of the Access Hollywood audio tape, Trump responded via Twitter: "This was **locker-room banter**, a private conversation that took place many years ago. Bill Clinton has said far worse to me on the golf course — not even close. I apologize if anyone was offended."

For most, that wasn't a sincere apology, and later that night, Trump released a video tape in which he said he had never said he was a perfect person, and that he had said and done things he regretted. He said the words on the "more than a decade-old video" were one of them. **He said the words didn't reflect "who I am." He said his travels across the country had changed him and he would pledge to be a better man in the future.** But **then the taped "apology" veered into his usual attacks on Hillary** about how she and her kind had "run our country into the ground."

He then went back to the subject of the Access Hollywood audio tape, dismissing it and saying **Bill Clinton had done much worse.** He then went on to say **Hillary had bullied, at-**

tacked, shamed, and intimidated Bill's victims. It was a clear indication that his response to the damaging audio tape was going to be, as usual, to counterattack.

For many of his supporters, the videotaped apology/attack was exactly what they wanted; they all began joining him to say it was nothing but "locker room talk."

But the Democrats were not willing to dismiss it so easily and neither were a lot of Republicans. **Not wanting their own careers to be tied to a presidential candidate bragging about sexual assault, a large number of elected Republicans withdrew their support from Trump**. Others just refused to talk about it. House Speaker, Paul Ryan, avoided withdrawing his endorsement of Trump merely saying **he was no longer going to campaign for Trump**.

But then it got worse: dozens of elected Republicans actually called for him to withdraw his name from the ticket, despite the fact that we were in the late stages of the campaign.

That set off a series of Twitter tweets from Trump accusing them of disloyalty. **He called Ryan "Our very weak and ineffective leader."**

In addition, **hundreds of newspaper across the country immediately endorsed Hillary. Only a few newspapers were now willing to go on the record as supporting Trump**. Even the newspapers that had formerly always endorsed Republicans, refused to endorse Trump. For example, **the Phoenix Arizona Republic (which was founded in 1890 and was originally named "The Arizona Republican") endorsed Hillary**. It was the first time in the newspaper's history that they had ever endorsed a Democrat. (It resulted in outrage from local Trump supporters and even some **death threats to the newspaper staff**.)

However, Trump's vice-presidential nominee, Mike Pense, and some politicians from the so-called "very red states" said they would continue to support Trump. Some of Trump's paid staff appeared on TV and radio news programs and talk shows to reiterate his claim that it was "only locker room talk." They said they had frequently heard men talk like that.

Although many well-known athletes came forward to say they had never heard such talk in any locker room they had ever been in, the "only banter" argument was a fairly clever strategy, giving Trump supporters a reason to dismiss the audio tape. (Remember the earlier discussion about reducing cognitive dissonance?)

Even some Christian Evangelist leaders came forward to say they would continue to support Trump.

However, that was **not true in Mormon Utah**. Although the state had long been voting Republican, **most of the state's Republican leaders immediately withdrew their support for Trump and said they would not vote for him (some of them, under intense pressure from Republican voters, later reversed course and said that although they could not endorse him, they would vote for him). The state's newspapers also withdrew their support for Trump, including the Deseret News, a newspaper owned by the Mormon Church.**

Soon the polls were indicating Trump might even lose traditionally Republican states like Utah, Arizona, and Georgia.

With all the news about Trump's words on the Access Hollywood audio tape, many were wondering how it would affect the second presidential debate.

Most everyone agreed that Trump would have to be very contrite and make a sincere apology during the debate. However, they also agreed that it would not be in Trump's nature to do that.

STORY

There is always more to the story when a candidate like Trump tries to move the discussion away from his own transgressions by staging an event to discredit his opponent. Minutes before the start of the second debate, Trump brought out three women that he had paid to come to the debate in order to accuse Bill Clinton of sexual abuse. One of them, in the late 1970s, had signed a deposition stating that no sexual contact had occurred with Bill Clinton. But years later, after hearing Hillary speak about accusations of sexual abuse, she changed her mind and accused him of rape.

The second women said Bill Clinton groped her in the White House Oval Office back in 1993, but nothing had ever come out of that accusation.

The third women said she had accompanied Bill Clinton to his hotel room in 1991 where he had propositioned her. In 1994, she filed a federal lawsuit against Clinton, alleging sexual harassment. The case was dismissed.

Trump brought in the fourth woman for a completely different reason: Trump claimed that Hillary had been the defense attorney for a man accused of attacking the woman back when she was twelve years old. Trump said Hillary had gotten the guilty man off. (Actually, the man had been found guilty and was sentenced to prison.)

The facts were that it was a rape case that took place when Hillary was a 27-year old attorney working at a legal aid clinic that provided free legal advice for the poor. The case involved a twelve-year old girl who claimed she had been raped after she went for a ride in a car with three men. She said she had consensual sex with one of the men, but she said after that, one of the other men had raped her. The accused man said she had consensual sex with both of them. Hillary was assigned to defend the man, but she tried to get out of it. However, she was unsuccessful, and after the man passed a lie detector test, she finally agreed to defend him. At the trial, on her advice, the man agreed to plead guilty. He was sentenced to five years in prison, but the judge, as part of the agreement to plead guilty, reduced his prison term to only one year.

After the conviction, the girl said she bore no ill will toward Ms. Clinton because she was just "doing her job" to represent the man.

However, later she said she blamed Hillary and a taped interview was found in which Hillary can be heard laughing about the case. Trump used segments of that tape to attack Hillary, even though the interviewer said Hillary was only laughing about the validity of lie detector tests.

Some called Trump's event a "stunt" that used women whose stories had long been known and previously investigated. Everyone agreed that it was a desperate attempt to divert attention away from the Access Hollywood audio tape before it was brought up in the debates.

The Second Debate

The first question at the second presidential debate was about whether the candidates were modeling appropriate and positive behavior for today's youth. The moderator said to Trump, "You described kissing women without consent, grabbing their genitals. That is sexual assault. You bragged that you have sexually assaulted women. Do you understand that?"

Trump replied, "No, I didn't say that at all. I don't think you understood what was — this was locker room talk. I'm not proud of it. I apologized . . . But this is locker room talk." Then he quickly tried to change the subject to talk about ISIS.

The moderator tried again to get Trump to answer the question, but Trump would only say, over and over again, that he had great respect for women. He then quickly changed the subject to illegal immigration and law and order.

The moderator then asked Hillary about it.

She said she had disagreed with prior Republican nominees for president, but she had never questioned their fitness to serve. She went on to say, "Donald Trump is different . . . What we all saw and heard on Friday was Donald talking about women, what he thinks about women, what he does to women . . . I think it's clear to anyone who heard it that it represents exactly who he is." She went on to point out that Trump had also insulted many others, immigrants, African-Americans, Latinos, people with disabilities, POWs, and Muslims.

To that, Trump said, "It's just words, folks. It's just words." He went on to say she had failed as a senator and that she had done "a terrible job for the African-Americans."

The moderator then said they had to move on to another question from the audience, but Trump complained that Hillary was getting more time to respond than he was.

The next audience question was also about the Access Hollywood audio tape. It was, "When you walked off that bus at age 59, were you a different man or did that behavior continue until just recently?"

Trump simply repeated what he had said before, that it was only "locker room talk." He again attacked Bill Clinton, saying that what he had done was much worse. He said four women who had accused Bill Clinton of sexual misconduct were there in the debate audience.

Hillary responded to Trump's attack on her husband by simply saying, Trump could "run his campaign any way he chooses. "She went on to quote Michelle Obama's advice: "When they go low, you go high." Despite warnings from the moderators to keep quiet, that statement drew loud applause from the audience. Hillary went on to say the audience could draw their own conclusions about whether or not the man in the video or the man on the stage respects women. She said Trump never apologizes, reminding them that he never apologized to Mr. and Mrs. Khan, the distinguished federal judge from Indiana, the disabled reporter he had mimicked, and he never apologized for the racist lie that President Obama was not born in the United States.

To that, Trump responded by saying Hillary should apologize for starting the birther movement. He then went on to once again refer to the 33,000 e-mails that he said she had deleted, and he said if he was elected president, he would instruct his attorney general to get a special prosecutor to look into Hillary.

Hillary replied, "Everything he just said is absolutely false, but I'm not surprised."

Trump interrupted with, "Oh, really?"

Hillary continued, saying that if she spent all her time fact-checking everything Trump said, she'd never get to talk about how to make lives better for people. She added, "It's just awfully good that someone with the temperament of Donald Trump is not in charge of the law in our country."

Trump interrupted with, "Because you'd be in jail."

That comment drew loud applause from the Trump supporters in the audience.

The moderator then turned to Hillary to ask her about her handling of e-mail when she was Secretary of State.

Hillary answered that she took responsibility for that, and it was a mistake. She said she was sorry about it. However, she said that after a year-long investigation, there was no evidence that any classified material ended up in the wrong hands.

Trump responded by saying, "She's lying again, because she said she — you know, what she did with the e-mail was fine. You think it was fine to delete 33,000 e-mails? I don't think so." He then launched into an attack on President Obama and the U.S. Attorney General, implying that they had colluded to keep Hillary from getting into trouble about her e-mails.

At this point, the moderators tried to move on to the next question, but Trump tried to continue talking about Hillary's e-mails.

When it was Hillary's turn, she started to talk, but Trump again interrupted, continuing to talk about her e-mails.

The moderator asked him to let her talk.

She tried again, but again Trump interrupted with the same charges about her deleting e-mails, and again the moderator asked him to let her talk. This went on for quite a while with Hillary trying to talk and Trump not letting her and the moderator unsuccessfully trying to get him to stop interrupting, saying, "Please allow her to respond. She didn't talk while you talked."

Hillary said, "Yes, that's true, I didn't."

Trump again interrupted with, "Because you have nothing to say."

And it continued. Hillary trying to respond, Trump continuing to interrupt, and the moderator unsuccessfully trying to get him to stop.

Finally, Hillary gave up and asked if they couldn't just move on to questions from the audience.

The moderator tried to read a question from the audience about health care, but Trump wouldn't let it go. He challenged the moderator, saying, "I'd like to know why aren't you bringing up the e-mails? I'd like to know. Why aren't you bringing . . . it hasn't been finished at all."

When the moderator again tried to move on to another question, Trump complained "It's nice—one on three."

When a question about the Affordable Care Act came up, Hillary was asked to respond.

Trump said he would let her reply because, "I'm a gentleman."

That got a round of loud laughter from the audience.

Hillary said she knew Trump would say he was going to just get rid of it, but she said she was going to fix the Affordable Care Act. She said it had allowed 20 million people to get insurance who didn't have it before.

When it was Trump's turn to answer the question, he said, "Obamacare is a disaster. You know it. We all know it." He said he would replace it with a health program that was "the finest health care plan there is."

The moderator asked Trump for more specifics, but Trump just went back to criticizing Obamacare.

The next question was from an audience member who said she was one of the 3.3 million Muslims in the United States. She asked how the candidates would deal with Islamophobia and with Muslims being labeled as a threat to the country.

Trump said she was right about Islamophobia, and it was a shame. But he said, "There is a problem. I mean, whether we like it or not, and we could be very politically correct, but whether we like it or not, there is a problem. And we have to be sure that Muslims come in and report when they see something going on. When they see hatred going on, they have to report it . . . in San Bernardino, many people saw the bombs all over the apartment of the two people that killed 14 and wounded many, many people. Horribly wounded. They'll never be the same. Muslims have to report the problems when they see them." He went on to mention Orlando, San Bernardino, the World Trade Center, and Paris, describing them as "radical Islamic terrorists." He said, "She won't even mention the word, and nor will President Obama. He won't use the term "radical Islamic terrorism."

When Hillary was invited to respond, she moved closer to the person who had asked the question and said she had heard the same question from a lot of Muslim-Americans. She said, "Unfortunately, there's been a lot of very divisive, dark things said about Muslims. And even someone like Captain Khan, the young man who sacrificed himself defending our country in the United States Army, has been subject to attack by Donald." She added that there had been Muslims living in America since George Washington, and that there had been many successful Muslims. She said it was "short-sighted and even dangerous to be engaging in the kind of demagogic rhetoric that Donald has about Muslims. We need American Muslims to be part of our eyes and ears on our front lines." She said that in order to defeat ISIS, we need to work with majority Muslim nations. "A lot of those nations are hearing what Donald says and wondering, why should we cooperate with the Americans?"

She said Trump's words were "a gift to ISIS and the terrorists, violent jihadist terrorists."

The moderator asked Trump a follow-up question about his call for a "total and complete shutdown of Muslims entering the United States."

Trump said Captain Khan is an American hero, but then he added if he was president at that time, Khan would be alive today. He said he would not have sent troops to Iraq. Finally, he said the Muslim ban had "morphed into a extreme vetting."

The moderator asked why it morphed, and Trump replied by saying, "Why don't you interrupt her? You interrupt me all the time."

When the moderator persisted, Trump said, "It's called extreme vetting." He said Hillary wanted "to allow a 550 percent increase," and he added it was going to be "the great Trojan horse of all time."

When the moderator asked Hillary if we should take the risk of having those refugees come into the country, she answered by saying she wouldn't let anyone into the country that posed a risk. She went on to point out that Trump had said he was going to ban people based on a religion, and she asked how could that be done. "We are a country founded on religious freedom and liberty." She added that Trump's insistence that he had been against the Iraq War from the beginning had been debunked by many press sources.

Trump interrupted to say, "That's not been debunked."

Hillary tried to go on, but Trump again said, "That has not been debunked."

Hillary said the viewer could go to her web site to see the evidence.

Trump said, "I was against — I was against the war in Iraq. Has not been debunked. And you voted for it. And you shouldn't have."

The moderator said there had been a lot of fact-checking on that and it was time to move on to another question.

Trump said, "Excuse me. She just went about 25 seconds over her time."

After a bit of back and forth, the moderator allowed him to respond. However, Trump did not respond to the question. Instead, he talked about all the criminal illegal aliens that were coming into the country, murderers, drug lords, drug problems. He said that when Hillary Clinton was Secretary of State, she said it was okay.

The moderator next asked about WikiLeaks release of purported excerpts of Secretary Clinton's paid speeches in which she said you need both a public and private position on certain issues.

Hillary replied that as she recalled, she was talking about how, in the movie, "Lincoln," Abraham Lincoln was able to get the Congress to approve the 13th Amendment by strategically using a different argument with different people. She said she thought that was a great display of presidential leadership. She then went on to criticize WikiLeaks as being part of Russia's attempt to influence the U.S. election to try to help Trump get elected. She then said Trump should release his tax returns so the people could find out what his relationships with Russia were.

Trump said she had been caught in a lie and was trying to blame her lie on the late, great Abraham Lincoln.

That got a round of laughter from the audience.

He went on, "Honest Abe, Honest Abe never lied. That's the good thing. That's the big difference between Abraham Lincoln and you. That's a big, big difference. We're talking about some difference." He then went on to say he didn't know Putin, but there was no way to say it was Russia doing the hacking. "Maybe there is no hacking. But they always blame Russia." He again said he couldn't release his taxes until the audit was complete, and he said many of Hillary's friends took the same kinds of tax deductions as he had.

The next question from the audience was also about taxes, and both candidates took some time to claim their economic policy would be the best for the country. Hillary, referring to recently-released copy of Trump's 1995 taxes in which he had claimed a

$916 million loss to avoided paying personal federal income taxes, said it was unfortunate that Trump paid zero in taxes and was therefore not helping the country.

Trump said Hillary's donors had also taken massive tax write-offs." But when the moderator pressed him about whether he had actually paid personal federal income tax, he said a lot of his write-offs had been depreciation, things that Hillary as a senator had allowed. He said, "See, I understand the tax code better than anybody that's ever run for president."

The moderator then asked him how many years he had avoided paying federal income taxes.

Trump wouldn't answer that question, but he said he did pay some taxes. He then repeated that Hillary had been "doing it" for thirty years and doesn't do anything but talk. "With her, it's all talk and no action."

The moderator tried to ask another question but Trump interrupted by bringing up Bernie Sanders, saying she had "really bad judgment," not only about taxes but also about Libya and Syria and Iraq. He said the way her and Obama got out of Iraq left a vacuum and that's why ISIS formed in the first place. "They started from that little area, and now they're in 32 different nations, Hillary. Congratulations. Great job."

Hillary responded by saying, "He has now said repeatedly, '30 years this and 30 years that.' So let me talk about my 30 years in public service. I'm very glad to do so." She went on to recount some of her accomplishments.

The moderator tried to move on to the next audience question but Trump interrupted with, "She said a lot of things that were false. I mean, I think we should be allowed to maybe—"

The moderator said, "No, Mr. Trump, we're going to go on. This is about the audience."

But Trump again interrupted with, "Excuse me. Because she has been a disaster as a senator. A disaster."

The moderator said, "Mr. Trump, we're going to move on."

The next question was about the humanitarian crisis in Syria.

Hillary said the situation in Syria "was catastrophic," and after describing the situation there, she added that Russia hadn't been paying any attention to ISIS and that she would advocate a no-fly zone and safe zones.

Trump accused Hillary of being involved in the so-called line in the sand in Syria, even though it was after she was no longer Secretary of State. He also criticized her for being "in favor" of the rebels in Syria, suggesting that they might be worse than the people in charge. He also criticized the agreement with Iran, saying we gave them enough cash to "fill up this room."

The moderator said Trump's time was up, but Trump said he had one more thing to say. The moderator repeated that his time was up, but Trump went on to say, "Russia is killing ISIS. And Iran is killing ISIS. And those three have now lined up because of our weak foreign policy."

The moderator repeated that his time was up, but Trump wouldn't stop talking: "I don't like Assad at all, but Assad is killing ISIS."

The moderator said, "Mr. Trump, let me repeat the question."

That got a lot of laughter from the audience.

The moderator finally got the question in, she again asked about Syria and reminded Trump that his running mate said if provocations by Russia continue, the U.S. should be prepared to use military force to strike the military targets of the Assad regime.

Trump said he disagreed with that.

The moderator said, " You disagree with your running mate?"

Trump wasn't willing to answer that question, and instead said we should focus on ISIS. He said, "Syria is fighting ISIS . . . Syria is Russia and it's Iran who she made strong." He added that he believed Aleppo had already fallen, and then he switched to talk about Mosul, saying he had a big problem with the stupidity of our foreign policy, and he said he had 200 generals and admirals and 21 Congressional Medal of Honor recipients who endorsed him.

The moderator asked Trump about what his strategy would be.

Trump again mentioned the 200 admirals and generals that

supported him, and he said, "General George Patton, General Douglas MacArthur are spinning in their grave at the stupidity of what we're doing in the Middle East."

The moderator then asked Hillary what she would do about Syria.

Hillary said she would not use American ground forces in Syria. She said she preferred the use of special forces as trainers, target the leaders of ISIS, and consider arming the Kurds.

Trump said, "You know what's funny? She went over a minute over, and you don't stop her. When I go one second over, it's like a big deal . . . It's really - it's really very interesting."

The moderator moved on to another question from the audience about whether the candidates would be "a devoted president to all the people in the United States?"

Trump said he would, and then he reminded the audience that Hillary had called "our people deplorable, a large group, and irredeemable." He then changed the subject to trade policies, specifically NAFTA, which he called "perhaps the greatest disaster trade deal in the history of the world." He then said he would be a president for all of the people and said, "African-Americans, the inner cities. Devastating what's happening to our inner cities. She's been talking about it for years. As usual, she talks about it, nothing happens. Same with the Latino-Americans, the Hispanic-Americans. The same exact thing. They talk, they don't get it done. You go into the inner cities and — you see it's 45 percent poverty. African-Americans now 45 percent poverty in the inner cities. The education is a disaster. Jobs are essentially nonexistent."

The moderator thanked him and tried to move on, but Trump continued with, "She's all talk. It doesn't get done."

The moderator said his time was up, but he added, "It turned out to be a disaster."

When Hillary got her chance to respond, she recounted some of her accomplishments including her two terms in the Senate. She went on to say she gets letters from immigrants who are worried that Trump would send them back to their countries of origin. She said kids were uneasy, bullying was up, and teachers and parents were calling it "the Trump effect."

The moderator said her time was up, but she added, "Democrats, Republicans, independents, people across our country. If you don't vote for me, I still want to be your president."

The moderator then asked about her comment that half of Donald Trump's supporters were deplorables, racist, sexist, homophobic, xenophobic, Islamophobic.

Hillary replied that she was sorry about the way she stated that. She added that her argument was not with his supporters but with him and his hateful and divisive campaign. She said he was inciting violence at his rallies, and making very brutal kinds of comments about not just women, but all Americans.

When it was Trump's turn to respond, he said, "We have a divided nation." He mentioned Charlotte, Baltimore, Chicago, and Washington, D.C. as examples. He said we have a divided nation, because "She has tremendous hate in her heart . . . when she said deplorables, she meant it . . . She's got tremendous hatred."

The moderator then asked Trump about discipline, and reminded him about his series of tweets from 3 AM. to 5 AM, including one that told people to check out a sex tape.

Trump said, "No, there wasn't check out a sex tape. It was just take a look at the person that she built up to be this wonderful Girl Scout who was no Girl Scout."

The moderator said, "You mentioned a sex tape."

Trump replied, "Just so you understand, when she said 3 o'clock in the morning, take a look at Benghazi. She said who is going to answer the call at 3 o'clock in the morning? Guess what? She didn't answer it, because when Ambassador Stevens—"

The moderator interrupted him to say, "The question is, is that the discipline of a good leader?" Trump replied, "Who's going — the famous thing, we're going to answer our call at 3 o'clock in the morning. Guess what happened? Ambassador Stevens — Ambassador Stevens sent 600 requests for help."

When it was Hillary's turn, she said it was not only her opinion that Trump would not be a good leader, it was also the opinion of many Republicans and former Republican members of Congress.

Trump said, "We have the slowest growth since 1929."

The moderator tried to stop him but Trump added, "It is our country has the slowest growth and jobs are a disaster."

The moderator said, "Thank you very much both of you," which drew loud laughter from the audience.

The next question from the audience was about what kind of person the candidates would appoint to the Supreme Court.

Hillary said she would appoint a Supreme Court justice who had real life experience, a justice that had actually tried some cases. She said she wanted the Supreme Court to maintain the Roe v. Wade decision and marriage equality. She criticized the names of the judges Trump had suggested, and she said she thought the Congress had been derelict in their duty when they failed to even consider the Supreme Court candidate the president had put forward.

Trump said he would appoint a justice in the mold of Justice Scalia, a person who would respect the Constitution and the Second Amendment. He then went on to criticize Hillary for taking contributions from corporations and asked why she didn't fund her own campaign like he was doing.

Hillary said she respected the Second Amendment, but believed there should be comprehensive background checks, and that the gun show and online loopholes should be closed.

The next question was from an audience member who asked about the candidates energy policies.

Trump replied that energy is under siege by the Obama administration. He said the EPA was killing energy companies. He accused China of dumping steel and said Hillary wanted to put coal miners out of work.

Hillary replied that Trump had used illegal Chinese steel to build his buildings.

She went on to say that when she was a senator she had voted to make sure that we didn't get taken advantage of by China on steel or anything else. She pointed out that the U.S. is now energy-independent and no longer dependent upon the Middle East.

The final question from the audience was, "Regardless of the current rhetoric, would either of you name one positive thing that you respect in one another?

At that, the audience applauded loudly.

Hillary said she respected Trump's children as incredibly able and devoted, and "that says a lot about Donald."

Trump said, "I will say this about Hillary. She doesn't quit. She doesn't give up. I respect that. I tell it like it is. She's a fighter. I disagree with much of what she's fighting for. I do disagree with her judgment in many cases. But she does fight hard, and she doesn't quit, and she doesn't give up. And I consider that to be a very good trait."

The moderators thanked the candidates and ended the debate.

Discussion of the Second Debate

Within hours, a national poll came out indicating that Hillary had won the debate, 57% to 34%.

Nevertheless, Trump was quick to dispute that: he said he won the debate "in a landslide," and that every poll proved it (he didn't provide any poll results).

There was post-debate talk about Trump's assertion that Hillary had **"hate in her heart,"** and his apparent "stalking " of her around the stage.

And of course, there was a lot of talk about **Trump's statement that if he was elected he would appoint a special prosecutor to try to have Hillary put in jail**. In fact, he said if he was in charge of the country's law enforcement agencies, Hillary **"would be in jail."** It reminded many of the kinds of post-election events they had seen in some of the darker parts of the world where losers in elections were routinely put in prison.

The most focused-on topic after the debate was Trump's response to questions about what he had said on the Access Hollywood audio tape. Trump had dismissed them as "nothing but locker room banter," and he said he had never actually done the things he bragged about doing on that audio tape. If Trump thought that would be the end of that story, he was sadly mistaken. **Soon after the conclusion of the second debate, women began to come forward to describe Trump's behavior toward them that matched what he had bragged about in the audio tape.** They all described incidents in which Trump had made unwanted sexual advances toward them.

Trump was again put on the defensive, no longer just being accused of inappropriate "locker room" talk, but now being accused of actual sexual assault. As more and more women came forward, people began to talk about a "pattern of behavior" that was going to be hard for Trump to deny. **But Trump did deny it, every bit of it. He said all of the women were liars. He said they were being directed by Hillary's forces as part of a vast conspiracy against him.** He said all you had to do was "look at the women" to see that he wouldn't have made advances on them. He said he would soon present evidence to disprove their accusations.

However, as time went by, no real evidence from Trump was forthcoming. In fact, **some of the women backed up their testimonies with testimonies from their friends and relatives who confirmed that they had been told about the incidents at the time they happened.**

As many of the women who were making accusations against Trump were being interviewed on TV, some people were insisting a man "like that" should never become president. They asked the voters to **imagine Trump's picture on the front wall of elementary schools and the teachers telling the kids that this was the man they should look up to for inspiration and guidance**.

When the news media continued to file stories about Trump's relationships with women and his poll numbers continued to drop, **Trump started saying the election was "rigged."**

That was the heated environment going into the third debate. Hillary was pulling farther and farther ahead in the polls, and most everyone agreed that the third and final debate would be Trump's last chance to somehow pull out a miracle win.

STORY

Just before the start of the third and final presidential debate, **WikiLeaks began releasing what they said were hacked e-mails from members of Hillary's campaign staff** and some transcripts from speeches she had made after she had left office.

Trump made much of the hacked e-mails, implying that they proved Washington "insiders" like Hillary **said one thing in public and then said something quite different in their private e-mails**.

Hillary's campaign staff said they could not verify the accuracy of the information in the supposedly hacked e-mails, and pointed out the fact that **U.S. intelligence officials had said they believed the e-mail hacking had been done by someone with connections to the Russian state**. Therefore, even if some of the e-mails were real, they might have been "doctored."

To some, it reminded of Trump's earlier statements saying he admired Vladimir Putin, and of the time Trump had invited the Russians to hack into Hillary's e-mail system.

They also remembered the prior hacked e-mails that had been embarrassing to the Democrats during their national convention. Some members of Hillary's campaign staff said **it was obvious that the Russians were interfering in the U.S. presidential election to try to help Trump get elected**.

Nevertheless, Trump continued mentioning the hacked e-mails in almost every public statement. Many wondered if he would bring them up in the final debate.

In the end, if people believed what they were hearing about the hacked e-mails, all it did was provide a glimpse into the inner workings of a political campaign. Since none of the hacked e-mails were from Hillary, the information probably didn't affect the election as much as the Republicans hoped.

The Third Debate

The third and final presidential debate of 2016 began with a question about who the candidates would put on the Supreme Court.

Hillary said she would like to have a Supreme Court that would maintain Roe v. Wade and "stand up against Citizens United."

Trump said we needed a Supreme Court with "a conservative bent" that would protect the Second Amendment.

After Hillary said she supported a woman's right to choose, Trump said late-term, partial-birth abortions were "terrible." He said if you go with what Hillary wants, you could "Rip the baby out of the womb of the mother just prior to the birth of the baby."

Hillary called that "a scare tactic," and she said she didn't believe the government should be making those kinds of decisions for a mother.

The moderator tried to go on, but Trump interrupted to say they were doing it as late as one day prior to birth."

The moderator then moved to the subject of immigration, and Trump accused Hillary of wanting "to give amnesty, which is a disaster." He then went on to say that there were four mothers in the audience whose children had been killed by illegal immigrants. He added, "We have no country if we have no border."

Hillary responded by talking about the 11 million undocumented people that had 4 million American citizen children. She said Trump's plan to deport them would mean "a massive law enforcement presence" that would go from school to school, home to home, business to business, to round up people. She said we are "a nation of immigrants." She said Trump had "started his campaign by bashing immigrants and calling Mexican immigrants rapists and criminals and drug dealers."

Trump responded by talking about the need for "a wall" and said Obama had deported millions. He said citizenship for those who had entered the country illegally was unfair to those who were waiting to enter legally. He accused Hillary of wanting open borders, but she immediately denied it.

The moderator then asked Hillary about a WikiLeaks report that she had given a speech in which she was in favor of open borders.

Hillary said she was only talking about open borders with regard to energy. And then she went on to say what was really important about the WikiLeaks report was that the Russian government was engaging in espionage against Americans by hacking American web sites and American accounts of private people and institutions. She said 17 U.S. intelligence services had confirmed that the Russians where trying to influence the U.S. presidential election. She then asked Trump to condemn that.

Trump responded that he was willing to talk about Putin. He said that although he didn't know Putin, he had said "nice things about me. If we got along well, that would be good." He then tried to switch the topic to how many more nuclear warheads Russia had than us, but the moderator tried to interrupt.

Hillary jumped in to say Putin favored Trump because "He'd rather have a puppet as president of the United States."

Trump replied, "You're the puppet."

Hillary went on to say that it was unprecedented to have a foreign government trying to interfere in our election."

Trump replied that "She has no idea whether it's Russia, China, or anybody else."

Hillary said she was quoting 17 intelligence agencies.

Trump said, "Our country has no idea."

Hillary said, "He'd rather believe Vladimir Putin than the military and civilian intelligence professionals who are sworn to protect us."

Trump said, "She doesn't like Putin because Putin has outsmarted her at every step of the way."

The moderator tried to bring the discussion back to the topic, but Trump wouldn't stop talking. He kept saying, "Putin has outsmarted her in Syria . . . He's outsmarted her every step of the way."

The moderator asked Trump if he condemned any interference by Russia in the American election?

Trump said he did condemn, but if the United States got along with Russia, it "wouldn't be so bad." He then went back to saying Russia had outsmarted Hillary and they had more nuclear weapons.

Hillary replied that she found it ironic that Trump would want to talk about nuclear weapons because he had "been very cavalier, even casual about the use of nuclear weapons."

Trump interrupted with, "Wrong."

Hillary went on to say there is only about "four minutes between the order being given and the people responsible for launching nuclear weapons to do so. And that's why 10 people who have had that awesome responsibility have come out and, in an unprecedented way, said they would not trust Donald Trump with the nuclear codes or to have his finger on the nuclear button."

Trump said he had "200 generals and admirals, 21 endorsing me, 21 congressional Medal of Honor recipients." He went on to say we needed to renegotiate our defense agreements.

The moderator tried to intervene, but Trump went on to say, "She's been proven to be a liar on so many different ways. This is just another lie."

Hillary said she was only quoting him.

Trump said, "There's no quote. You're not going to find a quote from me."

Hillary went on to say the United States had kept the peace through alliances. "Donald wants to tear up our alliances."

The moderator than asked about business regulations.

Hillary responded by outlining her plan to create jobs and improve economic growth in a way that would help small business. She said that people who work full time "should not still be in poverty." She added that women should get equal pay, and that there should be more technical education and apprenticeships in schools. She said her economic plan had been analyzed by independent experts who said that it could produce 10 million new jobs. "By contrast, Donald's plan has been analyzed to conclude it might lose 3.5 million jobs." She said his whole plan was to give the biggest tax breaks ever to the wealthy and to corporations, which would add $20 trillion to our debt and cause the kind of dislocation that we have seen before. She said it would be "trickle-down economics on steroids."

Trump replied that Hillary's plan would raise taxes, "even double your taxes. Her tax plan is a disaster." He then went back to talking about why our NATO allies were not paying their fair share.

Hillary said, "Well, let me translate that, if I can."

Trump interrupted to say, "You can't."

She went on to say she would not raise taxes on anyone making $250,000 or less, and that she would not "add a penny to the debt." She also pointed out that when her husband was president "We went from a $300 billion deficit to a $200 billion surplus."

Trump replied that the U.S. economy was only growing at "right around the 1 percent level. And I think it's going down." He then started talking about NAFTA and how it had caused jobs to leave the U.S. He said it was "because of the bill that her husband signed, and she blessed 100 percent . . . She lied when she said she didn't call the Trans-Pacific Partnership the gold standard. She totally lied."

Hillary replied that she had voted against the Trans-Pacific Partnership and went on to say, "There's only one of us on this stage who's actually shipped jobs to Mexico, because that's Donald. He's shipped jobs to 12 countries, including Mexico." She said that she fought against the Chinese illegal dumping of steel and aluminum into our markets, but "Donald has bought Chinese steel and aluminum. In fact, the Trump Hotel right here in Las Vegas was made with Chinese steel. So he goes around with crocodile tears about how terrible it is, but he has given jobs to Chinese steelworkers, not American steelworkers."

Trump said, "She's been doing this for 30 years. Why the hell didn't you do it over the last 15, 20 years? . . . I say the one thing you have over me is experience, but it's bad experience . . . if you say that I use steel or I use something else, I -- make it impossible for me to do that." He then went on to say that when she ran the State Department, $6 billion was missing. "If you become president, this country is going to be in some mess. Believe me."

Hillary replied that what he said about the State Department had been debunked numerous times, and she went on to recount some of the important things she had done for the country while he was getting sued by the Justice Department for racial discrimination." She said that while she was working to reform the schools in Arkansas, Trump was borrowing $14 million from his father to start his businesses. She added that she had worked on women's rights, while he was insulting a former Miss Universe, Alicia Machado. "He called her an eating machine."

Trump interrupted to say, "Give me a break."

Hillary went on, saying, "On the day when I was in the Situation Room, monitoring the raid that brought Osama bin Laden to justice, he was hosting the Celebrity Apprentice."

Trump replied that he had "built a massive company, a great company, some of the greatest assets anywhere in the world . . . if we could run our country the way I've run my company, we would have a country that you would be so proud of." He went on to mention Syria, Libya, and Iraq. "She gave us ISIS, because her and Obama created this huge vacuum."

The moderator then mentioned the fact that Trump had said his talk about grabbing women was just talk, but since then, nine women have come forward to say that you either groped them or kissed them without their consent. He asked why would "so many different women from so many different circumstances over so many different years, why would they all in this last couple of weeks make up -- you deny this -- why would they all make up these stories?"

Trump said the women's stories had been largely debunked. He then switched to an accusation that all the violence at his rallies were being caused by her and Obama. He said they paid people to "be violent, cause fights, do bad things." He then said he hadn't even apologized to his wife because he didn't do anything to those women and he didn't know any of those women, and that they were either doing it for fame or else Hillary's campaign had put them up to it. He said it was "all fiction . . . all lies."

Hillary said, "We heard Donald talking about what he did to women. And after that, a number of women have come forward saying that's exactly what he did to them. Now, what was his response? . . . he said that he could not possibly have done those things to those women because they were not attractive enough for them to be assaulted.

Trump interrupted with, "I did not say that. I did not say that."

The moderator told Trump to give Hillary her two minutes to respond, but Trump again interrupted with. "I did not say that."

The moderator again told Trump to give Hillary her two minutes.

Hillary went on with more quotes: "He went on to say, 'Look at her. I don't think so.' . . . wouldn't be my first choice.' He attacked the woman reporter writing the story, called her "disgusting," as he has called a number of women during this campaign. Donald thinks belittling women makes him bigger. He goes after their dignity, their self-worth, and I don't think there is a woman anywhere who doesn't know what that feels like. So we now know what Donald thinks and what he says and how he acts toward women. That's who Donald is."

Trump said, "Nobody has more respect for women than I do." That got a laugh out of the audience, but Trump continued, saying, the women's stories were "all fiction." He added, "But what wasn't fiction was her e-mails. "33,000 e-mails criminally, criminally." We have a great general, four-star general . . . going to potentially serve five years in jail for lying to the FBI. One lie. She's lied hundreds of times to the people, to Congress, and to the FBI . . . That's really what you should be talking about, not fiction, where somebody wants fame or where they come out of her crooked campaign."

Hillary responded, she said whenever he is "pushed on something which is obviously uncomfortable, like what these women are saying, he immediately goes to denying responsibility. And it's not just about women. He never apologizes or says he's sorry for anything. So we know what he has said and what he's done to women. But he also went after a disabled reporter, mocked and mimicked him on national television."

Trump interrupted with, "Wrong."

Hillary continued, "He went after Mr. and Mrs. Khan, the parents of a young man who died serving our country, a Gold Star family, because of their religion. He went after John McCain, a prisoner of war, said he prefers "people who aren't captured." He went after a federal judge, born in Indiana, but who Donald said couldn't be trusted to try the fraud and racketeering case against Trump University because his parents were Mexican. So it's not one thing. This is a pattern, a pattern of divisiveness, of a very dark, and in many ways dangerous vision of our country, where he incites violence, where he applauds people who are pushing and pulling and punching at his rallies. That is not who America is."

Trump replied, "So sad when she talks about violence at my rallies, and she caused the violence."

The moderator then asked Hillary about the Clinton Foundation. He said, "Why isn't it what Mr. Trump calls pay to play?"

Hillary responded that everything she did as Secretary of State was in furtherance of our country's interests and our values. She went on to say she was very proud of the Clinton Foundation and the great work it had done.

The moderator interrupted her to say the question had been about pay to play.

Hillary tried to respond that there had been no evidence of that, but Trump interrupted, saying it had been very well studied. He said the Clinton Foundation "is a criminal enterprise, and so many people know it."

Hillary responded that the foundation had the highest rating and that it gave 90 percent of the money to charity. She said she was happy to compare it with the Trump Foundation that took money from people and bought a six- foot portrait of Trump himself. She said, "I mean, who does that? It just was astonishing."

Trump replied that the Trump Foundation was a small foundation and that 100 percent of the money goes to charity instead of buying boats or airplanes. The moderator said, "Wasn't some of the money used to settle your lawsuits, sir?"

Trump said, "No, it was -- we put up the American flag. And that's it. They put up the American flag. We fought for the right in Palm Beach to put up the American flag."

The moderator said, "Right. But there was a penalty that was imposed by Palm Beach County, and the money came from your foundation."

Trump replied that the money "went to Fisher House, where they build houses for veterans and disabled vets."

Hillary interrupted to say, "But, of course, there's no way we can know whether any of that is true, because he hasn't released his tax returns." She said what was really troubling was that he hadn't paid a penny in federal income tax. She said half of all undocumented immigrants in our country actually pay federal income tax. "So we have undocumented immigrants in America who are paying more federal income tax than a billionaire. I find that just astonishing."

The moderator tried to go on, but Trump interrupted with, "We're entitled because of the laws that people like her passed to take massive amounts of depreciation on other charges, and we do it." He said her donors did the same thing.

The moderator tried to move on, but Trump persisted, saying, "And you know, Hillary, what you should have done, you should have changed the law when you were a United States senator."

The moderator again tried to move on, but Trump kept on repeating the same thing about her donors and how she should have changed the law. He said he sits in his apartment in his very beautiful Trump hotel down the street "watching ad after ad after ad, false ad. All paid for by your friends on Wall Street that gave so much money because they know you're going to protect them. And, frankly, you should have changed the laws."

The moderator again tried to go on, but Trump repeated, "If you don't like what I did, you should have changed the laws."

When the moderator was finally able to break in, he mentioned what Trump had been saying at his rallies, that the election was "rigged." He then asked Trump if he would accept the result of the election.

Trump said, "I will look at it at the time. I'm not looking at anything now. I'll look at it at the time.

The moderator tried again to ask the same question, would Trump accept the result of the election.

Trump said if you looked at the voter rolls, you would see millions of people that are registered to vote that shouldn't be registered to vote. He then went on to talk about "the corrupt media." And then he said, "I'll tell you one other thing. She shouldn't be allowed to run. It's crooked, she's, she's guilty of a very, very serious crime. She should not be allowed to run. And just in that respect, I say it's rigged, because she should never she should never have been allowed to run for the presidency based on what she did with e-mails and so many other things."

The moderator said, "But, sir, there is a tradition in this country —in fact, one of the prides of this country—is the peaceful transition of power and that no matter how hard-fought a campaign is, that at the end of the campaign that the loser concedes to the winner. Not saying that you're necessarily going to be the loser or the winner, but that the loser concedes to the winner and that the country comes together in part for the good of the country. Are you saying you're not prepared now to commit to that principle?"

Trump replied, "What I'm saying is that I will tell you at the time. I'll keep you in suspense. OK?"

Hillary joined in to say, "Every time Donald thinks things are not going in his direction, he claims whatever it is, is rigged against him. The FBI conducted a year-long investigation into my e-mails. They concluded there was no case. He said the FBI was rigged. He lost the Iowa caucus. He lost the Wisconsin primary. He said the Republican primary was rigged against him. Then Trump University gets sued for fraud and racketeering; he claims the court system and the federal judge is rigged against him. There was even a time when he didn't get an Emmy for his TV program three years in a row and he started tweeting that the Emmys were rigged against him."

Trump interrupted to say, "Should have gotten it."

That got a laugh out of the audience.

Hillary went on to say, "This is a mindset . . . it's also really troubling . . . that is not the way our democracy works. We've been around for 240 years. We've had free and fair elections. We've accepted the outcomes when we may not have liked them. And that is what must be expected of anyone standing on a debate stage during a general election. You know, President Obama said the other day when you're whining before the game is even finished."

That got loud applause from the audience, but Hillary went on: "It just shows you're not up to doing the job . . . let's be clear about what he is saying and what that means. He is denigrating, talking down our democracy. And I, for one, am appalled that somebody who is the nominee of one of our two major parties would take that kind of position."

Trump replied, "I think what the FBI did and what the Department of Justice did, including meeting with her husband, the attorney general, in the back of an airplane on the tarmac in Arizona, I think it's disgraceful. I think it's a disgrace."

The moderator tried to intervene, but Trump added, "I think we've never had a situation so bad in this country."

That got applause from the audience.

The moderator moved on to the next topic, foreign hot spots. He asked the candidates how they would deal with the situation in Syria.

Hillary said she was encouraged by the efforts of the Iraqi army and their American advisors. She went on to say she would not support putting American soldiers into Iraq as an occupying force. She said she would push for a no-fly zone and safe havens within Syria.

Trump said, "We lost Mosul in the first place because she took everybody out." He said there was no chance of getting the ISIS leaders because they had lost "the element of surprise." He said Douglas MacArthur and George Patton would be "spinning in their graves when they see the stupidity of our country." He went on to imply that the only reason the Iraqis were trying to retake Mosul was to help Hillary win the election.

When it was Hillary's turn, she tried to talk about Trump's prior position on Iraq, but Trump kept on interrupted her, saying "wrong" over and over again.

When she was finally able to continue, she said, "Mosul is a Sunni city. Mosul is on the border of Syria. And, yes, we do need to go after Baghdadi, just like we went after bin Laden while you were doing Celebrity Apprentice." She then said she was amazed that he would think "the Iraqi government and our allies and everybody else launched the attack on Mosul to help me in this election. But that's how Donald thinks. You know, he always is looking for some conspiracy."

Trump then interrupted her several times, but she kept on talking, saying, "He has all the conspiracy theories." She said he was unfit to be president, and "he proves it every time he talks."

Trump interrupted with, "No, you are the one that's unfit." Then he mentioned WikiLeaks and how it showed people were saying bad things about her.

The moderator then turned to the subject of Aleppo, but each time, he tried to ask a question, Trump interrupted. Finally, the moderator said, "Sir, if I may finish my question."

But Trump wouldn't stop. "OK, so it hasn't fallen. Take a look at it."

The moderator was finally able to speak, he said, "Well, there are a quarter of a million people still living there and being slaughtered."

Again, Trump interrupted him, saying "That's right. And they are being slaughtered because of bad decisions."

The moderator said, "If I may just finish here," and then he went on to ask Trump about his prior statement that Syria and Russia were busy fighting ISIS. He asked Trump if he would like to ""clear that up."

Trump replied that Aleppo is a disaster. Then he went on to say it was Hillary's fault. "A lot of this is because of Hillary Clinton, because what's happened is, by fighting Assad, who turned out to be a lot tougher than she thought, and now she's going to say, oh, he loves Assad, she's, he's just much tougher and much smarter than her and Obama. And everyone thought he was gone two years ago, three years ago. He aligned with Russia." Trump then turned to his prior statements about how much money the U.S. had given to Iran. "who we made very powerful." He went on to say, "We're backing rebels. We don't know who the rebels are. We're giving them lots of money, lots of everything. We don't know who the rebels are. And when and if, and it's not going to happen, because you have Russia and you have Iran now. But if they ever did overthrow Assad, you might end up with, as bad as Assad is, and he's a bad guy, but you may very well end up with worse than Assad. If she did nothing, we'd be in much better shape. And this is what's caused the great migration, where she's taking in tens of thousands of Syrian refugees, who probably in many cases -- not probably, who are definitely—"

The moderator tried to interrupt, but Trump continued to talk about the U.S. letting in refugees. The moderator again tried to talk, but Trump continued with, "Now have them in our country, and wait until you see. This is going to be the great Trojan horse. And wait until you see what happens in the coming years. Lots of luck, Hillary. Thanks a lot for doing a great job."

The moderator then asked Hillary about Aleppo, specifically about her saying there was a need for a no-fly zone there.

Hillary replied that she thought a no-fly zone could save lives and could hasten the end of the conflict. She added that "This would not be done just on the first day. This would take a lot of negotiation." She then responded to what Trump had said about refugees. She wasn't going to "slam the door on women and children," and she referred to the picture of a little 4-year-old boy who had been wounded in Aleppo. As far as letting terrorists into the country, she reminded Trump that the killer of the dozens of people at a nightclub in Orlando was born in Queens, the same place he had been born.

Trump replied that it was ridiculous to think "she will defeat ISIS. We should have never let ISIS happen in the first place. And right now, they're in 32 countries."

The moderator tried to move on, but Trump continued, saying,

"We should have, wait one second. They had a cease-fire . . . Russia took over vast swatches of land, and then they said we don't want the cease-fire anymore. We are so outplayed on missiles, on cease-fires. Nobody can believe how stupid our leadership is."

The moderator then moved on to the final topic, the national debt. He said under Hillary's plan, the national debt would rise to 86 percent of GDP. He said that under Trump's plan, it would rise to 105 percent of GDP.

Trump said the figures were wrong "because I'm going to create tremendous jobs, because we have a tremendous machine." He then went back to talking about how we were getting outsmarted by other countries.

Hillary responded, "When I hear Donald talk like that and know that his slogan is 'Make America Great Again,' I wonder when he thought America was great. And before he rushes and says, 'You know, before you and President Obama were there.' I think it's important to recognize that he has been criticizing our government for decades. Back in 1987, he took out a $100,000 ad in the New York Times, during the time when President Reagan was president, and basically said exactly what he just said now, that we were the laughingstock of the world. He was criticizing President Reagan. This is the way Donald thinks about himself, puts himself into, you know, the middle and says, 'You know, I alone can fix it.'" She went on to say her plan would not "add a penny to the national debt." She said, "You know, he started off with his dad as a millionaire—"

Trump interrupted with, "Yeah, yeah, we've heard, we've heard this before, Hillary."

Hillary said her dad was a small-business man—" but Trump again interrupted with, "We've heard this before."

Hillary finished her point about how differently they saw the world.

Trump then wanted to respond, but the moderator said they were running out of time.

Trump went on anyhow, defending himself by saying he did disagree with Ronald Reagan very strongly on trade.

The moderator then tried to go on, but Trump interrupted with, "And frankly, now we're going to do it right."

The moderator said the last topic was going to be about federal spending and about Medicare and Social Security. He asked the candidates how they were going to save them.

Trump said, "I'm cutting taxes. We're going to grow the economy. It's going to grow at a record rate of growth."

The moderator said, "That's not going to help in the entitlements."

Trump said, "No, it's going to totally help." He then went on to say we should repeal and replace the disaster known as Obamacare. He said, "It's destroying our country. You take a look at the kind of numbers that that will cost us in the year 17. It is a disaster. If we don't repeal and replace, now, it's probably going to die of its own weight. But Obamacare has to go. It's, the premiums are going up 60 percent, 70 percent, 80 percent. Next year they're going to go up over 100 percent."

Hillary answered the question by saying we needed to put more money into the Social Security Trust Fund. She said she would do that by raising taxes on the wealthy. She said, "My Social Security payroll contribution will go up, as will Donald's, assuming he can't figure out how to get out of it. But what we want to do is to replenish the Social Security Trust Fund—"

Trump interrupted with, "Such a nasty woman."

Hillary went on to say what Trump was proposing with his massive tax cuts would result in a $20 trillion additional national debt. That will have dire consequences for Social Security and Medicare, and if the Affordable Care Act was repealed, it would only make the Medicare problem worse.

At that point, Trump interrupted with, "Your husband disagrees with you."

The moderator then asked them both to make closing statements.

He asked Hillary to go first, and she said she wanted to reach out to all Americans, Democrats, Republicans, and independents. She said she wanted to grow the economy and make it fairer so it would work for everyone. She said, "We need your talents, your skills, your commitments, your energy, your ambition."

Trump said, "She's raising the money from the people she wants to control. Doesn't work that way." He said, "We're going to make America great. We have a depleted military. It has to be helped, has to be fixed. We have the greatest people on Earth in our military. We don't take care of our veterans. We take care of illegal immigrants, people that come into the country illegally, better than we take care of our vets. That can't happen. Our policemen and women are disrespected. We need law and order, but we need justice, too. Our inner cities are a disaster. You get shot walking to the store. They have no education. They have no jobs. I will do more for African-Americans and Latinos than she can ever do in 10 lifetimes. We cannot take four more years of Barack Obama, and that's what you get when you get her."

The moderator thanked them and closed the debate.

Discussion of the Third Debate

A national poll of debate watchers, taken right after the debate, indicated that most though Hillary had won the debate, 52% to 39%. Hillary also won on the question of who had the better understanding of the issues, 61% to 31%, and who was better prepared to handle the presidency, 59% to 35%. The two candidates were fairly even on all the other questions, except for the question about which of them was better able to handle foreign policy: Hillary won that one convincingly, 55% to 41%. However, there was a sharp divide about who won the debate based on education. Those who held a college degree said Clinton won by a wide margin, 58% to 33%. But those who did not have a four-year degree said Trump won by a 48% to 41% margin. Once again, the results showed how everyone was seeing this election through their own cognitive-reducing perspective.

The first polls that came out after the debate also indicated that Hillary had gained ground because of her debate performance.

Nevertheless, Trump and his supporters claimed Trump had

won the debate convincingly. They continued to say the polls were all wrong.

Much of the post debate discussion was about Trump's refusal to say he would accept the outcome of the election. Many elected officials, including a number of Republicans, came forward to condemn his words. Nevertheless, back on the campaign trail, Trump continued to say he was worried about voter fraud and how it might make him lose the election.

After the debate, there was a lot of news coverage of the ferocious fighting taking place in the on-going attack on Mosul by the Iraqi Army, and that led to talk about Trump's outrageous claim that the Iraqi Army's offensive against Mosul was only being done in order to help Hillary get elected, and how it revealed a lot about how Trump saw reality, how he believed the world revolved around him.

After the debate, even more women came out to accuse Trump of sexually molesting them, and Hillary made sure people didn't forget about that. In the debate, Trump had said the women's claims "had largely been debunked," but in fact, just the opposite was true: after the debate, friends and acquaintances of the women began coming forward to back up the accusations.

Even without Hillary's prompting, there was plenty of continuing commentary about how Trump felt about women, and both male and female Trump supporters were often being put on the spot with questions about why so many women would risk his wrath by coming forward with their stories. Trump and his supporters stuck to the story that they were all lying, having been "put up to it" by Hillary.

For weeks after the final debate, Wikileaks continued to post what they said were hacked e-mails from the Clinton camp, and several U.S. intelligence agencies continued to say the computer hacking was being done by the Russians. However, none of the hacked e-mails were attributed to Hillary herself, so it was not clear which of the candidates was being hurt by it—Hillary by the revelations about how a political campaign is actually run behind the scenes, or Trump by his continuing to appear that he was somehow alignment with Russia and that he approved of Russian cyber espionage.

People also wondered why Trump had said Hillary's forces were behind all the violence at his rallies. Apparently, he thought she was going to bring it up, and he had the reply that it was her fault ready.

Others found it odd that during the debate Trump had refused to say whether he wanted to see Roe v. Wade overturned, and there was a lot of talk about Trump's graphic descriptions of abortions that could occur one day before the birth of the child. Many doctors came forward to say that never happened.

One of the most talked about of Trump's word in the debate was his "Such a nasty woman" comment. It quickly became a hot topic on the internet, and somebody started printing signs and T-shirts that said, "I'm a nasty woman and I vote."

STORY

In 2016, there was more **voter polling** than ever. If polls were important in prior presidential elections, they were now seen as crucial. That's because **the polling data from all the prior elections was now available to the analysts for comparison**, and those comparisons were providing some valuable information. For one thing, the analysts now knew that the early polling data was not all that significant in terms of predicting who would win. In 1980, early on, the incumbent president, Jimmy Carter was way ahead in the polls, but eventually lost to Ronald Reagan. But in all the elections that followed, the data clearly showed that such a reversal was not likely; it would take significant world or national events (like the Iran hostages situation) to change people's minds once they had stated their preference in a poll.

The analysts had also learned that when voters read about poll results, it can influence voter behavior. When polled, people are more likely to say they are going to vote for the candidate that seems to be winning.

The polls that came out after the conclusions of the two conventions clearly indicated that Hillary had gotten a bigger "bounce" than Trump did. Among the key swing states, Hillary immediately pulled ahead in Florida, Ohio, Michigan, and North Carolina, and **the polls were now showing her with larger leads in New Hampshire, Virginia, and Wisconsin.** Trump had earlier proclaimed that he was going to win Pennsylvania, but the post-convention polls were showing that Hillary now had an even bigger lead there. **She was even leading in some polls taken in the so-called "red states" of Arizona, Georgia, and Utah.**

Before the two national conventions, the polls showed Trump was doing fairly well, and he often bragged about how great he was doing in those polls. But later, when he began to fall behind in those same polls, he disputed them or else blamed the news media for influencing the polls against him. He said, **"If the disgusting and corrupt media covered me honestly and didn't put false meaning into the words I say, I would be beating Hillary by 20%."** Also, Trump started saying the election was "rigged," and then, in the third debate, **he refused to say whether or not he would accept the outcome of the race.** He reiterated that at his rallies on the post-debate campaign trail and began talking about how the election might be stolen. **He didn't elaborate on how that could be done when elections were conducted by local people in tens of thousands of polling places.** He did talk about stricter voter identification requirements (a common Republican talking point). He said that without strict voter identification rule, people could walk in and vote for Hillary 15 times. **He didn't** explain how that could be done or why he was sure the voting cheaters would all vote for Hillary.

Democrats said the Republican push for strict voter ID rules was a ploy to intimidate minority voters, especially Hispanics, and keep them away from the polling places. If the Republicans hoped voter identification would keep Hispanics away from the polls, they had good reason: **the polls were indicating that support for Trump among Hispanics was at historic lows.** Undoubtedly, it was due to Trump's demeaning of Hispanic immigrants.

The polls were also indicating that Trumps' support among African-Americans were also startlingly low. Although most African-Americans usually voted Democratic, the pollsters were finding far fewer voters than usual in that subgroup willing to say they would vote for Trump.

Another startling result came out of the polling of young people. One survey that polled those under 35 found Hillary trouncing Trump 56% to 20%. That too was a historic low for a Republican candidate, dramatically lower even than the 35% of young people who had supported Nixon.

Among white groups, Hillary held a huge lead among those who were college educated (a group that had supported Romney in the previous election). But Trump help a solid lead among white voters who had not gone to college.

Trump had strong support from white evangelicals. And even after more and more information began to come out about how Trump treated women, and many leading Republicans began to ask Trump to withdraw from the ticket, many evangelicals still stuck by him. This was not true in Mormon-dominated Utah: all of the Republican political leaders in Utah eventually withdrew their support of Trump, and many came out publicly to say they would not vote for him under any circumstances.

Pollsters often asked people about the issue of restrictions on guns. Although the majority of Americans polled said they would favor more restrictions on gun ownership, those who said they were against gun restrictions strongly favored Trump.

Another very significant group that Romney had been unanimously supported by was Republican leaders. None of the former Republican presidents would support Trump, and many former officials in Republican administrations came out publicly against him. This was unprecedented in any prior presidential election.

A Gallup poll taken after the conclusion of the Democratic National Convention indicated a sizable increase in the number of voters who said they would be more likely to vote for Hillary. After the Republican National Convention, the same poll showed a dramatic *dn women came forecrease* in the likelihood that voters would vote for Trump.

From then on, the polls gave the news media something to talk about. At first the news media seemed more interested in the national polls (they were showing a close race). They didn't talk as much about the polls that were taken in the swing states, and they rarely, if ever, talked about the Electoral College. It is unlikely that they forgot it is the Electoral College, not the general election, that determines who our president will be; they couldn't have forgotten the lesson of 2000. More likely, they just wanted to keep the image of a close race going as long as possible. After all, who is going to tune into the election news on TV if the polls are indicating that the election is all but over?

But as Hillary started to move farther and farther into the polling lead in the swing states, the news media began to look more closely at the implications of swing state voting on the likely outcome. Some even began to focus on what it would take for the candidates to reach the magic 270 number (the majority) in the Electoral College. By late summer, looking only at the swing states in which Hillary had a solid lead, it was obvious that if she maintained the lead in those states she would far surpass the required 270 Electoral College votes, and she would become the forty-fifth president of the United States. Some then went back to look at the data to find out if any presidential candidate had ever come back from that big a lead that late in the campaign season. No one had.

You might think Hillary's supporters would have started broadcasting that fact, but few did. It was almost as if they were worried that if she was that far in the lead, people wouldn't bother to go out and vote for her.

Trump disputed the polls, and his supporters either didn't believe them or they tried to ignore them. The few Trump supporters that even mentioned the polling results said the huge crowds the Trump rallies were drawing proved the polls were wrong. The question was, were those large audiences attending Trump's rallies to spur on their candidate, or did they just want to get in on the daily drama of the "Trump show"?

By the middle of September, before the first presidential debate, Trump had narrowed Hillary's lead, at least in the national polls. She still led in most of the swing states, but the gap seemed to be closing.

After the first presidential debate, Hillary again moved ahead in the polls, and most took that as an indication that either she was perceived to have "won" the debate or else people had seen a side of Trump that they didn't like.

Then came the Hollywood Access audio tape and the many elected Republicans who began to suggest that Trump should withdraw from the race, and it was a central discussion in the debates that followed. When a number of women came forward to accuse Trump of sexually molesting them exactly as he had described in the audio tape, Trump denied it all and said the women were being put up to it by Hillary's people. Nevertheless, Trump's standing in the polls began an even more precipitous drop. For a while, it looked like Hillary was going to win big. Hillary's supporters were buoyed up, and Trump started saying the election was "rigged" against him.

But then, only eleven days before election day, James Comey, the director of the FBI, sent a letter to Congress saying there had been a new development in the investigation of how Hillary had handled her e-mail when she had been Secretary of State (see the later discussion of the "October Surprise"). Hillary's poll numbers immediately began to drop, and it began to look like it was going to be a much closer race than anyone thought.

However, two days before election day, Comey sent another letter to Congress saying the FBI had found nothing new. Nevertheless, with only two days to go before the election, and with millions having already cast their ballots in early voting, it was hard to judge the impact of Comey's new "never mind" letter. Many thought it was too late; the damage to Hillary's campaign had already been done.

Back on the campaign trail, Trump continued to hold his large boisterous rallies, often repeating his claim that the election was rigged and saying that he might not accept the results of election.

Hillary mostly just stayed the course she had been on all along, talking about her experience. When she did mention Trump, it was only to say that his words and his behavior proved he was **"not fit to be president of the United States."**

The polls continued to show that although Hillary was in the lead both nationally and in the swing states, there was a solid base of **Trump supporters whose faith in him was unshakable, no matter what he did or said**.

Near the end of the campaign, information came out about impending rate hikes for some of the people who were on the Affordable Care Act insurance program, and for a short time, Trump focused on what he called **"Obamacare," calling it "a complete disaster," a catastrophic event** that is making it impossible for families to pay their bills." However, that tactic didn't seem to affect the polls one way or the other, so Trump soon turned back to attacking Hillary as "corrupt."

At the annual Alfred E. Smith Memorial Foundation Dinner, a Catholic charity event which gave the two candidates a chance to poke friendly jabs at each other, Trump used the opportunity to once again talk about how corrupt Hillary was. He was roundly booed by many of the dignitaries in attendance for violating the friendly spirit of the event, but Trump, as usual, was not interested in apologizing. It showed once again that Trump was not about to "play by the established rules."

STORY

Every four years, as the presidential campaign season is winding down, many are waiting for an **"October surprise," some last minute bit of information that has the potential to change the outcome of the election**. In 2016, an announcement from the director of the FBI looked like it might be that October surprise.

On Friday, October 28th, only ten days before the election, the director of the FBI, James Comey, sent a letter to key members of Congress saying **new e-mails had been found** that might have relevance to the prior investigation of Hillary's use of a private e-mail server. Because Comey didn't say what was in those e-mails or why he was notifying Congress about it, many said it must mean there was something explosive in them, or else why would he be notifying Congress about it.

Trump, of course, made it out to be a *very* big deal, saying **the new emails would prove what he had been saying** all along, that Hillary was "totally corrupt," so corrupt that she **"should never have been allowed to run for president."** He immediately put out a new TV ad saying **Hillary's e-mail had been found on the laptop of "a pervert."** The ad said, Hillary was under FBI investigation, and that **"Decades of lies, cover-ups and scandal" had finally caught up with her.**

For over a week, Trump talked about little else, saying we were "finally going to learn the truth about Hillary's "crooked" email usage. He characterized it as a "reopening" of the e-mail "scandal."

The FBI said that was not true; they said it was merely that some new e-mails had come to light that might have relevance to their prior investigation of Hillary's private e-mail server. Sure enough, Trump operatives were immediately hitting all the talk shows to mischaracterize it as a "reopening" of the criminal investigation of Hillary and that she might be about to be "indicted." Trump was noticeably excited by the news. He made a sudden and dramatic change of course—instead of constantly castigating the FBI as corrupt, as he had been doing for months, he started saying the FBI was doing a good thing in "going after" Hillary. At his rallies, his **very mention of the FBI brought excited cheers from the boisterous audience**, and many started yelling "Lock her up," or "Hang the Bitch." Trump responded to their excitement by saying, **"Clinton's corruption is on a scale we have never seen before**." He said,

"We must not let her take her criminal scheme into the Oval Office."

The news media grabbed onto the issue, there were new headlines about it daily.

Hillary was upset that Comey had made that kind of vague announcement so close to the election. It soon came out that the head of Justice Department (Comey's boss) had been against him doing it, but he went ahead and did it anyhow.

Some suggested Comey's revealing information about an ongoing FBI investigation was unprecedented, and others suggested he might be in violation of the Hatch Act, a law that forbids prohibits employees in the executive branch of the federal government (except the president and vice-president) from engaging in political activity.

Democrats criticized the timing of the Comey's announcement, pointing out that the FBI is also investigating connections between the Trump campaign and Russian hacking, but they had not releasing any information about that investigation because they knew it might influence the election.

Under intense pressure, Comey did make a follow-up statement, saying, "We don't know the significance of this newly discovered collection of emails," and he said he was aware "there is significant risk of being misunderstood" in sending Congress such a letter in the middle of an election. And it did have an affect on the election, at least on the polls. Hillary's poll numbers immediately began to drop, making the race much closer. In addition, with the improved chances of a Trump victory, the stock market went down for days.

And then, more than a week later, only two days before election day, Comey sent another letter to Congress saying they had found nothing to suggest any wrongdoing by Hillary. Stock markets all over the world went up dramatically. But

Hillary's supporters were still upset; they said Comey's earlier announcement had negatively influenced those who had voted early, and it had unnecessarily cast a shadow over Hillary's campaign.

Trump said she was "guilty" no matter what the FBI said, and that Hillary was "being protected by a rigged system."

The Outcome

Election night was a nail biter. In most of the swing states, first Hillary and then Trump pulled into the lead. As it went back and forth, it became obvious the election was going to be a lot closer than anyone thought.

Still, most of the analysts continued to believe Hillary would win because **Trump would have to win *all* the swing states** in order to win in the Electoral College, and he was losing in the key states of Virginia, Colorado, and Nevada.

Even when it looked like Trump was going to squeak out wins in Florida, North Carolina, and Ohio, **most assumed Hillary would win all the states that traditionally voted Democratic and that would still be enough for her to be the winner**.

The analysts didn't count on Trump's appeal in the so-called "rust belt" states of Pennsylvania, Michigan, and Wisconsin. Trump won all three of those states, but by the tiniest of margins.

While Hillary was racking up large numbers of votes in the big cities, Trump was managing to win most rural counties.

Even though Hillary ended up winning the popular vote, the final vote tallies in those three historically Democratic states gave Trump just enough votes to win in the Electoral College.

STORY

After the election of 2016 was over, there was **a lot of analysis** of what had caused such a monumental upset. Some blamed the low turnout of African-Americans (as compared to the two previous presidential elections). But that was to be expected after the huge turnouts Obama had gotten in African-American communities.

Others blamed the low turnout of young voters. Many of them said they were "turned off" by the tenor of the attack-oriented campaigns.

Of course, **Hillary won the women's vote, but not by as much as expected.** She did poorly among white, non-college-educated women. Many of them said they just didn't want a woman to be their leader.

Non-college-educated voters turned out to be Hillary's Achilles heel: she won overwhelmingly among college-educated voters, especially among college-educated women voters, but did very poorly among white voters who had not been to college.

After Trump's many negative comments about Mexicans and illegal immigrants, many expected a huge turnout of Hispanic voters. And although there was an increase in their numbers, there was not enough of them in the "rust belt" states to make a difference there.

In the end, with such a close race in a few "surprise" states, it was the "energized" voters that made the difference.

The election of 2016 became the fifth time in U.S. History when the winner of the general election did not get to be president.

After the election results were in, there was a lot of analysis about **campaign strategy**. Most analysts had seen **Hillary's two-pronged approach** of staying upbeat and talking about togetherness, mixed in with comments about Trump's character (often using his own words against him), as a winning strategy.

Trump's campaign strategy on the other hand, was harder to define. **He mostly ran an attack-oriented campaign**, and he liked to shoot from the hip and make seemingly outrageous off-the-cuff statements and Twitter tweets that often got him into trouble. **A great deal of his campaign was based on trying to associate his opponent with negative concepts like "crooked" and "corrupt."** Without any supporting evidence, he often called Hillary "a liar" or "a world-class liar." He called her "the most corrupt candidate in history." Maybe a lot of people, including the news media, got so used to hearing such outlandish statements from Trump that they stopped paying attention. But **in a few keys states, some people were listening, and apparently, believing**.

From the start, Trump seemed to have adopted an entertainer's **all-news-is-good-news** approach, and his extreme statements and outrageous Twitter tweets, did keep him in the news.

Despite all the focus on Trump's seemingly off-kilter statements, what undoubtedly got him the victory was **his description of himself as "an outsider"** who was going to go to Washington to "fix things" (he said he was going to go there and "drain the swamp"). That approach cost him the support of many mainstream Republicans, but that **only further supported his outsider status**.

After the election, there was a lot of talk about how effective his attack-oriented, propaganda-filled campaign had been at polarizing the country.

During the Republican primaries, he had uncovered a vein of anger among the Republican base, and he used it to sweep to victory over his better-known Republican rivals. What now seems clear, in retrospect, is that the Republican base—as evidenced by the Tea Party Movement—had been steadily moving farther to the right for some time, and they were looking for a new candidate that reflected their values.

Many analysts felt Trump's campaign, if nothing else, demonstrated how effective a no-holds-barred, down-and-dirty style of campaigning can be. The question is, will propaganda-oriented campaigning be **the new normal in future presidential campaigns**?

INDEX

About The Author

Dr. Everett Murdock is an Emeritus Professor at California State University, Long Beach. He is a recipient of that university's Distinguished Faculty Teaching Award (the university's teacher of the year award).

37420183R00203

Made in the USA
Middletown, DE
27 November 2016